Palgrave Macmillan Series in International Political Communication

Series Editor: Philip Seib, University of Southern California (USA)

From democratization to terrorism, economic development to conflict resolution, global political dynamics are affected by the increasing pervasiveness and influence of communication media. This series examines the participants and their tools, their strategies and their impact. It offers a mix of comparative and tightly focused analyses that bridge the various elements of communication and political science included in the field of international studies. Particular emphasis is placed on topics related to the rapidly changing communication environment that is being shaped by new technologies and new political realities. This is the evolving world of international political communication.

Books Appearing in this Series

Media and the Politics of Failure: Great Powers, Communication Strategies, and Military Defeats
By Laura Roselle

The CNN Effect in Action: How the News Media Pushed the West toward War in Kosovo
By Babak Bahador

Media Pressure on Foreign Policy: The Evolving Theoretical Framework
By Derek B. Miller

New Media and the New Middle East
Edited by Philip Seib

The African Press, Civic Cynicism, and Democracy
By Minabere Ibelema

Global Communication and Transnational Public Spheres
By Angela M. Crack

Latin America, Media, and Revolution: Communication in Modern Mesoamerica
By Juanita Darling

Japanese Public Opinion and the War on Terrorism
Edited by Robert D. Eldridge and Paul Midford

African Media and the Digital Public Sphere
Edited by Okoth Fred Mudhai, Wisdom J. Tettey, and Fackson Banda

Islam Dot Com: Contemporary Islamic Discourses in Cyberspace
By Mohammed el-Nawawy and Sahar Khamis

Explaining News: National Politics and Journalistic Cultures in Global Context
By Cristina Archetti

News Media and EU-China Relations
By Li Zhang

Kurdish Identity, Discourse, and New Media
By Jaffer Sheyholislami

Al Jazeera English: Global News in a Changing World
Edited by Philip Seib

Civic Engagement, Digital Networks, and Political Reform in Africa
By Okoth Fred Mudhai

Egyptian Revolution 2.0: Political Blogging, Civic Engagement, and Citizen Journalism
By Mohammed el-Nawawy and Sahar Khamis

The Dispute over the Diaoyu/Senkaku Islands: How Media Narratives Shape Public Opinion and Challenge the Global Order
Edited by Thomas A. Hollihan

Media Evolution on the Eve of the Arab Spring
Edited by Leila Hudson, Adel Iskandar, and Mimi Kirk

The EU Foreign Policy Analysis: Democratic Legitimacy, Media, and Climate Change
By Cristian Nițoiu

Media and Political Contestation in the Contemporary Arab World: A Decade of Change
Edited By Lena Jayyusi and Anne Sofie Roald

Migration, Media, and Global-Local Spaces
By Esther Chin

Migration, Media, and Global-Local Spaces

Esther Chin

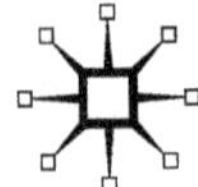

MIGRATION, MEDIA, AND GLOBAL-LOCAL SPACES

First published 2016 by
PALGRAVE MACMILLAN

The author has asserted their right to be identified as the author of this work in accordance with the Copyright, Designs and Patents Act 1988.

Palgrave Macmillan in the UK is an imprint of Macmillan Publishers Limited, registered in England, company number 785998, of Houndmills, Basingstoke, Hampshire, RG21 6XS.

Palgrave Macmillan in the US is a division of Nature America, Inc., One New York Plaza, Suite 4500, New York, NY 10004-1562.

Palgrave Macmillan is the global academic imprint of the above companies and has companies and representatives throughout the world.

Hardback ISBN: 978–1–137–55856–5
E-PUB ISBN: 978–1–137–53223–7
E-PDF ISBN: 978–1–137–53227–5
DOI: 10.1057/9781137532275

Distribution in the UK, Europe and the rest of the world is by Palgrave Macmillan®, a division of Macmillan Publishers Limited, registered in England, company number 785998, of Houndmills, Basingstoke, Hampshire RG21 6XS.

Library of Congress Cataloging-in-Publication Data

Names: Chin, Esther, author.
Title: Migration, media and global-local spaces / Esther Chin.
Description: New York City : Palgrave Macmillan, [2016] | Series: The Palgrave Macmillan series in international political communication | Includes bibliographical references and index.
Identifiers: LCCN 2015030192| ISBN 9781137558565 | ISBN 1137558563
Subjects: LCSH: Emigration and immigration—Social aspects. | Transnationalism—Social aspects. | Mass media and minorities | Group identity. | Space—Social aspects. | Singaporeans—Australia—Melbourne (Vic.)—Social conditions.
Classification: LCC JV6225 .C45 2016 | DDC 304.8—dc23 LC record available at http://lccn.loc.gov/2015030192

A catalogue record for the book is available from the British Library.

Contents

List of Illustrations vii
Acknowledgments ix

Introduction 1
1 Migration, Media, and Social Space 11
2 Relational Glocalities 41
3 Singaporean Cultures of Migration and Media 73
4 Geographies 89
5 Cartographies 115
6 Glocal Cosmopolitanism 157

Appendix 1: List of Interviewees 175
Appendix 2: Methodological Details 181
Notes 193
Bibliography 199
Index 221

Illustrations

Figures

4.1 Geographics 91
A2.1 Stages of interpretation 190

Tables

3.1 Where do Overseas Singaporeans live? 82
3.2 Where do Singaporean international students live? 83
3.3 Where do international students in Australia come from? 83
A2.1 Links between conceptual framework and interview questions 183

Acknowledgments

This book is based on my PhD thesis, entitled *Relational "glocalities": a study of "cartographies" of media and migration through the approach of "glocal" cosmopolitanism* (2012). My PhD was done at the University of Melbourne, Australia, and it was fully funded by University of Melbourne scholarships. I would like to acknowledge the excellent research environment of the School of Culture and Communication, Faculty of Arts, The University of Melbourne. Many academics, administrative staff, and research students have contributed to this environment over the years. I have received support in my training and work in research and academic publication, through the colloquium convened by my PhD supervisor Ingrid Volkmer and through *PLATFORM: Journal of Media and Communication*, an international graduate journal based at the School of Culture and Communication. I thank all the people who have invested time and energy to support my work at the University of Melbourne.

Ingrid Volkmer (Associate Professor in Media and Communications at the University of Melbourne) has been my professional mentor since 2007. She has guided me to develop an academic career specializing in global communication. Ingrid has supervised my PhD and encouraged the publication of my PhD thesis as a book. Those of us who are familiar with Ingrid's work may observe how her work has influenced my own.

Scott McQuire (Associate Professor in Media and Communications at the University of Melbourne) was the Associate Supervisor of my PhD. As Head of the Media and Communications Program from 2013 to 2014, Scott supervised my post-PhD employment as a sessional lecturer at the University of Melbourne. I thank my colleagues in the Media and Communications Program for giving me responsibilities and recognition that have built up my experience and confidence as an academic.

Ingrid, Scott, and Audrey Yue (Associate Professor in Cultural Studies at the University of Melbourne) gave me feedback on my proposal for this book.

Teaching has helped me to communicate in an accessible way, and to relate theory to current events, issues, and professional practice. As I revised my PhD thesis for publication as a book, I pitched my writing at my undergraduate students. I thank all my students and industry contacts who have kept my work relevant and engaging, and value our ongoing relationships. I am grateful to Ingrid, Audrey, and Dr Wendy Haslem (Lecturer in Screen Studies at the University of Melbourne) for encouraging me to teach well by their examples and encouragement. I also thank my colleagues from across the University of Melbourne who have contributed to my professional development in teaching through the Graduate Certificate in University Teaching.

As this book shows, my thinking has been significantly informed by the work of Ulrich Beck, Professor of Sociology at Ludwig Maximilian University of Munich, British Journal of Sociology Visiting Centennial Professor at the London School of Economics, and Professor at the Fondation Maison des Sciences de l'Homme, Paris. Ulrich Beck was the international examiner of my PhD thesis and he recommended that my PhD thesis be considered for the University of Melbourne Chancellor's Prize for Excellence. Professor Beck led the world in developing the approach of "methodological cosmopolitanism," and I feel very honored that he read and appreciated my work. Professor Beck passed away in January 2015, but I trust that future generations of scholars will build on his legacy.

Gerard Goggin (Professor of Media and Communications at the University of Sydney, Australia) was the other examiner of my PhD. He recommended that my PhD thesis be passed without amendment, but he also gave me feedback on how I might develop it for publication. Professor Goggin, thank you for your generosity in reading my work and in your feedback. I hope you enjoy reading this book.

I finalized this book as part of my new employment as a Lecturer in Media and Communications at Swinburne University of Technology, Australia. The Department of Media and Communication funded the indexing of this book through an internal grant. After a very positive experience of work at the University of Melbourne, I feel very amazed to find myself in another outstanding working environment. My academic and administrative colleagues in the Department of Media and Communication are generous and diligent, and working at Swinburne reminds me of how valuable people and relationships are. I am glad to meet our students and to contribute my research in global communication to our work in media and communications.

I would like to thank Palgrave Macmillan, in particular the New York office and its staff, for publishing this book. Thank you, Sara Doskow

(Editor, International Relations, Regional Politics & Development Studies) and Chris Robinson (Editorial Assistant) for your generosity and patience with this first time book author. Thanks also to the following staff at Palgrave Macmillan: Rachel Crawford (production editor), for coordinating the production process; and the designer, for creating a beautiful book cover that reflects my preferences. It is my honor and joy to publish my first book with Palgrave Macmillan.

Thank you, Newgen, for packaging this book. Thanks to Deepa John (Project Manager) for coordinating the packaging process; the copyeditor, Kamlesh Pant, for your meticulous work; and the typesetter, Newgen Knowledge Works.

Thank you, Teri Lefever, for creating the index for this book.

As Editor of The Palgrave Macmillan Series in International Political Communication Philip Seib (Professor of Journalism and Public Diplomacy and Professor of International Relations, University of Southern California, USA) considered my book proposal, forwarded it on to the publisher, and advised on the revision of the manuscript. Thank you for all your support. I hope this book adds value to the series.

I would like to say a big thank you to the anonymous reviewer who read and gave feedback on my sample chapters and the revised manuscript. Your comments have made a positive difference to this book.

Thanks also to the editorial board who accepted my book proposal and recommended the title of this book.

I would like to thank the following individuals for reading and endorsing this book: Ingrid Volkmer, Gerard Goggin, and Karen Farquharson (Associate Dean (Research & Engagement) and Associate Professor Sociology, Swinburne University of Technology).

Chapters 4 and 5 would not be possible without the open sharing of my interviewees. Thank you for giving me your time and for trusting me with your personal experiences of migration and media. Please know that I appreciate your participation in my research, and your involvement has contributed to the knowledge of migration and media in Singaporean and global contexts.

I experienced a significant breakthrough in the book's theoretical framework and data analysis when I was in Europe in 2011 for exchange and the International Communication Association annual conference. I would like to thank the Institute for Media and Communication Studies at Freie Universität Berlin, Germany, for hosting me as a guest PhD student. Particular thanks to Ansgar Koch (Program Coordinator and Academic Advisor at the Institute for Media and Communication Studies) for helping with the arrangements of my visit. Thank you to all the people who included me in your work. Special thanks to Elfriede Fürsich (Research Associate Professor at Boston College, USA, and Visiting Professor at Freie Universität Berlin) for the opportunity to share the findings of this research in the seminar "Media, Mobility, and Meaning."

Thank you, Professor Daniel Dayan, Professor Andreas Wimmer, and Professor Thomas Faist for meeting me to engage in intellectually constructive conversations.

Thank you, dad and mum, Drew and Jeanette, gujie, and popo, for remembering me and showing me your love across geographical distance. I honor my family as a stable network of love and support.

Thank you, Xin Yi, Nat, and Akina, for close friendships that we sustain through circular migration and media.

Thank you, Nola and Monica, for caring for me through major life events in Australia and for encouraging me to manage new experiences confidently.

Ultimately, thank You, Jesus, for Your unconditional love and for giving me the capacity to enjoy and extend Your goodness in the world. In a more personal reflection on the purpose of our positions in local and global societies, the following verses resonate:

> From one man he made all the nations, that they should inhabit the whole earth; and he marked out their appointed times in history and the boundaries of their lands. God did this so that they would seek him and perhaps reach out for him and find him, though he is not far from any one of us.
>
> (Acts 17:26–27, The Bible, New International Version)

Introduction

As the United Kingdom entered the 2015 election year, the national significance of international students became evident in public debate on migration. Theresa May, the political leader in charge of UK national security and a potential leader of the governing political party, proposed to cut net migration by requiring non-European Union (non-EU) university students to depart the United Kingdom once they graduate, and to apply for any further right to study or work from outside the United Kingdom. However, prominent political, business, and community leaders opposed this proposal. They expressed concerns that the United Kingdom could lose its competitiveness in the global market for international education because foreign students could view the United Kingdom as less attractive than other potential study destinations if it became harder for them to access poststudy opportunities there. In addition, restricting the right of non-EU citizens to work in the United Kingdom could reduce UK companies' access to foreign talent and hurt the United Kingdom's competitiveness in the global economy more generally.

The opinions on this prominent news story reveal that there are overlaps in public discussion about distinct forms of migration (such as student and skilled migration, as well as mobility within and into the EU); that established narratives of student migration are reconstructed by a wide range of stakeholders and actors (such as politicians with different political affiliations, business leaders, locals, and international students); that many of these diverse stakeholders and actors participate in multiple polities and societies (such as the United Kingdom, the EU, countries where UK multinational corporations operate, and international students' countries of origin); and that these stakeholders negotiate the continuously changing relationships between the global and the local spaces of the United Kingdom and other countries.

I have written this book to share information, research, and ideas on how our experiences of migration might be related to our experiences of media. We may experience migration first-hand, be familiar with the migration of loved ones, and encounter foreigners face to face and through media. How are our thoughts and feelings about migration informed by our engagement with news, entertainment, social and mobile media? How are migration and media relevant to our views of the world, its countries, and its cities? How do we draw our own maps of the world and its places, as we try to construct meaningful relationships between the various places we see through migration and media? Besides countries and cities, what other social spaces do we consider important, and how do we use a range of media platforms to create these social spaces?

These questions are rarely asked, but in asking them, we begin to consider the reality that we live not just transnationally across particular countries of origin and residence, but in a much broader global society, across multiple countries and local units of space other than nation-states. We experience our global society as a set of local spaces, spaces that are connected to one another through migration, but especially through media.

Through our various forms of communication about places and people, we access alternative templates of how we might draft our personal maps of the world. Reading news from the websites of the BBC and *The Guardian*, for example, I saw that commentators related the regulation of student migration to the United Kingdom's position in the world—as a competitor to countries such as the United States, Canada, Australia, and Germany, which also attract a huge proportion of the global market for international education.

As a major exporter of international education, the United Kingdom has been marketing to and providing education to students from many countries, especially China and India. These "source countries" were ranked—an established way of defining hierarchical relationships between countries in student migration and international education.

On the one hand, if the United Kingdom required foreign students to leave shortly after graduation as Theresa May proposed, it might play an essential and ethically compelling role in the development of emerging economies by training foreign talent and then encouraging them to return to contribute to their countries of origin. On the other hand, by making it more difficult for skilled foreigners to stay in the United Kingdom to work after their studies, the United Kingdom would not retain international talent. It might also lose its capacity to import talent from the international market, consequently becoming less competitive in the global economy.

As might be expected in the national news of UK politics, these maps of the world, though different, were all UK centric. The comments on Theresa May's proposal presented different views of the

United Kingdom's relationships to other countries within the global economy.

In contrast to these economic maps of the world, a political map was also evident. Although Theresa May's proposal targeted the migration of non-EU university graduates, the proposal was discussed with reference to the issue of freedom of movement within the EU, specifically the economic migration of Rumanians and Bulgarians into the United Kingdom, an issue raised by the UK Independence Party as part of its sustained campaign for the United Kingdom to withdraw its membership of the EU.

In just one news debate on student migration in the United Kingdom, the intersections between multiple global and local spaces were defined, problematized, and negotiated.

We don't often consider how our experiences of migration and media reflect relationships between local spaces and the world as a whole. More frequently, we talk about migration with reference to national societies, particularly migrants' countries of origin and residence. This focus on national societies is evident not only in everyday conversations about migration, but also in academic studies. Scholars use the term "methodological nationalism" to criticize our assumption that the societies we research are national societies.

We take for granted that society is national when we evaluate migration using national criteria (such as the priorities of the national labor market and national values), when we refer to the crossing and transgression of national geographical and jurisdictional borders (through *im*migration, *em*igration, and *il*legal migration), and when we view diaspora as the geographically distributed segment of a national population (see A. Wimmer and Glick Schiller, 2003, pp. 598–599).

In the first chapter of this book, I argue that three forms of methodological nationalism are evident in research on migration and media. I use the terms "minority," "transnational," and "diaspora paradigms" to conceptualize these forms of methodological nationalism.

The minority paradigm focuses on the role of minority media in encouraging assimilation into the host society (Zhou and Cai, 2002), divergence between minority and mainstream spaces of representation (Silverstone and Georgiou, 2005), as well as the relevance of media for integration and segregation between ethnic minority groups and the native population (D'Haenens and Ogan, 2007). In the minority paradigm, media is mainly viewed within a national context of inequality. Migration is not just associated with cultural, political, and social difference from the society of settlement, but related to exclusion and marginalization.

Whereas the minority paradigm is oriented to the country of settlement, the transnational paradigm considers the significance of satellite television for the experience of proximity to a geographically distant country of origin (Aksoy and Robins, 2003a). The transnational paradigm views diasporas as "imagined communities" (cf. Anderson, 1991) which connect across societies of origin and settlement (Tsagarousianou, 2004). The transnational paradigm explores the construction of cultural spaces through national and transnational lenses (Bailey, Georgiou, and Harindranath, 2007), often considering transnational spaces as a counterpoint to national societies of origin and settlement.

The emphasis on societies of origin and settlement is less evident in the diaspora paradigm. The diaspora paradigm studies the creation of globalized ethnic communities around diasporic media (Cunningham, 2001). It conceptualizes diasporas as "deterritorialized nations" which are oriented toward the homeland territory through shared media (Karim, 2007). For example, within the diaspora paradigm, we might discuss how the technological properties of the Internet can be used for "diasporic nationalism" (Kim, 2011). The diaspora paradigm considers the importance of globalized communication for a globally distributed national population, especially an ethnic group that is associated with a country of origin.

Across the minority, transnational, and diaspora paradigms, we tend to study culture, identity, and community with reference to the spaces and territories of countries of origin and settlement (e.g., Ogan, 2001; Sinclair and Cunningham, 2001). Current research rarely explores the ways in which multiple perceptions of the global and the local are configured in experiences of migration and media.

One of the distinctive arguments of this book is that today's globalized experiences of migration and media are characterized by diverse configurations of global and local spaces. These spaces include countries other than countries of origin and settlement, and are not limited to national units of social space.

Through processes of globalization such as worldwide migration and communication, cultures, identities, and communities are situated in media and communication "networks" between the local and the global (Castells, 2009, 2010). Social spaces that appear at a particular scale (such as the national scale) are often "assemblages" of the "subnational," the national, the global, and the digital (Sassen, 2006).

Having critiqued nation-centric perspectives on migration and media in chapter 1, I show, in the rest of this book, how we might instead think about migration and media in the context of "global interdependencies" (Beck and Grande, 2010, p. 412) and locally specific (e.g., "Western" and "postcolonial") expressions of "entangled modernities" and "reflexive modernization" (Beck, Bonss, and Lau, 2003; Beck and Grande, 2010; Beck and Sznaider, 2006). For example, how do we perceive East-West relations and histories of colonization within our experiences of migration and media?

In chapter 2, I develop Ulrich Beck's seminal theory of "methodological cosmopolitanism" (Beck, 2006) for a non-nation-centric study of migration and media. I use diverse "local," "translocal," and "global" lenses to conceptualize the relationship between migration, media, and the construction of "local-global," "trans-local," and "global-global" social relations (Beck, 2006, pp. 76–77, 81–82).

The central contribution of this book is a new conceptualization of migration and media, a conceptual approach I call "glocal cosmopolitanism." This approach builds on Beck's theory of "methodological cosmopolitanism" in relation to Roland Robertson's (1992, 1995) theory of "glocality" as a "universalism-particularism nexus." The main argument I develop in this book is this: in order to fully understand today's globalized experiences of migration and media, we must view social spaces as "relational glocalities"—"glocal" (R. Robertson, 1995) social spaces that are locally and unequally differentiated in relation to one another within "global fields" (Glick Schiller and Çağlar, 2009; R. Robertson, 1992). We can construct these relational glocalities through dialectical negotiation between "universalism" and "particularism"—through the two processes of "universalization of particularism" and "particularization of universalism" (R. Robertson, 1992). I use Beck's terms "cosmopolitan gaze" (Beck, 2000a, p. 79) and "cosmopolitan vision" (Beck, 2006) in a new way—to conceptualize the "universalization of particularism" and the "particularization of universalism" (R. Robertson, 1992), respectively.

My concept of "glocal cosmopolitanism" is informed by the social theory of cosmopolitanism and prominent initiatives to apply this theory to the study of migration and media (Beck, 2006; Beck and Beck-Gernsheim, 2009; Beck and Grande, 2010; Georgiou, 2007c; Jansson, 2009). Leaders in the scholarship of migration and media have been shifting our thinking toward a cosmopolitan worldview. For example, they have analyzed how multilingual audiences "relativize" interpretations of globalized conflict events through diverse satellite television news sources (Gillespie, 2006). They have viewed migrant and diasporic relations of belonging through a non-"nation-centric" perspective (Georgiou, 2007c, p. 19), as well as examined ethical negotiations of "attachment" and "detachment" toward places of origin and residence (Christensen, 2011).

I have developed my concept of "glocal cosmopolitanism" in today's "transmedial" context of migration (Hepp, 2009a, p. 330). Rather than limiting my scope to particular media technologies or genres (such as satellite television and news), I prefer to explore how we perceive migration within our holistic experiences of all media. Whereas most studies of migration and media focus on specific types of media (such as mass, social, and interpersonal media), I elaborate on the relationship between migration and "polymedia" (Madianou and Miller, 2012, 2013). How might we shape our experiences of migration through the implicit and subtle distinctions we make between media (such as different applications and functions), within various contexts of media convergence (Castells, 2010, Chapter 5) (such as the simultaneous use of multiple screens, as well as engagement with social and Internet television)?

"Glocal cosmopolitanism" is my attempt to conceptualize how we experience diverse "global interdependencies" (Beck and Grande, 2010, p. 412) through migration and media. In the public debate around Theresa May's proposal, migration was primarily defined as a process that significantly impacts economic relations between the national (the United Kingdom) and the global. According to public opinion, the national migration management strategy should mainly enhance the relative position of the national economy within the global economy, as well as promote mutual engagement between national businesses and global talent. In contrast, research on migration and media is typically concerned about how we sustain and transform cultural and political relations such as community and citizenship.

As a sociologist, I am interested in social relations more broadly, which includes how we relate with one another economically, culturally, politically, and ethically. I seek to discover "ways of being" and "ways of belonging" in "transnational social fields" (Levitt and Glick Schiller, 2004).

As a media scholar, I explore how people imagine places and spaces through media—not only places and spaces of migration (such as our countries of origin and residence, "home," and "diaspora"), but also the many territories and networks of global media events (such as the United States, Germany, Iraq, India, North Korea, and the global financial market, all of which are prominently represented in news). In the interviews I have conducted with Singaporean university students in Melbourne, Australia, my interviewees and I have not limited our conversations to what it means to be Singaporean in Melbourne.

Instead, these students have mentioned a variety of public issues, events, and places relevant to our lives in globalized society, globalized lives that are enabled by migration and media. In chapters 4 and 5, I present the findings of my interviews and analyze how experiences of migration intertwine with experiences of media.

My concepts of "glocal cosmopolitanism" and "relational glocalities" are empirically supported by my interviews with Singaporean university students in Melbourne, Australia. These interviews offer not only localized perspectives on globalization (e.g., experiences of the Internet and climate change, compared across Singapore and Melbourne), but also globalized perspectives on localization (e.g., perceptions of different countries in global news). The media culture of Singapore is both similar to and different from the media cultures of other East Asian cities, such as Hong Kong, Seoul, Taipei, and Tokyo (W.-Y. Lin, Cheong, Kim, and Jung, 2010). The Singaporean students in Melbourne have contributed to a distinctive dialogue between Western and Asian cultures of migration and media (Iwabuchi, 2010), a dialogue that might help us to refine our established models of globalized societies (Beck and Grande, 2010).

In 2015, Singapore celebrates its 50th year as an independent nation-state. With a year-long public campaign known as SG50, the state is leading the people to articulate a sustainable national identity. However, in recent years, our expressions of citizenship reflect growing resentment between self-identified Singaporeans and foreign residents. Migration is a major issue in Singapore public opinion, and most of the debate is about immigration rather than short-term emigration such as overseas study. But how do "Overseas Singaporeans" experience migration and media?

There is some research on Overseas Singaporeans' first-hand experiences of migration. These studies have systematically discovered how Singaporean "transnational elites" negotiate difference while working in China (B. S. A. Yeoh and Willis, 2005), how Singaporean creative professionals in Perth, Australia connect Singapore and Perth through cultural organizations (T. Lee, 2006), and how the Singapore state manages the transnational citizenship and family relations of Singaporean highly skilled workers in London (Ho, 2008d).

I explain Singaporean cultures of migration and media in chapters 3–5. Which experiences of migration and media are distinctively Singaporean? Which experiences are less locally specific? How do Singaporean cultures compare with other local cultures?

In chapter 3, I provide an overview of research on Singaporean cultures of migration and media. I also analyze how the Singapore government has developed these cultures through strategic public relations.

In chapters 4 and 5, I share the results of my fieldwork with Singaporean university students in Melbourne, Australia. I contribute deep insight into various experiences that have not been methodically explored: Overseas Singaporeans' experiences of media, Singaporean experiences of student migration, and Overseas Singaporeans' second-hand experiences of the migration of people we know personally.

According to the 2015 QS ranking, Melbourne is the second best "student city" in the world and the best in terms of student diversity (QS, 2015). What do Singaporean students think about studying in Melbourne? How do we view Melbourne within our individual maps of the world? What are our experiences of cultural diversity and how do we compare different configurations of multiculturalism in Singapore and Australia?

I use the terms "geographies" and "cartographies" to conceptualize the two types of world maps that we create through migration and media. The spatial units of geographies are literal places, such as countries and cities. In contrast, cartographies are new units that I have invented to identify new types of social spaces. I conceptualize geographies in chapter 4 and cartographies in chapter 5.

In chapter 4, I show that we cannot assume that the geographies of migration consist of only one place of origin and one place of residence. Many of my interviewees have lived in multiple countries and cities, know people who have migrated to other places, and aspire to migrate to a new country, whether in the near future or in the long term. We can group individual geographies and identify broader patterns across individual experiences of migration and media by asking the following questions:

- When is migration experienced—childhood, young adulthood?
- Are close personal relations (such as family members, romantic partners, and friends) relevant for the experience of migration and media? How are they relevant? Do the parents decide that the family will migrate? Is a particular place seen as an attractive migration destination because the aspiring migrant knows and has a personal relationship with someone who is already there?
- Is migration experienced first hand or second hand?

Having analyzed our world maps of actual places in chapter 4, I propose, in chapter 5, new units of social space that we can use to create alternative maps of the world. Unlike the spatial units in chapter 4, these new units are not primarily based on geographical, national, or state coordinates. Instead, they are "relational spaces"—emergent configurations of media, social relations, place, and space. I call these spaces "cartographies," inspired by Brah's (1996) work *Cartographies of Diaspora*. Brah has used the term "cartographies" to conceptualize the construction of diasporic subjectivity across multiple types of social relations—multiple "axes of differentiation" (Brah, 1996, pp. 13–14). Building on Brah, I use the term "cartographies" to highlight the ways in which we subjectively construct spaces of social relations in our experiences of migration and media.

This book is about how we experience migration and media. I intentionally use the phrase "experience of migration and media" to describe the focus of my work, rather than other common terms of reference such as "migrant," "minority," "transnational," and "diaspora." In my view, "migrant," "minority," "transnational," and "diaspora" are examples of terms that we use to position ourselves in relation to one another and in relation to space. These terms represent specific and different types of positioning in relation to social space. If we use these terms to label who and what we are researching at the start of our research, we risk only considering spaces associated with nation, state, and specific countries of origin and settlement. Instead, starting with a more general topic like "experience of migration and media" opens us to seek information about a wider range of social spaces and to see much more diverse types of social spaces. When we have gathered this information and are in the process of analyzing it, we can then use terms like "migrant," "minority," "transnational," and "diaspora" to make sense of it.

CHAPTER 1

Migration, Media, and Social Space

On November 20, 2014, US President Barack Obama used his authority as president to act toward a reform of the US immigration system. Through his actions, President Obama segmented the undocumented immigrant population and defined national priorities for the regulation of illegal immigration. Targeting potential and recent undocumented immigrants, the president directed more resources to the territorial border between the United States and Mexico to prevent illegal immigration and to deport illegal immigrants. In contrast, the president developed schemes to promote the authorization of undocumented immigrants who had lived continuously in the United States for the past five years and who had either migrated to the United States as a child or who had at least one child who is an American citizen or legal permanent resident. Through these schemes, eligible immigrants could obtain amnesty from deportation as well as permission to stay and work in the United States, for a renewable period of three years.

President Obama justified these actions in a national context of sustained political opposition and ongoing division in public opinion. Announcing these actions in an address to the American public (Obama, 2014), the president said that the national debate on immigration is significant because it is about "who we are as a country and who we want to be for future generations." He argued that America was, is, and "always will be a nation of immigrants" and "a nation that values families" (Obama, 2014).

Similarly in Singapore, immigration is a topic of intense political and public debate, as well as a deeply personal issue. This is because our opinions on immigration reflect our perceptions of, and aspirations for, the societies we live in. Who are we? Who do we want to be? We express our diverse responses to these broader questions as we take specific positions and actions on a current issue of immigration. In a Leadership in Asia Public Lecture at Singapore Management University on June 30, 2015 (H. L. Lee, 2015), Singapore's Prime

Minister Lee Hsien Loong said that Singapore's capacity to act has increased as "we have become so open, so cosmopolitan, our people can adapt anywhere and be at home in many places in the world." At the same time, PM Lee cautioned that like other small countries with a significant proportion of the population residing overseas (e.g., New Zealand, Greece, and Ireland), the territorial "centre" of our society "cannot hold" if many of us leave Singapore (permanently or temporarily) and we could risk "los[ing] that special sense of being distinctive Singaporeans, different from non-Singaporeans" as our national identity "can dissolve with globalization."

In this chapter, I identify the main paradigms that inform our experiences of migration and media. I hope that as we understand the distinctions and overlaps between these paradigms, we will develop insight into our own and other points of view, appreciate dialogue and debate between multiple perspectives, and create a broader space of shared understanding and consensus with other stakeholders in our global and local societies.

When President Obama spoke repeatedly of "who we are as a country" (Obama, 2014) and when PM Lee highlighted that "identity" is "the most profound challenge we have" for the next 50 years (H. L. Lee, 2015), they were appealing to American and Singaporean visions of what Benedict Anderson (1991) calls "imagined communities." Anderson uses the term "imagined communities" to conceptualize the mental construction of strong collective belonging among complete strangers. Such a collective

> is *imagined* because the members...will never know most of their fellow-members, meet them, or even hear of them, yet in the minds of each lives the image of their communion....It is imagined as a *community*, because,...[it] is always conceived as a deep, horizontal comradeship.
>
> (Anderson, 1991, pp. 6–7, original emphasis)

How do we similarly and differently imagine America and Singapore as communities? To what extent is the "deep, horizontal comradeship" among fellow Americans and among fellow Singaporeans extended to our immigrants and emigrants?

Anderson (1991) argues that at a specific historical point of cultural transformation (p. 36), new forms of collective imagination were enabled by the development of new mass media systems, differentiated by culture (especially language) and geopolitical territory. He views print mass media systems as critical for the construction of national forms of "imagined communities" (Anderson, 1991). This association between print mass media systems and modern nationalism was made by Marshall McLuhan 25 years earlier (McLuhan, 2011[1962], pp. 226–227).

Anderson offers historical evidence to support his argument that the rise of commercial print publishing in popular languages for a mass readership was crucial for the formation of national collectives situated in a particular time and in a particular territory (Anderson, 1991). Each collective was constructed through its representation in, and its shared consumption of, novels and newspapers, published in a common written language and distributed within a limited geographical space (Anderson, 1991). Given that the boundaries of the collective tended to correspond to the linguistic and geographical reach of the newspaper, "the very conception of the newspaper implies the refraction of even 'world events' into a specific imagined world of vernacular readers" (Anderson, 1991, p. 63).

Anderson's concept of "imagined communities" emphasizes the centrality of media for the perception of cultural similarity within groups and cultural difference between groups. To sustain Singapore's unique national identity in a globalized world and to prevent it from fragmenting into mutually exclusive subnational groups (H. L. Lee, 2015), it is helpful to consider how Singaporeans experience migration and media. Although Anderson (1991) developed the concept of "imagined communities" based on an analysis of territorial nations, this concept is often used to frame the scholarly discussion of minority, mobility, and diasporic cultures of migration and media (Appadurai, 1996; de Leeuw and Rydin, 2007a; Georgiou, 2007c; Bailey, 2007; Sinclair and Cunningham, 2001; Tsagarousianou, 2004).

The Minority Paradigm

Minority and National Forms of Imagination

Around the same time as, and in the same territories (in particular, North America) where, print media facilitated the surfacing of "national consciousness" (Anderson, 1991, Chapter 2–3), the establishment of minority media infrastructures enabled a conscious, minority form of imagination of the nation. From the eighteenth to the mid-twentieth centuries, thousands of European foreign-language newspapers, publishing in tens of languages, were introduced to the United States, Canada, and Australia (Zubrzycki, 1958). These newspapers covered news pertaining to immigrants' countries of origin (e.g., Southern and Eastern European countries such as the former

Austria-Hungary and Poland), countries of settlement, and the world; however, they were (increasingly) oriented toward news in countries of settlement, such as America and Britain (Zubrzycki, 1958). The survival of these newspapers depended on the sustained inflow of first-generation immigrants (Zubrzycki, 1958).

If we compare Anderson's and Zubrzycki's historical accounts of early national and foreign-language newspapers, we see that in both cases, "the very conception of the newspaper implies the refraction of even 'world events' into a specific imagined world of vernacular readers" (Anderson, 1991, p. 63). The readers of a newspaper share in a "specific imagined world," a world that is constructed in the language and content of the newspaper.

Influential studies of historical and contemporary forms of minority media point to the creation of a "specific imagined world" through minority media. This idea is evident in the claim that immigrant-specific socialization into the country of settlement is the "principal function" (Zubrzycki, 1958, p. 77) and significance of minority media (Zhou and Cai, 2002).

For example, Zubrzycki argues that foreign-language newspapers served primarily to integrate new immigrants into their country of settlement by using a familiar language to teach them about "good citizenship" in the country of settlement (Zubrzycki, 1958, p. 77). Similarly, Zhou and Cai argue that Chinese-language media in the United States encourages an "immigrant community"-specific orientation toward upward socioeconomic mobility in the country of settlement, as well as the adoption of new lifestyle routines and behavior associated with the country of settlement (Zhou and Cai, 2002). Chinese-language media in the United States also provide new immigrants with a "roadmap . . . to navigate unknown and foreign territories" by offering practical advice on housing, employment, and education in the country of settlement (Zhou and Cai, 2002, p. 435). As for Russian-speaking Jews in Israel:

> the Russian-language media played a central role in their process of settling in, since they provided them with a symbolic anchor to be clung to during the period of rapid changes resulting from the immigration to a new country, thus contributing to their sense of psychological comfort and wellbeing.
>
> (Elias, 2008, p. 144)

These studies show that minority media offers a distinctive service to first-generation immigrants by advising them about life in the country of settlement and easing their transition to life in this country. Minority media is beneficial because it promotes assimilation,[1] "the narrowing of differences between immigrants and the native-born majority population in certain aspects of social life" (Bloemraad, Korteweg, and Yurdakul, 2008, p. 163). By addressing new residents' relative deficits in information and sense of stability, minority media enables a temporary form of imagination of the nation, an imagination that is essential in the early stages of settlement but that becomes progressively irrelevant as immigrants assimilate into the country of settlement.

Today, *Meld Magazine* is an example of minority media for Singaporean and other international students in Melbourne, Australia. Continuing the tradition of minority media in its functions and content, *Meld Magazine* targets first-generation immigrants, in this case international students in Melbourne. The magazine addresses "the need to provide relevant news and information to international students who make up a sizable community in Victoria" (Meld Magazine, 2015). It also aims to "help international students feel at home in Melbourne" by enabling them to communicate with the "local community" and by motivating them to "explore the city and greater Melbourne" (Meld Magazine, 2015). *Meld Magazine* not only facilitates international students' interaction with the local people and place; it also offers practical opportunities for international students to progress from education to employment by supporting them to "get a leg up in their careers" through voluntary work experience with *Meld Magazine* (Meld Magazine, 2015).

Toward the end of his speech on November 20, 2014, President Obama said, "My fellow Americans, we are and always will be a nation of immigrants. We were strangers once, too" (Obama, 2014). The president conflated immigrants and nationals by imagining America in terms of generations of immigrants.

The idea that we can bridge the divide between illegal immigrants and citizens is also evident in American public opinion. In a 2013 Gallup poll, 88 percent of national adult respondents (87 percent of whom were born in the United States) favored "allowing illegal immigrants already in the country the opportunity to become U.S. citizens if they meet certain requirements over a period of time, including paying taxes and a penalty, passing a criminal background check and learning English" (Gallup, 2015). Similar percentages of non-Hispanic Whites (87 percent), Blacks (89 percent), and Hispanics (92 percent) favored this statement (Gallup, 2015).

The above studies of minority media, the case of *Meld Magazine*, President Obama's statement, and the Gallup poll result express common ideas: Minority and national experiences of migration and media are compatible, and immigrants may progressively become nationals within the "imagined community" (Anderson, 1991) of the country of settlement.

Research on minority media balances two considerations: we show how minority and national experiences are compatible, but we also raise awareness of the challenges we need to address if we are to ethically integrate minority voices within national imaginations. Such research can help minority media such as *Meld Magazine* work more effectively as they seek "to give international students a voice" and contribute to a more holistic representation of "the full picture of the overseas student experience" (Meld Magazine, 2015).

Newer research on minority media focuses on such a politics of imagination (Siapera, 2010, pp. 106–110). The nation is routinely constructed in national forms of mainstream media (Anderson, 1991; Billig, 1995). There are three challenges to minority representation within this construction of the nation: nonrepresentation (Morawska, 2008; Parker and Song, 2007), stereotypical misrepresentation (Alia and Bull, 2005, pp. 157–162), and limited self-representation "on one's own terms" (Silverstone and Georgiou, 2005, p. 437).

Mass forms of collective imagination may limit minority representation. Even when state media policies aim for multicultural public service broadcasting (e.g., in Australia), it may not be feasible to represent minority worldviews in national mass media without a critical mass of minority audiences (Sinclair and Cunningham, 2001). Even when minority groups represent themselves in minority mass media, they often do not communicate the needs and concerns of minority subgroups such as Muslim youth in Britain (Ahmed, 2006) and working-class Chinese women in the United States (Shi, 2009). Singaporean international students in Melbourne can include themselves in larger publics while raising more culturally specific issues by using a combination of minority media such as *Meld Magazine* as well as the media of Singaporeans of Victoria and its affiliated Singapore Students Societies.

The contested and changing realities of "mass" and "minority" imaginations (Madianou, 2005) are often simplified within established national and state frames. For example, in the United States, public opinion on immigration is mainly divided by racial category (White, Black, Latino, and Asian) and political affiliation (Democrat, Republican, and Independent). Who is the dominant group? Our instinctive answer might be American-born Whites; in contrast, immigrants and other races are often considered as "ethnic minorities." But although economic models show that immigration benefits the national economy, working-age lower- to middle-class White American men have been leaving the labor market in response to competition from immigrants (Frum, 2015). Given their White ethnicity and American citizenship, these men are usually subsumed within the mass American population. However, their experiences as a class minority are especially sensitive to immigration. If we are to accurately evaluate the national impact of immigration, we must account for how the benefits and costs of immigration are distributed across the national population, and how these benefits and costs are experienced across various types of social relations and "axes of differentiation" (Brah, 1996, pp. 13–14). The citizenship rights of individuals in the lower to middle classes require protection where immigration significantly increases the demand and competition for public goods that address basic needs (such as housing, health, transport, education, and employment).

By facilitating undocumented immigrants' access to work, President Obama acted in alignment with the general will of the "Latino community" (Latino Decisions, 2014). However, given that the president acted without the support of Congress, his actions did not represent the national will.

How socially equitable are the president's actions? On the one hand, these actions could benefit ethnic minority American citizens and legal permanent residents, by targeting their families and communities. On the other hand, these actions could make it harder for precariously employed American citizens and legal permanent residents to compete for jobs, especially in states with a high proportion of undocumented immigrants.

How do we value the distinctive relationship between minority and national cultures without over-emphasizing cultural difference? We might critique how we use language (e.g., signifiers of ethnicity) to distinguish members of minority groups from the dominant group in the nation (Lacatus, 2007; Mainsah, 2011; Ogan, 2001, p. 178). For example, a comparative study by Nickels and his colleagues (2009) found that British news on terrorism distinguishes between the Irish Republican Army and the Irish minority in Britain, but the distinctions between Muslim terrorist organizations and British Muslims are not as clearly presented. As a result, the news gives the impression that the Muslim minority is opposed to British culture and not part of the British national community (Nickels et al., 2009).

How might such an exclusionary discourse inform minority modes of national imagination? Minority subjects may internalize these negative representations (Mai, 2005). Those who affiliate themselves with one minority group may also act according to the exclusionary logic of these discourses and exclude people from other minority groups (Banaji and Al-Ghabban, 2006). In addition, being aware that exclusionary discourses can powerfully influence national public opinion (Aly, 2007), minority subjects might decide to efface signifiers of difference from the national culture (King and Mai, 2009) by conforming fully to national norms (Mai, 2005) or conforming in public but consuming minority media in private (Elias, 2008, p. 143; Morawska, 2008).

Exclusionary discourses can be especially harmful when they are not problematized by alternative perspectives. However, it may be challenging to access alternative perspectives when there is an "[im]balance of insider, outsider and collaborative representations" (Alia and Bull, 2005, p. 147) and when there is no dialogue between dominant and subaltern representations (Harindranath, 2007). Minority media can address this challenge by directly challenging exclusionary forms of national discourse and thereby enabling coalitions to form within national society (Kosnick, 2004). For example, the not-for-profit organization Transient Workers Count Too (TWC2) advocates for more inclusive policies and public opinion on migrant workers in Singapore through its engagement with policymakers, media organizations, employers, and schools (Transient Workers Count Too, 2011). TWC2 also comments on related news in Singapore and other countries like Qatar and Kuwait (Transient Workers Count Too, 2015a, 2015c).

"Long Distance Nationalism" and "Ethnicization"

President Obama initiated to reform immigration through two main actions: reinforce the policing of the United States-Mexico border, and help long-term undocumented residents to obtain legal rights to reside and work in the United States. We could say that President Obama planned to manage undocumented immigration through a differentiated strategy: keep nonresidents out of the country, remove short-term residents from the country, and assimilate long-term residents into the country.

How does living in a country inform our relationship with it?

We don't necessarily have to be in a country to participate in its politics and public events, especially when we can gather with fellow citizens abroad and establish a sense of connection with the nation through media. In response to the passing away of Singapore's founding Prime Minister Lee Kuan Yew on March 23, 2015, Overseas Singaporean organizations collaborated to organize public memorial events across Australia (Singapore High Commission in Canberra, 2015, March 22 to April 7 posts). Overseas Singaporeans in Australia also gathered to watch the state funeral of the late leader, which was streamed live through the Singapore Prime Minister's Office YouTube channel (Singapore High Commission in Canberra, 2015, March 22 to April 7 posts). We remembered the late leader on social media and on the international student news website *Meld Magazine* (K. Y. Wong, 2015), and we signed condolence books arranged by the Singapore High Commission in Canberra (Singapore High Commission in Canberra, 2015, March 22 to April 7 posts).

During a major national event like an election, we can decide who we want to represent us in government through overseas voting. Even though we do not live within the geographical boundaries of our countries of origin, we can construct an "imagined heimat" (p. 11) and express our relationship with it as we participate in its politics (Anderson, 1992). Benedict Anderson (1992) conceptualizes this form of national imagination as "long distance nationalism."

The Italian Parliament has established this form of national imagination by creating electorates outside Italy. Having inherited Italian citizenship, Italian citizens who do not live in Italy can participate formally in politics in Italy by exercising their voting rights. The 2006 Italian national elections proved that long-distance nationalism can have a major influence on national politics: "For the first time in Italian history, representatives of Italian citizens resident outside Italy arguably held the balance of power in the Italian Senate" (Arcioni, 2006, p. 2).

Arcioni's (2006, p. 2) experience of overseas voting in the Italian election demonstrates how we might practice long-distance nationalism through various forms of communication and media platforms. Prior to the election, the Italian government and political parties helped overseas Italians to know how to vote and whom to vote for, through public information, mass advertising, and interpersonal communication:

> Leading up to the election, material was sent to me by post. In addition to official information regarding the election process, in both English and Italian, I also received printed electoral advertising from the two main coalition groups vying for my vote, as well as phone calls asking whether I needed any further assistance.
>
> (Arcioni, 2006, p. 3)

The Italians in Australia could gather information about the election from diverse sources—print publicity in the local neighborhood, the multicultural public service broadcasting of the country of settlement, online news from the country of origin, and discussions within the local segment of the diaspora:

> Living in a part of Australia with a noticeable Italo-Australian population, the official channels of communication were added to by posters on streets and in shop windows. I received further information from occasional reference to the SBS [Special Broadcasting Service, the Australian multicultural public service broadcaster] television broadcast of Italian news, Italian newspapers available online and discussions with fellow dual citizens in Australia.
>
> Finally, the voting papers arrived.... The ballot papers were posted and I and the world waited for the result.
>
> (Arcioni, 2006, p. 4)

Arcioni's account of overseas voting shows how a minority community in a country of settlement can be constructed as an extraterritorial constituency of the imagined heimat of a country of origin. This segment of the imagined heimat may be defined by bilingual and interpersonal communication (and not just imagined relations) with "fellow dual citizens" in the "noticeable Italo-Australian population."

Although we do not need to physically be in a country to participate in its politics, our physical presence and absence do inform how we imagine this country and how we participate in it. If we compare Anderson's concepts of "imagined communities" (1991) and "long distance nationalism" (1992), we can speculate that as we live in a country, we may progressively develop a greater stake in it and become more likely to personally invest in it.

In our country of settlement, our corporeal and mediated modes of national imagination are mutually referencing, as we see the place we live in represented in the media, and see others around us consuming national media (Anderson, 1991). We develop such a strong sense of community with our co-nationals that we are willing to make personal sacrifices, even to put our lives at risk (Anderson, 1991), for example, when we act as part of a national army in international conflict.

In contrast, we mainly experience and act on our geographically distant country of origin through media. The geographical distance may be a comfortable distance that allows us to act without having to experience the personal costs and consequences of our actions:

> His political participation is directed towards an imagined heimat in which he does not intend to live, where he pays no taxes, where he cannot be arrested, where he will not be brought before the courts and

> where he does not vote: in effect, a politics without responsibility or accountability.
>
> (Anderson, 1992, p. 11)

We might be tempted to apply this critique to those of us who have left Singapore (whether temporarily or permanently) but who continue to comment on its public issues. However, in relation to territories such as Singapore where the capacities to communicate and act on public issues are significantly restricted by political, legal, and cultural mechanisms, we may only be able to safely and freely participate from a position of geographical distance. Cherian George, a highly regarded academic who researches, teaches, and comments on political communication in Singapore, relocated to Hong Kong in 2014 after his contract with Nanyang Technological University (NTU) in Singapore ended following the repeated denial of tenure (George, 2014). From Singapore to other parts of the world, many media organizations, academics, students, and other members of the public communicated about George's experience of NTU's tenure process (Kuek, 2013). Many people called for George to be granted tenure, believing that he had been unjustly denied tenure on political rather than academic grounds, and that this denial of tenure raised issues of academic freedom in Singapore (K. Han, 2013). Reaffirming "my sense of belonging to my country [and] my vocation," George described his new appointment in Hong Kong as "a move that will let me continue my journalism research, teaching and advocacy while remaining in Asia. . . . I can't do so in my homeland" (George, 2014).

How do different segments of our population (e.g., resident citizens, overseas citizens, permanent residents, temporary residents, and undocumented residents) contribute to our society in exchange for rights such as residency, employment, and voting? How should different segments of our population contribute to our society in exchange for their rights?

"Long distance nationalism" (Anderson, 1992) can be based on nonreciprocal relations to the country of origin—we can choose to act toward our countries of origin without being vulnerable to the effects of our political action or inaction. However, the risk of political action increases as we establish our lives and relationships in a country, invest our material possessions (e.g., cash, assets, and taxes) in its economy, and subject ourselves to keep all its laws or pay penalties for breaking them.

But although we mainly experience our countries of origin through media, we are likely to also experience it corporeally. Mediated and corporeal mobilities are interdependent (Urry, 2007, p. 47), and corporeal mobility has become a lifestyle of "both rich and even for some poor" (p. 4).

Whereas we used to view migration patterns as linear, unidirectional, and finite, today we observe "a more complex range of patterns, which includes seasonal, itinerant, recurrent, and incessant movements" (Papastergiadis, 2010, pp. 246–247). The emergent trend of super commuting (Bearce) and the practice of fly-in fly-out (FIFO Families) show that for many people, "shuttling between two or more places plays a significant role in the contemporary condition of working and social life" (cf. Papastergiadis, 2010, p. 247). Social and mobile networking enables us to keep in touch and to complete tasks when we regularly spend a lot of time on long-distance travel.

In the nineteenth century, we started to imagine the societies we live in as nations (Anderson, 1991). National imagination was shaped within a print media system (Anderson, 1991) and in a context where people migrated from "dynastic states (which were not primarily defined in either national or ethnic terms) towards still new, still labor-scarce republics" (Anderson, 1992, p. 9).

Transformation in this context of media and migration enabled "long-distance nationalism" to emerge (Anderson, 1992). As nation-states were established worldwide, we could now perceive migration as relocation from one "nation-state" to another; as national modes of identification increased, we could now negotiate between multiple "nationalities" (in particular, nationalities associated with our countries of origin and settlement); and with the advancement of electronic communication technologies, we could now simultaneously communicate with social relations in our countries of origin (Anderson, 1992).

"Long distance nationalism" was our response not only to this global transformation, but also to transformation at a local level (Anderson, 1992). At the local level of the nation-state, "long distance nationalism" was our direct response to the "ethnicization of…nationalities" (Anderson, 1992, pp. 9–11), the increasing perception and construction of national modes of identification in ethnic terms. As we construct our identities between multiple nationalities, "the emphasis has been shifting from, say, Irish-*American* to *Irish*-American" (Anderson, 1992, p. 10, original emphasis).

Together, "long distance nationalism" and "ethnicization" (Anderson, 1992) constitute a particular mode of imagining our countries of origin and settlement in relation to each other. More generally, "long distance nationalism-ethnicization" is a way of imagining the geographically distant in relation to the geographically proximate.

We can use various forms of media and communication to practice long-distance nationalism. For example, we might use the phone, fax, email, and video to discuss political issues with people we know personally (Anderson, 1992, p. 7).

Historical research on migration and media shows that we have constructed an "imagined heimat" (Anderson, 1992, p. 11) through minority and diasporic media, personal technologies of self-representation (e.g., diaries), and mass technologies of communication (e.g., radio). For example, in the nineteenth century, an Irish-New Zealand minority was conscious of events in Ireland and of a worldwide Irish diaspora as they consumed Irish literature, which was published worldwide and advertised in the Irish newspaper in New Zealand (Molloy, October 2003–October 2004). In addition, in the early twentieth century, Russian exiles in China wrote personal diaries that positioned Russia within a European political geography, the Soviet Union and China within an Asian political geography, and the city of Harbin in China as a Russian colonial outpost (Hsu, 2010). Also, since 1932, a South Asian version of "imperial…imaginings" has been negotiated through the BBC World Service (Gillespie, Pinkerton, Baumann, and Thiranagama, 2010, p. 16).

These examples all show how territorially situated ethnic groups (Irish-New Zealand, Russian-Chinese, and South Asian) have been constructed within broader globalized political networks (e.g., national, regional, and colonial), networks that are centered on geographically distant territories (Ireland, Russia, and Britain).

Is "long distance nationalism" only a response to "ethnicization" (cf. Anderson, 1992, pp. 9–11)? Will we discover other coexistent, complementary, and/or contradictory relationships between "long distance nationalism" and "ethnicization" (Anderson, 1992)?

More recent studies focus on how we represent and promote an "exilic" imagination of the nation through the mass media technology of television (Johnson, 2010; Naficy, 2003).

Different types of "minority television" reflect different spaces of production, distribution, and reception: "ethnic television" is produced by indigenous minorities; "transnational television" is imported from a geographically distant country of origin; whereas "diaspora television" is produced in the country of residence but positioned between the countries of residence and origin (Naficy, 2003, pp. 51–53).

These spaces are both local and global, since these types of "minority television" reflect "centralized global broadcasting" and "decentralized global narrowcasting" models of television (Naficy, 2003, p. 51). For instance,

> diaspora television, to which Middle Eastern programmes primarily belong, is an example of the decentralised global narrowcasting model. The programmes are produced in diaspora, usually by local, independent, minority entrepreneurs for consumption by a small, cohesive population which, because of its diaspora status, is cosmopolitan, multicultural and multilingual. Such decentralised narrowcasting is thus simultaneously local and global.
>
> (Naficy, 2003, p. 53)

Broadcasting reaches mainstream audiences, whereas narrowcasting reaches niche audiences:

> Even though ethnic television networks . . . are primarily focused on the cultural concerns and personalities of segments of the USA population, they also reach mainstream audiences because their programmes are delivered in English. As such, ethnic television is a form of 'broadcasting'. Transnational and diaspora television, on the other hand, are examples of 'narrowcasting' because they are aired in foreign languages, which limits their reach considerably.
>
> (Naficy, 2003, pp. 52–53)

From a national perspective that takes the country of residence as its reference point, we can distinguish "ethnic television" from "transnational" and "diaspora television" by the language of its programs, by whether or not programs are communicated in the national language or in "foreign" languages.

We tend to view migration as a phenomenon that we experience between nations, between particular countries of origin and settlement. However, migration is a globalized phenomenon that is constitutive of imagination of the nation. It is often overlooked that Anderson (1991) developed his concept of "imagined communities" in the context of settler colonialism. Yet "national consciousness" emerged in territories shaped by colonial migration (Anderson, 1991). In other words, territorial nations were imagined in an early globalized context of migration (cf. Bayart, 2007; Papastergiadis, 2000).

We often assume that we belong primarily to nations, to our countries of origin and settlement. But with the shift from mass to networked communication in advanced globalization, our social relations look less like "imagined communities" (cf. Anderson, 1991); rather, they are "materially constructed" from common aspects of "history, geography, language, and environment" in a mediated "global network society" (Castells, 2009, p. 69).

The Transnational Paradigm

Whereas the minority paradigm tends to focus on social life in and from the country of settlement, the transnational paradigm broadens our perspective of migration by showing how we extend and negotiate social relations across two or more societies. Whereas the minority paradigm looks at our experiences of immigration and resettlement, the transnational paradigm helps us to understand our experiences of "transmigration"—the development of "simultaneous embeddedness" and transnational connections in and across at least two societies through migration (Glick Schiller, Basch, and Szanton Blanc, 1995, p. 48).

The transnational paradigm is especially relevant for thinking about the position of international students within Singapore-Australia diplomatic relations. At the end of June 2015, Singapore and Australia signed a Comprehensive Strategic Partnership (CSP) that outlined our plans to strengthen bilateral relations over the next ten years. In his comments on the CSP, Australian Prime Minister Tony Abbott said that through the significant participation of Singaporeans and Australians in international education, Singapore and Australia have developed close links that can extend into other spheres such as defense:

> I want to see an intimate defence partnership with Australia and Singapore and I know that building on the very long educational relationship that Singaporeans have had with Australia, and the much newer but rapidly deepening educational relationship that Australians have had with Singapore, that our two peoples will walk arm in arm into a brighter future.
>
> (Australian Broadcasting Corporation, 2015)

Since the 1990s, a substantial field of research on migration and transnationalism has been addressing the relationship between migration and cross-border phenomena in economic, political, social, cultural, and religious spheres (Ho, 2008a; Levitt and Jaworsky, 2007). But although many of us integrate media deeply into our experiences of business, politics, society, culture, and religion, the field of migration studies rarely investigates how we sustain diverse cross-border relations through media and communication technologies (but see Vertovec, 2004 for an exception).

How do we use different types of media (e.g., mass, interpersonal, online, digital, social, and mobile media) to create our lives in and across multiple societies? How do we use media in everyday life, as well as during planned and unexpected major events such as elections and crises? How do we combine the use of mass transport (such as air travel and international shipping) and communications technologies, to establish transnational "grass-roots" practices of caring for dependents and sustaining connections across multiple societies (Madianou and Miller, 2013; Portes, Guarnizo, and Landolt, 1999)? How do we use media to cultivate our perceptions of "multi-locality" (Vertovec, 1999, pp. 450–451) and to "(re)construct[ ] 'place'" (pp. 455–456)?

Singapore-Australia organizations such as the Singapore-Western Australia Network (SWAN) might address these questions as they aim to develop relationships between Singaporeans and Australians through mediated events such as Singapore Film Festivals (Singapore-Western Australia Network, SWAN, 2015).

Whereas migration studies have explored transnationalism in a wide range of economic, political, social, cultural, and religious spheres (Levitt and Jaworsky, 2007), research on the relevance of media for transmigration often focuses on our changing experiences of cultural space (Aksoy and Robins, 2003g; Georgiou, 2005a, 2005e; Gillespie, 1995; Ogan, 2001). Through this research, we have gained insight into the cultural politics we engage in when we define and structure national and transnational spaces:

> The growing visibility of diasporas, as expressed in their numerical presence, but even more so in their cultural practices and the development of projects of cultural particularity and expression, challenge ideologies of cultural homogeneity and imaginings of ethnic and cultural hierarchies in national and transnational spaces.... Transnational media become outlets and means for transporting and translating ideologies and cultural repertoires beyond bounded physical places.
>
> (Bailey et al., 2007, pp. 2–3)

As we extend our media environments across multiple cultures, we can broaden our resources for self-expression and collective representation. By drawing on these resources, we can empower ourselves to "challenge... cultural hierarchies in national and transnational spaces" and to "open up new possibilities for expression and representation and thus of imagining the self and belonging within and across space" (Bailey et al., 2007, p. 2).

What spaces might we position ourselves in? How are these spaces related to one another? Chapter 5 details how Singaporean students in Melbourne rank places in the world and how their personal hierarchies of places are related to global geographies of media power.

We often process our experiences of migration and media by reflecting on and discussing the cultural differences between our countries of origin and settlement (de Leeuw and Rydin, 2007a). Although many of us use a wide range of media and prefer global commercial media, we tend to use these media to grow our relationships with people in our countries of origin and settlement (de Leeuw and Rydin, 2007a).

"Transnational Fields" Incorporating Countries of Origin and Settlement

We are all situated within a "social field"—"a set of multiple interlocking networks of social relationships through which ideas, practices, and resources are unequally exchanged, organized, and transformed" (Levitt and Glick Schiller, 2004, p. 1009). Through migration and media, we extend these unequal connections and flows across territorial borders. Within these networks, we relate with a variety of actors, including different types of states, social institutions, and groups (Levitt and Glick Schiller, 2004, pp. 1023–1024). Whether we have experienced migration first-hand or second-hand, we construct and inhabit these spaces through "ways of being" ("social relations and practices") and "ways of belonging" (more specific practices that express conscious identification with a collective) (Levitt and Glick Schiller, 2004, p. 1010).

We shape our "social fields" (Levitt and Glick Schiller, 2004) as we negotiate our social relations with other actors. We hold different positions in our "social fields" and relate with one another unequally, depending on the power we have relative to one another, the extent to which we consciously relate with one another, our motives for developing our social relations, the extent to which our relations are institutionalized, and our modes of experiencing the "social field" (e.g., through media, as well as through first-hand and second-hand experiences of migration).

Our countries of origin and settlement can both benefit from their connection in "transnational social fields" (Levitt and Glick Schiller, 2004). Incorporation into countries of origin and settlement can be complementary (Portes, Escobar, et al., 2009), for example, through "co-development" (Faist and Fauser, 2011).

In a speech to 300 Singaporeans in Beijing in July 2015, Singapore's President Tony Tan said that the growth in bilateral trade between Singapore and China "reflect[s] the ability of…Singaporeans to make an impact wherever we are" and "you play an important role in strengthening ties between Singapore and China with the bonds of friendship that you form here" (Teo, 2015). These statements recognize that Singaporeans can make a major contribution to economic growth in, between, and across both our countries of origin and settlement as we establish ourselves in positions of influence overseas.

Within "transnational social fields" (Levitt and Glick Schiller, 2004), particular polities may be especially significant because our relations with them are institutionalized. A major institutionalized relation that informs our experiences of migration and media is citizenship, which is both a legal and an affective relation to a society (Ho, 2008a). How do we think and feel about different types of legal membership, such as citizenship and residency? What does it mean to be a legal member of multiple polities, and how does our legal membership of one polity inform our legal membership of another?

If we view citizenship as an exclusive relation to a single state, it will be challenging to adapt it to our diverse relations with multiple states (Fox, 2005). But citizenship has been increasingly "transnationalized" as we have increased the overlap between the membership spaces of different states (Faist, 2010c, p. 17).

Although dual citizenship is currently recognized in Australia but not in Singapore, the membership spaces of the two states are increasingly overlapping. Singaporean is one of only eight nationalities (including Australian) which are eligible for automated passport processing at Australian airports (Australian Government Department of Immigration and Border Protection), and Australian Prime Minister Tony Abbott stated in June 2015 that "I want to see Australians and Singaporeans with the same kind of work and residency situation in our two countries as Australians and New Zealanders have long had" (Chong, 2015).

We bring the membership spaces of different states together by creating a "citizenship constellation"—a "citizenship opportunity structure" in which we are legally bound to multiple political units through migration and "political integration" (Bauböck, 2010). Within "citizenship constellations," political units may be "nested" (Bauböck, 2010, p. 856) at different scales (e.g., municipality, state, federal, and supranational).

How do we define our personal "citizenship constellations" (Bauböck, 2010)? How does our membership of multiple polities inform our "citizenship opportunity structures" (Bauböck, 2010)? How do our perceptions of different "citizenship opportunity structures" inform our experiences of migration?

In post-Yugoslavian Croatia, Serbia, and Macedonia, we can discern two definitions of transnational citizenship: "post-territorial nationalism" and "territorial, multi-ethnicism" (Ragazzi and Balalovska, 2011). According to "post-territorial nationalism," citizenship is based on ethnicity, not residence; it is transnational in that it is extended to co-ethnics who reside in different countries (Ragazzi and Balalovska, 2011, p. 2). In contrast, "territorial, multi-ethnicism" defines citizenship based on residence, not ethnicity; it is transnational in that it is extended to residents regardless of their ethnicity, based on a logic of pluralism (Ragazzi and Balalovska, 2011, pp. 2, 22). According to "post-territorial nationalism," one cannot gain or lose citizenship through migration; however for "territorial multi-ethnicism," one can change one's citizenship through migration.

Where particular countries have been connected through mass migration, transnational media networks have also been institutionalized. For example, transnational economies have been established between particular countries of origin and settlement (e.g., United States-Mexico, United Kingdom-India, Germany-Turkey, etc.) in response to the high demand for calls among family members who are distributed across these countries (Vertovec, 2004).

Whereas we have historically used ethnic media to cultivate our orientation toward the country of settlement (Zhou and Cai, 2002; Zubrzycki, 1958), we are increasingly using ethnic media to position ourselves in relation to both countries of origin and settlement. However, our use of ethnic media reflects different levels and forms of transnational engagement. For example, whereas Chinese and Korean communities in the United States prefer news about their home countries, Latino communities in the United States have more transnational connections and a greater preference for "transnational news, defined here as news that has implications for both home and the host countries" (W.-Y. Lin, Song, and Ball-Rokeach, 2010, p. 210).

In contrast to Chinese and Korean media in the United States, Latino media in the United States represent a larger transnational news space. This is because compared to China and Korea, Latin America is geographically closer to the United States (W.-Y. Lin, Song, et al., 2010, p. 224). Over a long period of time, Latinos have been migrating and communicating between Latin America and the United States, establishing a "transnational field" that incorporates Latin America and the United States (Basch, Glick Schiller, and Szanton Blanc, 1994; Portes, Escobar, et al., 2009; Rouse, 1991; Vertovec, 2004).

Are we more likely to incorporate geographically proximate places into our constructions of transnational space? Maybe geographical distance is becoming less relevant for our connections to one another as we invent and adopt new technologies for travel and communication.

On the other hand, we are also likely to reinforce existing transnational networks, rather than create new ones. Perhaps the transnational networks of geographically proximate places are more established, having been founded in older environments of migration and media when geographical distance significantly limited the extent to which we could connect to one another.

Contemporary ethnic media incorporate particular countries into a "transnational field" (Levitt and Glick Schiller, 2004) in different ways, for example through their content, their operations, and how they are interpreted. Ethnic media in the United States cover news that impacts both the countries of origin and settlement (W.-Y. Lin, Song, et al., 2010). Chinese-language media in Australia operate in a transnational policy context, evolving in response to China's policy of cultural globalization and Australia's policy of multiculturalism (Sun, Yue, Sinclair, and Gao, 2011). Even though ethnic media may be branded as representing minorities who are completely situated in their country of settlement, they may actually be interpreted as expressing positions in the cultural politics of both the countries of origin and settlement (Kosnick, 2007).

Our transnational social spaces often reflect the places where we live, as well as the places where our parents and grandparents have lived. In addition to particular countries of origin and settlement, we may incorporate other places into a "transnational field" (Levitt and Glick Schiller, 2004), for example, by living in multiple countries or by experiencing multiple countries through media.

Premigration "Aspiration" to Potential Countries of Resettlement

How do we use media before and after migration? Most of the research on migration and media explores how we use media after migration. However, a few studies reveal how we use media to imagine life in a geographically distant place and to encourage migration. Governments and universities can use the findings of such studies to inform the design of marketing strategies that are effective in attracting immigrants and international students.

Many of us first became aware of foreign places through transnational media. We then projected ourselves in these places and aspired to migrate there. Using the "diasporic function" (Mai, 2005, p. 552) of transnational media, we inspired ourselves to create a "migratory project," a plan to migrate for self-actualization (Mai, 2004).

We see many foreign places through media. Why do we decide to migrate to some of these places, and not others? Migration occurs between places with different levels of "symbolic power," from symbolic peripheries to symbolic centers (Sabry, 2004, p. 2). When places are more prominently and positively represented in everyday media, we are more likely to perceive them as more attractive migration destinations.

When there is mass migration between particular countries, transnational media networks are often established across these countries. Within these networks, the country of settlement is well represented in the media environment of the country of origin, encouraging chain migration. Many Albanians are motivated to migrate to Italy when they see Albanians in Italy represented in Italian media (Mai, 2004). Following a similar logic, Cuban-American exilic media represent Cuban-American identity as a more authentic, actualized, and therefore preferred version of Cuban national identity, in order to invite Cubans to migrate to America (Johnson, 2010).

But we cannot assume that media representation of place is related to aspiration to migrate. We may be more aware of places that are represented more often in media. We may have a more positive opinion of places that are represented more positively in media. But we may not plan to migrate to these places.

We interpret media representations of place in relation to our personal situations. As young adults in Japan view foreign media representations of the "imagined West," some choose to migrate to "the popular, contemporary West" of America, whereas others select the "cultural, classical West" of Europe (Fujita, 2004). These people aspire to migrate to different destinations in order to realize their different personal goals for socioeconomic status (Fujita, 2004).

Research on media and aspiration to migrate enables us to understand how we use media to construct potential places of settlement, within a transnational space of migration. We unequally position these places in our personal maps of the world, depending on our personal situations as well as how places are positioned in migration trends and global media structures. Chapter 5 shows how Singaporean students in Melbourne perceive distant places through media, and elaborates on how Andrew, a Singaporean student in Melbourne, has developed a strong motivation to migrate to Japan through Japanese media.

Postmigration Familiarity to Country of Origin

Having migrated, we use media to maintain our connection with what is familiar. As we use transnational media to access familiar content in a new setting, we incorporate both old and new places of representation and reception into a transnational space of experience.

We experience migration as a sustained "disturbance of lifeworlds," as corporeal relocation from a familiar environment to a less familiar one (Moores, 2007, p. 16). But by effectively incorporating media technologies such as satellite television into our everyday routines, we can keep accessing and enjoying updated images of the environments we are familiar with (Aksoy and Robins, 2003a; Karanfil, 2007). When Turkish migrants consume media from Turkey, they consider how familiar their experiences are compared to their previous experiences in Turkey (Aksoy and Robins, 2003a; Karanfil, 2007). Migrants' consumption of media from the country of origin may reflect notions of familiarity rather than perceptions of segregation and integration in the country of settlement (Trebbe, 2007).

Singaporeans who have migrated to Australia can continue to access Singapore newspapers and the TV news channel *Channel NewsAsia* through their websites. For Singaporeans who are used to reading Singapore print newspapers, the *Straits Times* and *Today* websites even offer "print editions" of the news in PDF format. These "print editions" simulate the appearance of the print newspaper and the preferred reading experience of "itching to flip a page" (The Straits Times Print Edition, 2015).

However, we can only partially sustain our premigration experiences through transnational media. The satellite television programs that migrant audiences view are often "displaced broadcast television" (Sinclair and Cunningham, 2001, p. 28), originally produced and distributed not for a diasporic audience but for a mass audience who resides in the territory of the original broadcast (Morley, 2000, Chapter 5). Compared to local audiences in the country of origin, diasporic audiences are likely to experience greater disjuncture between the spaces that are represented in media and the spaces where media are received (Aksoy and Robins, 2003a). Content that is broadcast on free-to-air television in Singapore is also available online through the Toggle platform, but users who are not geographically located in Singapore cannot access some of this content as a result of geoblocking.

Although we can now use transnational media to be aware of changes in our geographically distant countries of origin, we may find it difficult to adjust to these changes (Karanfil, 2007). We may experience these adjustment difficulties especially if we have not been keeping up to date with our countries of origin through return visits or media (Karanfil, 2007). In previous generations of migration and media, it was much more challenging to keep up to date with transformation in a geographically distant country of origin (Karanfil, 2007, pp. 67–68) and to deeply engage with it (Hall, in Hall and Werbner,

2008, pp. 349–350). In order to maintain a sense of familiarity after migration, we used to develop nostalgic relations to our countries of origin by maintaining unchanging mental images of homeland (Karanfil, 2007). But these idealized mental images of homeland are problematized in a "process of de-mythologization" when, later on, we are able to view updated images of our countries of origin through media technologies such as satellite television (Aksoy and Robins, 2003a, p. 95). We may already feel disconnected from our countries of origin, having experienced departure and a sense of geographical distance. These feelings of disconnection can be exacerbated when we perceive that the television images of our countries of origin are unfamiliar (Karanfil, 2007).

The Diaspora Paradigm

We draw relationships between spaces at different scales ("the local," "the national," and "the transnational") in our maps of the "triangular spatial context of diasporic belonging:...the host country,...the country of origin and the global diasporic community" (Georgiou, 2005e, p. 47). The minority paradigm focuses on local-national relations in the host country; the transnational paradigm broadens our perspective to consider transnational relations between the host country and the country of origin; and the diaspora paradigm expands our sense of community to include national and transnational relations within a global diaspora.

"Diasporic Nationalism" in Configurations of Media and Geographical Spaces

The European Union has just introduced a new version of Erasmus, its popular program for overseas study, training, and work. Erasmus promises to help participants develop an international worldview, to "improve their foreign language skills and develop greater intercultural awareness" (European Commission, 2014, p. 4).

We can use statistics to obtain a general overview of Erasmus participants' transnational practices, such as the use of more than one language, mobility between countries, and participation in international exchange. But how do these participants experience learning and life abroad? How are their overseas experiences relevant for their perspectives on culture and cultural diversity—national, regional, and global?

It may be inaccurate to infer from an observation of transnational practices that international, intercultural, and/or transnational worldviews are being developed. On the contrary, we may respond to experiences of transnationalism and cultural difference by cultivating an imagination of a global, ethnic nation, an imagination which Youna Kim conceptualizes as "diasporic nationalism":

> Diasporic nationalism . . . emerges as reactionary ethno-nationalism within global knowledge diasporas of those who appear to be bilingual cross-cultural negotiators moving regularly between different cultures and participating in exchanges across national borders.
>
> (Kim, 2011, p. 136)

We may imagine that we participate in a global ethnic nation when we feel that we are excluded from others, marginalized, and unable to express ourselves in our new countries (Kim, 2011). As the Internet is a technology with "simultaneously dis-embedding and re-embedding capacities," we can use it not only to create a comfortable distance from the challenging environments we are immersed in, but also to connect selectively to familiar environments across geographical distance (Kim, 2011, p. 133).

We use the Internet not just as a "tool," but as a "distinct new environment of connectivity," when we create online networks that extend across "peripheries" and bypass the "centre," connecting with mostly overseas rather than resident co-nationals within national communities (Hanafi, 2005, pp. 582–584). For example, although the Overseas Singaporean Portal ("Overseas Singaporean Portal," 2015) has been set up by the Singapore government to preserve Overseas Singaporeans' affection for Singapore, it does so mainly by networking Overseas Singaporeans with one another through stories, events, and a database of "Overseas Singaporean Organisations," rather than by connecting Overseas Singaporeans with Singaporeans in Singapore.

We can also view online spaces such as the Twitter thread #singaporean as "cyber-place[s]" (Parham, 2004, p. 205), the online presence of national civic spaces, where some of us may debate our relations to our national societies.

We use media to connect not only with others who have migrated from the same country of origin, but also with people with different types of migration experience. Whether we consider ourselves "pre-migrant," "post-migrant," or "settled migrant," we can develop a sense of community based on our shared experiences and cultural knowledge of language and places of previous residence and/or birth (Hiller and Franz, 2004).

If we consider different media platforms as distinctive technologies of "simultaneous dis-embedding and re-embedding" (Kim, 2011, p. 133) and spaces of connectivity, we might want to explore different configurations of geographical and media spaces. For example, we might investigate how we converge the Internet and other media platforms (e.g., in our use of Internet television, social media, social television, and mobile Internet) to create different types of "online territories" (Christensen, Jansson, and Christensen, 2011) that reflect:

> the extensions and reconfigurations of pre-existing means of territorialization . . . as well as the potential for new types of social territories to take shape, enabled by online connectivity and sociability.
>
> (Christensen et al., 2011, p. 5)

The social spaces we create are likely to vary depending on which media and geographical places we bring together. What relationships do we create between media spaces and geographical places, between "cyber-place" and "geographic place" (Parham, 2004, pp. 204–205)?

We experience geographical places as social contexts (Parham, 2004) and contexts of corporeal experience (Alinejad, 2011; Hiller and Franz, 2004). Based on our perception that our country of origin is a shared context of corporeal experience, we refer to it to define the symbolic boundaries of our diasporic community (Alinejad, 2011; Hiller and Franz, 2004). For example, Iranians who live outside Iran use blogs to express "transnational embodiment," a form of imagination and affective relation to their geographically distant homeland that is informed by a sense of "embodied" or corporeal experience (Alinejad, 2011).

How do we shape exclusive and inclusive relations within our "citizenship constellations" (Bauböck, 2010), as we communicate about our corporeal experience and create connections between media and geographical places?

Distinctions between Diasporic and National Spaces

Whereas most studies of media and diaspora seek to discover the links between diasporic and national spaces, Hepp's concept of the "localities of diasporic communicative spaces" helps us to conceptualize diasporic spaces without necessarily referring to national coordinates.

"Diasporic communicative spaces" and their "localities of media appropriation" are "communicative thickenings" (Hepp, 2009a, pp. 329–331), particular confluences of communication networks and flows that have unclear and "disappearing" boundaries (Hepp, 2008, p. 41). "Diasporic communicative spaces" are spaces where we develop collective relations with our co-ethnics through communication. These spaces are "*transmedial*, i.e., articulated by the meshing of very different media" (Hepp, 2009a, p. 330, original emphasis). They should not be understood in terms of the "national community of origin," but as "deterritorial in the sense that they spread *across* different national territories and that their meaning horizon lies *beyond* a national territoriality" (Hepp, 2009a, p. 330, original emphasis).

"Localities of media appropriation" are the "material" bases that enable us to access "diasporic communicative spaces" (Hepp, 2009a). There are three types of "localities": the "domestic world," the "elsewhere" (predetermined places of routine media use outside the domestic world), and the "somewhere'" (ad hoc places of mobile media use) (Hepp, 2009a). Besides our own homes, we routinely access media at our educational institutions, workplaces, cafés, and the homes of our loved ones (Hepp, 2009a). We also use mobile media technologies (such as mobile phones and car radios) to create spaces "somewhere" where we communicate with locals we know personally and access ethnic content such as ethnic news and music (Hepp, 2009a).

By investigating the types of media spaces used in relation to migration, we can conceptualize diaspora in non-national terms, "as social figurations *of their own*" (Hepp, 2009a, p. 330, original emphasis).

We can also learn to critically relate with national spaces of "identity," "knowledge," and "society" by developing a transnational context of experience through migration and media (Aksoy and Robins, 2003g). This critical perspective is reflected in the ways transmigrants use media:

> Scepticism and experience of multiple belonging influences news consumption practices so that they differ significantly from those practiced by the majority population.
>
> (Christiansen, 2004, p. 189)

When our sense of belonging extends beyond a single country, we will have news needs that we cannot fully address through national news media, perceive that news coverage is limited, access a broader range of news sources (including national but especially transnational television), and use multiple sources to critically interpret national news (Christiansen, 2004).

There are three reasons why we are increasingly establishing our lives across countries: our countries have become more insecure in the context of "global restructuring of capital," we experience racial discrimination in our host societies, and we respond to "the nation building projects of both home and host society" (Glick Schiller et al., 1995, p. 50). Since migration and transnationalism are shaped by the contemporary context of neoliberal globalization (Glick Schiller et al., 1995; Glick Schiller and Çağlar, 2009), we must study how we experience migration and media within "global fields of power" (Glick Schiller and Çağlar, 2009).

Although we have situated migration and media in a worldwide context of globalization (see, e.g., W.-Y. Lin, Song, et al., 2010; Ong, 1999; Tsagarousianou, 2004), we have studied a limited range of social spaces, such as a worldwide distribution of sending and receiving societies. Thomas Faist rightly critiques our narrow view of migration and social space:

> While the impact of globalisation is often assumed to be universal and worldwide, approaches linked to the concepts of diaspora and transnationalism refer to phenomena that occur within the limited social and geographic spaces of a particular set of regions or states.
>
> (Faist, 2010a, p. 14)

When studying how we construct "boundaries" of social space, we need to be informed by not just concepts of the "transnational", but also "world" theories (Faist, 2010c). In this book, I analyze how, in our experiences of migration and media, we construct social spaces in relation to the global and the local. By examining our experiences of the global and the local rather than the nation and the state, I offer an alternative approach to the "methodological nationalism" that often informs "minority," "transnational," and "diaspora paradigms" of migration and media.

"Methodological Nationalism" in Concepts of Migration and Media

It is problematic to presume that social relations are coordinated within and between "nation-states" that are distinct and connected in an "international" system, to take for granted that "society" corresponds to the "nation-state" (Beck and Sznaider, 2006; Chernilo, 2007; A. Wimmer and Glick Schiller, 2003), and to assume that "modern society" is organized in terms of "the nation" and "the state" (Beck, 2006, p. 24).

We conceptualize this error as "methodological nationalism" when it is found in the "perspective of the scientific observer," and use the term "national outlook" when this error is evident in the view of other "social actors" (Beck, 2006, pp. 24, 27).

Ulrich Beck has defined the following "principles of methodological nationalism":

1. Each state encloses a society.
2. The world consists of state/societies. The boundaries of each state/society divide the "internal national" from the "external international."
3. We make general conclusions about "universal society" or global society based on what we know about a particular "national society" or based on an international comparison of "national societies."
4. We distinguish culture by its associated territorial boundaries. In doing so, we interpret cultural difference as cultural incompatibility.
5. Although polities and cultures have historically developed through mutual influence, we distinguish them based on their "essence."
6. We view "reality" in "either/or," rather than "both/and" categories. For example, an experience is either national or not.
7. Social relations are "either inside or outside," and cannot be "both inside and outside". (Beck, 2006, pp. 27–33)

Why do these expressions of "methodological nationalism" (Beck, 2006, pp. 27–33) reflect an inaccurate and limited view of the spaces where we relate with one another? It is not meaningful to locate our social relations in the "nation-state" by default, because what we call the "nation-state" has historically appeared in various forms and has been defined in various ways (Chernilo, 2006). We need to recognize and reveal the multiple, negotiated ways in which we have defined "society" and the "nation-state" as a specific concretization of society (Chernilo, 2006). Moreover, diverse visions of the nation-states are still being negotiated, so it is simplistic to conceptualize "*the* nation-state" as a singular, fixed, and "teleological" outcome of "nationalizing and homogenizing the population" (Brubaker, 2005, p. 10, original emphasis).

As a result of contemporary globalization, we have to update what we mean by the "nation-state" by illuminating "the transnationality that is arising inside [what we have conventionally described as] nation-states" (Beck and Sznaider, 2006, p. 9). In this book, I weave a discussion of Singaporeans' experiences of migration into a broader overview of how migration is experienced across the world, to offer alternative frameworks that we might consider as we redefine our national identities in the context of contemporary globalization.

We would still be thinking according to the logic of "methodological nationalism" if we assume that society used to be structured in terms of "nation-states" and viewed as such (Chernilo, 2006). So instead of saying that "[t]here is simply no way of turning the clock back to a world of sovereign nation-states and national societies" (cf. Beck and Sznaider, 2006, p. 10), I would like to discover how we view "society" and "space," and what we mean when we talk about "nation-states" and "national societies."

We have been moving beyond "methodological nationalism" (Beck, 2006, pp. 27–33) by developing transnational, diasporic, and globalization approaches to the study of migration:

> The study of diaspora, globalization and transnationalism has been pivotal in highlighting the significance of translocal processes, [although] a state-centred 'methodological nationalism'... has remained evident in many disciplines such as political science and development studies.
>
> (Knott and McLoughlin, 2010, p. 7)

However, to some extent, "the regional or transnational outlook is merely a variant of the national outlook" (Beck, 2006, p. 31). For example, although we often contrast "diaspora" with the "nation-state," we usually represent it in similar, "groupist" terms such as "community" or "identity," as a "non-territorial *form* of essentialized belonging" (Brubaker, 2005, pp. 11–12, original emphasis). It would be more productive to conceptualize diaspora as a "category of practice," a mode of constructing the identities and commitments of a population (Brubaker, 2005).

Our concept of "diaspora" is limited in helping us to think beyond "methodological nationalism" (Beck, 2006, p. 31), because of how we have based it on Anderson's (1991) concept of national societies as "imagined communities":

> 'Diaspora' is a category par excellence of the national imaginary, a category that subordinates the social world to the national logic. It is no surprise that the 'diasporic imagination' is isomorphic with the 'national imagination', we would say, for the ideal of 'imagined community' has been used as the basic template for capturing migrant experience and aspirations.
>
> (Aksoy and Robins, 2003g, p. 371)

The concept of "imagined communities" (Anderson, 1991) can inform the concept of "diaspora," but we have tended to apply it uncritically. With the exception of globalization approaches such as Appadurai's (1996) idea of "imagined worlds" and Georgiou's (2006) idea of a "hybrid imagined community," we have not discerned the limits of applying Anderson's (1991) concept of "imagined communities" to a different contemporary context of migration and media. For example, while Tsagarousianou recognizes that Anderson has developed his concept of "imagined communities" in a national context, she argues that "there is no reason why diasporas could not qualify as imagined communities too," given that they are formed through cultural homogenization and the definition of collective identity through discourse (Tsagarousianou, 2004, p. 60).

We conceptualize diaspora as a version of national society when we define diasporas as "deterritorialized nations" (Karim, 2007), associate diaspora with "double or ambivalent belonging" (Christiansen, 2004, p. 195), and write that "a relation to a homeland imagined as a bounded, geographical place with particular sites characterises diaspora identification" (Alinejad, 2011, p. 46).

"Methodological nationalism" (Beck, 2006, pp. 27–33) reflects "bound" rather than "unbound" "logics of seriality" (Anderson, 1998), categories that are closed and exclusive, rather than open and inclusive. Similar to national categories, diaspora is often imagined as a "bound series" (Anderson, 1998). In contrast, I would study social relations within a cosmopolitan worldview, the consciousness of being "a firmly local member of the unbounded series of the world-in-motion" (Anderson, 1998, pp. 131–132).

Whereas the minority, transnational, and diaspora paradigms tend to define social spaces in terms of "nation" and "state," a "cosmopolitan" paradigm helps us to understand social spaces as configurations of the global and the local. In the next chapter, I introduce my approach of "glocal cosmopolitanism" and my concept of social spaces as "relational glocalities," to address how we construct social spaces in our experiences of migration and media.

CHAPTER 2

Relational Glocalities

We have tended to view our experiences of migration and media with reference to "nation" and "state" spaces. With this focus in mind, we have not thought much about migration and media in the context of other social relations in the world.

However, the reality is that we experience migration and media in global society. We become aware of this reality especially when we debate how we address unauthorized maritime migration to Europe and Australia. How shall we respond when many people are risking and losing their lives as they flee to us for refuge? How shall we act in a way that simultaneously regards the universal moral values of human life and freedom, as well as international and national laws? How do our responses and actions reflect the ways we position ourselves in relation to global and local societies?

Different theories of globalization offer alternative ways of thinking about our relations with others as locally situated members of global society. In this chapter, I discuss how we can use these theories to develop a broader understanding of migration and media. Building on these theories, I conceptualize spaces of migration and media as "relational glocalities," and show how we can construct these spaces through an approach I call "glocal cosmopolitanism."

Global and Local Spaces

For a long time now, we have been developing worldwide relations and have been increasingly making media significant for our everyday lives (Krotz, 2008). These two processes of "globalization" and "mediatization" are independent, but they intertwine (Krotz, 2008). For example, we have used media to transform how we experience the world and relate with others in the world (Appadurai, 1996; Castells, 2000, 2010; Sassen, 2006; Tomlinson, 1999).

The concept of globalization enables us to reflect on how we develop a social space that is global in scale, broader in scope than local, national, and regional social spaces (Held, McGrew, Goldblatt, and Perraton, 2003, p. 67). Globalization is:

> a process (or set of processes) which embodies a transformation in the spatial organisation of social relations and transactions—assessed in terms of their extensity, intensity, velocity and impact—generating transcontinental or interregional flows and networks of activity, interaction and the exercise of power.
>
> (Held et al., 2003, p. 68)

We don't experience the global as a single space of society. Rather, we can define varieties of global social spaces by evaluating the relative reach, strength, speeds, and effects of our worldwide connections.

Global "Landscapes" of Flow and Local "Neighbourhoods"

We communicate global culture in and through the "disjunctures" between five "landscapes": "ethnoscapes," "mediascapes," "technoscapes," "financescapes," and "ideoscapes" (Appadurai, 1996). These global "landscapes" are constituted by global flows of persons, media technologies and images, technology, capital, and ideologies, respectively (Appadurai, 1996, pp. 33–37).

How do we relate these landscapes to one another in our maps of the world? Through migration, we position ourselves in "liminal placements in the interstices within and among nation-states" (Karim, 2010, p. 406), resulting in an overlap between particular "ethnoscapes" (Appadurai, 1996) and nation-states. If, from these positions, we want to efficiently and cost-effectively communicate within a group of co-nationals that is small but wide in geographical distribution, we might be motivated to be early adopters of new media technologies, such as Digital Broadcasting Satellite (DBS) in the 1990s (Karim, 2010). In this way, we might be encouraged to create new "mediascapes" when we experience an overlap between "ethnoscapes" and nation-states (cf. Appadurai, 1996).

As we adopt new media technologies to initiate transnational communication networks, we contribute to the transformation of global communication and promote "a self-reassessment on the part of the nation-state" (Karim, 2010, pp. 401, 406). Our "mediascapes" transform existing "ideoscapes" (cf. Appadurai, 1996).

In contrast to global "ethnoscapes," "neighbourhoods" are local "contexts" of "meaningful social action" (Appadurai, 1996,

p. 184). But "neighbourhoods" are also "ethnoscapes" (Appadurai, 1996, p. 182) in that they are not just "contexts" but also "context-generative"—the global ("ethnoscapes") is constructed in the "production" of the local ("neighbourhoods") (p. 184). We experience our "neighbourhoods" as "ethnoscapes" when we observe that the

> intensification of global mobility and interconnectedness has turned places...into spaces of juxtaposition and mixture, spaces where disparate cultures converge, collide, and grapple with each other, often in conditions of radical inequality.
>
> (Inda and Rosaldo, 2008, p. 5)

The construction of global "landscapes" and local "neighbourhoods" reflects the "production of locality" (Appadurai, 1996, Chapter 9), which is

> primarily relational and contextual rather than...scalar or spatial....a complex phenomenological quality, constituted by a series of links between the sense of social immediacy, the technologies of interactivity, and the relativity of contexts.
>
> (Appadurai, 1996, p. 178)

What are our experiences of "living in specific localities when more and more of [our] everyday lives are contingent on globally extensive social processes" (Inda and Rosaldo, 2008, p. 7)? Today, "localities, virtuality and sociality...would be the 'anchor-points' of a broad discussion about the new technologies of mediation, in their various applications" (Appadurai and Morley, 2011, p. 45) since we now produce "localities" in new types of virtual media environments (Appadurai and Morley, 2011, pp. 44–45) such as augmented realities enabled by mobile Internet.

In chapter 1, I showed that when we think through the "minority paradigm," we cultivate our awareness of how migration may challenge the participation of some of us in national society. The minority paradigm focuses our attention on addressing how we promote inclusive and full participation in national politics, culture, and society.

In contrast, Appadurai's (1996) concepts of global "landscapes" of flow and local "neighbourhoods" helps us to realize that migration and media are major flows that constitute spaces that are simultaneously global and local. These concepts reflect the "mobilities paradigm" (Sheller and Urry, 2006; Urry, 2007) in that they define that space is constituted by flows. Whereas the minority paradigm is concerned about how we may experience migration as a lag behind national standards, the "mobilities paradigm" (Sheller and Urry, 2006; Urry, 2007) appreciates how the experience of migration can lead to initiative and innovation in global communication and culture.

Global Networks of Connectivity and "Deterritorialized Localities"

As we share our experiences of diverse types of "mobilities" (cf. Urry, 2007), we develop networks of social relations. For example, we might actively reconstruct diasporas as "constellations of economic, technological, cultural and ideological and communication flows and networks" [sic] (Tsagarousianou, 2004, p. 61).

We experience globalization as "complex connectivity," "the rapidly developing and ever-densening network of interconnections and interdependences that characterise modem social life" (Tomlinson, 1999, p. 2). In this context of "complex connectivity," we experience sociability in new configurations of "proximity" (Tomlinson, 1999). Culture is a shared version of "'existentially significant' meaning" (Tomlinson, 1999, p. 19), a common sense of what life in the world means to us. As we share culture in networked configurations of "proximity," we decrease the overlap between physical places and cultural spaces. Through these practices of "cultural deterritorialization," we establish "deterritorialized localities" (Tomlinson, 2007, p. 154). We especially use media to develop cultural spaces beyond physical places, a process that John Tomlinson has conceptualized as "telemediatization," "deterritorialization" through media (Tomlinson, 2007).

"Global connectivity" results in both "physical" and "communicative deterritorialization" (Hepp, 2008). In "physical deterritorialization," we disassociate subjects and objects, cultures, and territories (Hepp, 2008, p. 43), disentangling "global ethnoscapes" from local "neighbourhoods" (Appadurai, 1996). In contrast, we disassociate media, cultures, and territories in "communicative deterritorialization" (Hepp, 2008, p. 43) or "telemediatization" (Tomlinson, 2007), disentangling "global mediascapes" from local "neighbourhoods" (Appadurai, 1996).

As our locales are "connected physically and communicatively to a very high degree," we develop "translocal" media cultures (Hepp, 2008, p. 45). Our media cultures are "translocal" in that they reflect both the continuing significance of our locales and the changes in our locales (Hepp, 2008, p. 45).

A "geolinguistic region" (Albizu, 2007) is a type of "translocal media culture." A global map of satellite television broadcasts shows that "geolinguistic regions" have broadened into and across national markets and state territories (Albizu, 2007). As satellite television is popularly used in diasporic communication, satellite television broadcasts have proliferated in places that have not historically used the language of the broadcast (i.e., places that are not "'natural' territories"; Albizu, 2007, p. 257). The incorporation of both "natural" and "non-natural territories" into "geolinguistic regions" based on satellite television networks is an example of how localities can be transformed into "deterritorialized localities" through "telemediatization" (Tomlinson, 2007).

We used to define community in terms of territory, thinking that the closer we are to the territorial center, the stronger our relations to the community and the more agency we have to shape community relations (Papastergiadis, 2000, p. 207). But we have moved beyond this "concentric and territorial construction of community" (Papastergiadis, 2000, p. 207) as we have improved our communication technologies and migrated in "multidirectional" patterns. Now a community space is a "cluster,"

> a space in which various participants gather, and in the process of assembly the respective identity of each member is respected, but at the same time a motion, shape and energy are generated by their proximity. Simultaneously a semi-porous boundary is formed and new sets of possibilities are established. Within such a space it may be necessary to hold a number of differences together, to arrange them in multi-directional and fluid orders, and, most importantly, not to reduce the identity of one as the negative of the other.
>
> (Papastergiadis, 2000, p. 210)

A "cluster" is a community space that emerges from proximity and from a specific holding together of multiple differences and inclusive identities (Papastergiadis, 2000, p. 210). Territorial modes of belonging need to hold differences together (Papastergiadis, 2000, p. 210) and they are complemented by nonterritorial modes of belonging (Papastergiadis, 2000, p. 208).

Whereas "imagined communities" (Anderson, 1991) are based on perceptions of cultural similarity, "clusters" (Papastergiadis, 2000, p. 210) are based on the recognition of both cultural similarity and difference.

In the "network society," we also create homogeneous "communes" based on "communal images" (Castells, 2009). For example, a homogeneous but historically and empirically inaccurate Chinese nation has been created online in response to globalization and migration (L. Wong, 2003).

Whereas our experiences of migration used to be fragmented by geographical and "temporal distance," new media, information, and communication technologies enable "a sense of contemporaneity and synchronicity" that facilitates "new ways of 'coexistence' and 'experiencing together'" (Tsagarousianou, 2004, p. 62). For a long time, we have used media to create "new possibilities of being in two places at once" (Scannell, 1996, p. 91), the place we represent in media content and the place where we experience media. However, today, we also create "'*new spaces* where remote localities and their experiences come together and become 'synchronised'" (Tsagarousianou, 2004, p. 62, original emphasis).

How do we use various media to synchronize our experiences of geographically distant localities in different ways? How do our constructions of localities change as we bring our localities closer together to the point of being synchronized? How do we blur and distinguish the boundaries between localities and relate localities to one another, in different spaces of experience?

Later in this chapter, I show how Saskia Sassen's concept of "assemblages" (Sassen, 2006) helps us to analyze what happens when diverse configurations of social space, time, and spatial scales are synchronized.

In chapter 1, I showed how the "transnational paradigm" broadens our perspective of migration and media by incorporating countries of origin and destination in a transnational space. The transnational paradigm helps us to analyze how multiple national and transnational spaces are transformed in relation to one another as they are integrated through migration and media.

However, when we situate migration and media within global networks of connectivity and "deterritorialized localities," we can explore a wider variety of configurations of "proximity" (Tomlinson, 1999). For example, when we use our mobile phones to discuss global news on social media, we synchronize different persons, places, and platforms, connecting with others in the world. How do our experiences of migration and media inform the persons, places, and platforms we engage with, and how we synchronize them?

Today, we structure our social relations in a global "network society" (Castells, 2000, 2004, 2007, 2008, 2009, 2010), "a society whose social structure is made of networks powered by microelectronics-based information and communication technologies" (Castells, 2004, p. 3). The "network society" promotes the logic of a "space of flows," a space of simultaneous communication over geographical distance (Castells, 2010, pp. 442–443). We experience a "space of flows" as a space of power, but continue to experience a "space of places" (a space of physical contiguity) as a space of meaning (Castells, 2010, pp. 453, 458–459).

When we synchronize a "space of flows" and a "space of places" (Castells, 2010, pp. 453, 458–459), we encourage "a sense of place which is extraverted, which includes a consciousness of its links with the wider world, which integrates in a positive way the global and the local" (Massey, 1993, p. 67). We transform the meaning of places in this way when we "generate" global "landscapes" of flow as part of our "production" of the local (Appadurai, 1996), developing "deterritorialized localities" (Tomlinson, 1999, 2007).

Whereas we used mass media to communicate "from one to many" in the "industrial society," the "network society" is based on "horizontal networks of interactive communication that connect local and global in chosen time" (Castells, 2007, p. 246). Through these networks, we now participate in "mass self-communication," communication that is "self-generated in content, self-directed in emission, and self-selected in reception by many that communicate with many" (Castells, 2007, p. 248). Today's global communication environments are no longer dominated by media flows between nation-states, but now comprise "supranational and subnational communication spheres," as well as direct connections between subjects (Volkmer, 2009, p. 447).

Enabled by this networked "global/local communication media system" (p. 89), we tend to discuss public issues and events at global rather than national levels (Castells, 2008). Rather than experiencing "media events" (Dayan and Katz, 1994, c1992; Katz and Liebes, 2007), narratives that are centrally distributed through mass media, we construct "live" narratives that develop unpredictably in "event-spheres," "decentred" forms of "discourse domains" in which we continuously exchange event-related images (Volkmer, 2008, pp. 92, 97). Today,

> new event-spheres create globalized discourse spaces in a global network society as 'spaces of connectivity' and shape discourse in a culture of the 'spatial reach'... it is not events but connectivity across globalized event spheres where the culture of the 'spatial reach' forms the mediated center of an event, and shapes and influences local happenings.
>
> (Volkmer, 2008, pp. 91, 98)

Although we have structured our social relations as networks for a long time (Krotz, 2008, p. 15), today's social networks are based on new convergences of digital, social, and mobile technologies that enable us to create new types of networked spaces (such as "spaces of flows" and media spaces characterized by "mass self-communication") (Castells, 2007, 2010).

With today's new technologies, we incorporate a vast range of cultural forms into a "culture of real virtuality" (Castells, 2010, Chapter 5) in which reality is not simply "communicated through symbols," but "fully immersed in a virtual image setting" and constituted in the images (p. 404). As we directly experience the "spatial reach" through "event-spheres," the "lifeworld [is] globalized" and "the ontological ground [shifts] from the clearly defined place of the nation to the open space of (global) 'virtuality'" (Volkmer, 2008, pp. 96–97).

The "transnational paradigm" expands our worldview to consider how we establish transnational lives in and across more than one country through migration and media. But today, we live global lives through media as well as through the migration of others and ourselves. We experience migration and media in global networks that synchronize various forms of proximity.

The Unequal Differentiation of Social Spaces in Local and "Global Fields"

We incorporate local places into global networks in a differentiated way, based on the relative significance of the places for the networks (Castells, 2010, p. 443). Glick Schiller and Çağlar's (2009) "comparative theory of locality" shows how we use migration to differentiate local places in global networks.

Glick Schiller and Çağlar's concept of "city-scale" enables us to categorize "the differential positioning of cities determined by the articulation of institutions of political, cultural and economic power within regions, states and the globe" (Glick Schiller and Çağlar, 2009, p. 188). We can compare cities based on whether they are "top-scale," "up-scale," "low-scale," or "down-scale" (Glick Schiller and Çağlar, 2009). Cities are positioned differently in the world because, historically and currently, they vary in the range and types of opportunities that they offer for "migrant incorporation" and transnational connection (Glick Schiller and Çağlar, 2009). Migration significantly contributes to the "differential positioning" (p. 188) of cities in "global fields of power" (Glick Schiller and Çağlar, 2009).

We use migration to differentiate not only places, but also people in the world. We occupy different positions in a "power geometry of time-space compression" (Massey, 1993) in which we can discern how we are positioned relative to others, by comparing our capacities to move, to be in control of movement, to influence others' capacities to move, and to influence others' capacities to be in control of movement (Massey, 1993).

These differentiated capacities are related to our positions in "global ethnoscapes" (Appadurai, 1996) and in local places of residence. Our positions in global spaces are strongly contingent on our positions in places of residence (de Blij, 2009, p. 4). We can categorize ourselves into "globals," "locals," and "mobals," based on our positions in the global and the local (de Blij, 2009, Chapter 1). An elite handful of us are "globals" who have the power to structure migration for others while enjoying free migration ourselves; the vast majority of us are "locals" who are exploited in our places of residence but are unable to migrate to improve our life chances; but a minority of "locals" can become "mobals" who mobilize our limited resources to migrate at personal risk (de Blij, 2009, Chapter 1).

As we simultaneously construct local "neighbourhoods" and global "landscapes" (such as "ethnoscapes") (Appadurai, 1996), we negotiate our positions and shape unequal social relations in local and "global fields of power" (Glick Schiller and Çağlar, 2009).

"Glocality": The Local in the Global, the Global in the Local

When we understand that global spaces are constructed in the process of developing local spaces (Appadurai, 1996), we are defining space as "glocality" (Meyrowitz, 2005; R. Robertson, 1992, 1994, 1995, 2003).

Globalization is "glocalization"; the construction of the local "in . . . global terms" (1994, p. 39) as culture is distributed and differentiated (R. Robertson, 1994, 1995, 2003). As we experience migration and media, we may participate in different "glocalization projects": "relativization," "accommodation," "hybridization," and "transformation" (Giulianotti and Robertson, 2007). In "relativization," we maintain local culture as distinct from host culture; in "accommodation," we maintain core components of local culture by selectively incorporating other cultures; in "hybridization," we creatively fuse local and other cultures; and in "transformation," we prefer other cultures over local culture (Giulianotti and Robertson, 2007, p. 31).

When we are conscious of "glocality," we are aware that we are "both inside and outside the locale at the same moment" (Meyrowitz, 2005, p. 27), and we experience place from both internal and external perspectives. Our perception of places as "glocalities" is distinctive to the contemporary era of migration and media:

> Today's consciousness of self and place is unusual because of the ways in which the evolutions in communication and travel have placed an interconnected global matrix over local experience. We now live in "glocalities." Each glocality is unique in many ways, and yet each is also influenced by global trends and global consciousness.
>
> (Meyrowitz, 2005, p. 23)

We perceive "our localities" relative to "other localities" in the context of "the generalized elsewhere" (Meyrowitz, 2005, pp. 22–23). "Each glocality is unique" (Meyrowitz, 2005, p. 23) because we distinguish "our localities," "other localities," and "the generalized elsewhere" according to where we position ourselves in the world. Depending on our "glocalization projects" (Giulianotti and Robertson, 2007), we might attribute greater, equal, or lesser significance to "our localities," relative to "other localities." We unequally differentiate our "glocalities" in relation to one another.

We have rarely studied migration and media from "glocal" (Meyrowitz, 2005; R. Robertson, 1992, 1994, 1995, 2003) perspectives, but recent cosmopolitan approaches to migration and media show us how we might develop "ethical glocalis[t]" (Tomlinson, 1999, pp. 194–198) perspectives.

In a rare study of migration and media through a "glocal" (Meyrowitz, 2005; R. Robertson, 1992, 1994, 1995, 2003) perspective, de Block and Buckingham view different places as "centres of different types of 'globalities'" (de Block and Buckingham, 2007, p. 7) and show how local, "here and now" experiences of media contribute to the "reconfiguration of relations between the global and the local" (2007, pp. 197–198). Based on their empirical research into how children experience forced migration and media, de Block and Buckingham found that our conceptual distinctions between "transnational," "national," and "global" media have little meaning in empirical contexts because

> unlike their parents, they [the children in the study] are growing up in a world in which globalised communications are a routine expectation, rather than a relatively novel development.
>
> (de Block and Buckingham, 2007, p. 112)

This finding supports Joshua Meyrowitz's argument (2005, p. 23) that the experience of "glocality" is distinctive to the contemporary era of globalization, migration, and media.

In the "power geometry of time-space compression" (Massey, 1993) in which our capacities for migration are differentiated in local (de Blij, 2009) and "global fields of power" (Glick Schiller and Çağlar, 2009), we experience forced migration as being "arrested in space" (Witteborn, 2011, p. 1144). Maybe the refugee children in de Block and Buckingham's study focused on local, "here and now" experiences (de Block and Buckingham, 2007, p. 198) of "glocality" (Meyrowitz, 2005; R. Robertson, 1992, 1994, 1995, 2003) because they had limited agency to migrate elsewhere. But where migration and the use of media are more independent and voluntary, we are likely to experience "glocality" (Meyrowitz, 2005; R. Robertson, 1992, 1994, 1995, 2003) across multiple places and time periods.

We have historically and conventionally constructed the "national" as a singular configuration of space and time by synchronizing particular "spatialities" and "temporalities" (Sassen, 2006, pp. 380–383, 402). However, as we migrate and use media, we develop "transboundary networks and formations connecting and articulating multiple local or "national" processes and actors" from within the local (Sassen, 2007, p. 7). In this "partial imbrication" of "global," "digital," "national," and "subnational" types of "spatio-temporal order," we contribute to the "partial denationalization" of the "national," the limited separation of previously synchronized "spatialities" and "temporalities" (Sassen, 2006, Chapter 8). We also constitute new "mixed spatio-temporal assemblages," "types of territoriality" that combine "national" and "global" components (e.g., financial centers that are situated in national territories but connected in a global network, and "global digital networks" that connect "localized activists" in "global public space") (Sassen, 2006, pp. 386–390).

These "mixed spatio-temporal assemblages" (Sassen, 2006, Chapter 8) are glocalities that configure the global, the local, media, and social relations. Since the "partial imbrication" of the "global," the "national," the "digital," and the "nondigital" is "specific," we need to conduct empirical research to explore varieties (Sassen, 2006, pp. 379, 390) in how we construct "glocalities" (Meyrowitz, 2005; R. Robertson, 1992, 1994, 1995, 2003) and unequally differentiate them in relation to one another through migration and media.

Relational Spaces

As social scientists have experienced changes in communication, migration, and the increasing importance of global issues, we have turned our attention to how society and space are connected in globalization (see Warf and Arias, 2008). For example, spatial sociologists intend to understand how subjects, societies, states, spaces, and scales are related in globalization. How can we conceptualize "space as the intersection between the underlying forces and surface appearances of social life in the age of globalisation" (Dahms, 2008, p. 97)? We can research "spatial inequality" by addressing three issues: how social actors, groups, and institutions at different scales appropriate and claim space; flows between, within, and across spatial units and scales (in particular the subnational scale); and how we develop space (Hooks, Lobao, and Tickamyer, 2007).

When social scientists refer to a "spatial turn" in our field, we are recognizing that we need to reconceptualize space as a significant social context that is relevant for not just where but also why and how social phenomena may be formed and developed (Warf and Arias, 2008). As we have established our concepts of space through diverse "genealogies" of thought (Hubbard, Kitchin, and Valentine, 2004), we have developed various approaches to space. For example, social geography is especially interested in the interplay between space, social relations, and structures of differentiation (S. J. Smith, Pain, Marston, and Jones III, 2010).

Whereas "sedentarist" and "nomadic" theories view social life as *either* enclosed by *or* emancipated from place, we can observe how *both* "materialities" *and* "mobilities" interplay in the configuration of people and places, as well as in the integration of "presence" and "absence" (Sheller and Urry, 2006). These combinations are especially diverse in experiences of migration and media.

But although social scientists have been increasing our attention to the spatial aspects of social life, our research is still "static" (Sheller and Urry, 2006). This "static" (Sheller and Urry, 2006) tendency is evident in how we address migration.

We think that migration is an important issue that needs to be managed and studied because we assume that migration is an exception (Kleinschmidt, 2006). Through a paradigm of "residentialism," we assume that we usually stay within state territorial boundaries, permanently associating each of us with a particular state territory by default (Kleinschmidt, 2006). Since migration challenges this assumption, we view it as a problem that we need to manage and a phenomenon that we need to justify (Kleinschmidt, 2006).

From a government or researcher's point of view, we often define migration with reference to state borders; however, if we were to take the perspective of a migrant, we might discover that we are forming and transforming "transnational social spaces" and facilitating regional integration (Kleinschmidt, 2006). Depending on whether our vantage points are external or internal, top-down or bottom-up, we might observe different relationships between migration, media, and social spaces. To what extent do the social spaces of state sovereignty and migrant agency overlap? How do we experience the distinctions between state and civic definitions of social space?

Since I have a background in the disciplines of media and communications and sociology, my contribution to our discussion of the changing relationships between society and space is especially informed by the emerging subfield of communication geography (Jansson and Falkheimer, 2006). Research in communication geography has four main foci: "place-in-media," "media-in-place," "space-in-media," and "media-in-space" (Adams, 2010). "Place" and "space" are not related in a dichotomy, but they fuse in a "scaleless" manner through communication (Adams, 2010).

In contrast to what Harold Innis conceptualized as "*time-biased*" and "*space-biased* media," "*hyper-space-biased communication*" restructures contemporary society (Jansson and Falkheimer, 2006, pp. 10–11, original emphasis). Through the "*mobility*" of subjects and media, "*convergence*," and "*interactivity*," we now live in an environment characterized by "*spatial ambiguities*" (Jansson and Falkheimer, 2006, pp. 11–13, original emphasis). These "spatial ambiguities" problematize our traditional notions of "*text*," "*context*," and "*text-context relationships*," as well as established paradigms of media studies that we formulated for an earlier "mass society" (Jansson and Falkheimer, 2006, pp. 11–13, original emphasis).

At the microlevel of the individual lifeworld, how is "hyper-space-biased communication" (Jansson and Falkheimer, 2006, pp. 10–11) relevant for the structuring of sets of social relations? How do we understand convergence and interactivity in relation to different configurations of media, social relations, and space?

There is a dialectical relationship between "media" and "space" (Couldry and McCarthy, 2004), between "communication" and "space" (Jansson, 2009), as well as between "space" and "place," and the "content" and "context of communications" (Adams, 2010).

We can elaborate on this idea of dialectical relationship by conceptualizing the relationship between different types of media and social space. For example, the concept of "MediaSpace" invites us to analyze:

1. how we represent space in media,
2. how we reorganize space through media flows,

3. how we produce and consume media in space,
4. how we use media to combine spaces at different scales,
5. how we interpret and experience these combinations of scale in specific places (Couldry and McCarthy, 2004).

We can also explore the "space-communication nexus" along three dimensions:

1. "Communication in space": How media and communication are arranged in space.
2. "Space in communication": How we structure representations of space.
3. "Space as communication and communication as space": How we construct meaningful space through imagination (Jansson, 2009).

The second, first, and fifth dimensions of "MediaSpace" correspond to the first, second, and third dimensions of the "space-communication nexus" respectively.

These multidimensional concepts expand our awareness of the possibilities of media-space configurations. We need to conduct empirical research to detect concrete expressions of diverse media-space configurations in specific cultures and contexts of migration and media.

My empirical research focuses on the final dimensions of the "MediaSpace" (Couldry and McCarthy, 2004) and "space-communication" (Jansson, 2009) models as I explore how Singaporean students in Melbourne experience social spaces through media and give meanings to these spaces. However, the other dimensions of the models also inform my analysis of how these students experience:

- hierarchies of places in news representation (how we represent space in media);
- distance and proximity in relation to different groups of social relations (how we organize spaces through media and how we organize spaces of media);
- fan spaces (how we produce and consume media in space);
- spaces of convergence (how we use media to combine spaces at different scales).

I present the findings of my empirical research in chapters 4 and 5.

As types of media-space configuration, the "media city" (McQuire, 2008) and "communication cities" (Gumpert and Drucker, 2008) are especially prominent in our experiences of migration and media. We can conceptualize all cities in terms of communication (Gumpert and Drucker, 2008, pp. 195–196) and comparatively analyze them through categories such as "Interaction," "Infrastructure," and "Politics/Civil Society" (pp. 197–200).

However, I would be careful not to use extensive lists of indicators to describe "communicative cities" and "disqualify" (cf. Gumpert and Drucker, 2008, pp. 199–200) other cities from being recognized as "communicative." Rather than viewing cities as being *either* "communicative" *or* not, "transparent" (cf. Gumpert and Drucker, 2008, p. 199) or not, it would be more culturally sensitive to explore cities as contexts in which notions of communication (such as "transparency") are given specific meanings. Gumpert and Drucker use "normative criteria" to distinguish "communicative cities," suggesting, for example, that a city is "communicative" when it is "a place to celebrate vice" and "disqualified" when it has "[m]andatory language requirements" (pp. 197–200). But these criteria are problematic. For example, "[m]andatory language requirements" (Gumpert and Drucker, 2008, pp. 197–200) do not necessarily hinder communication; rather, the institutionalization of a shared working language can promote intercultural communication. More importantly, whose normative criteria are reflected in definitions and differentiations of space? We must be informed by concepts of space, but not overly predetermine the spatial unit (e.g., a city), categories, and criteria of analysis from objective and normative viewpoints, so that we can recognize diverse subjective and alternative constructions of media-space.

We can create alternative maps of the world by viewing social space from "absolute," "relative," and "relational" perspectives (Harvey, 2009, pp. 133–141). We use fixed and closed boundaries to define "absolute" space; we frame "relative" space with reference to our positions, viewpoints, and criteria; and we construct "relational" space from "things, events, processes, and socio-ecological relations," including immaterial entities such as thoughts and memories (Harvey, 2009, pp. 133–141). Through a comparative interpretation of "relational" views of space, I seek to expand our concepts of space beyond "absolute" views of state and nation, as well as "relative" views of "home," "host," and "diaspora" (Harvey, 2009, pp. 133–141).

Space is "relational," an open-ended construction that results as we negotiate unequal sociopolitical relations in a global context (Massey, 2005, pp. 100–101). We negotiate the "openness" and "closure" of space in specific situations (Massey, 2005, p. 166). Today, we construct "relational space" when we relate with one another in everyday glocalities, configurations of "the global" and "the face-to-face":

> Relational space is the social space created by the contemporary imperative to actively establish social relations 'on the fly' across heterogeneous dimensions in which the global is inextricably imbricated with the face-to-face.
>
> (McQuire, 2008, p. 23)

"Locality" is "relational" in two senses: it is an open-ended construction based on social relations, and it is constructed in relation to other "localities." In the first sense, "locality" produces and is produced by "local subjects, actors who properly belong to a situated community of kin, neighbours, friends, and enemies" (Appadurai, 1996, p. 179). In the second sense, "as [global] ethnoscapes, [local] neighbourhoods inevitably imply a relational consciousness of other neighbourhoods" (Appadurai, 1996, p. 186).

This "relational consciousness" (Appadurai, 1996, p. 186) is routinely cultivated, particularly when we reflect on the many places we see through migration and media. For example, when migrants discuss what they watch on television, they facilitate a "multiple 'sense of place' that moves beyond one's immediate circumstances" (p. 133) and develop "continuities between the places in which they live, and which they imagine" (de Block and Buckingham, 2007, p. 11).

We practice "biographical glocalization" when we incorporate "glocalities" (Meyrowitz, 2005; R. Robertson, 1992, 1994, 1995, 2003) into an "individualized" narrative of one's "own life" (Beck, 2000d). Each place is a "glocality" (Meyrowitz, 2005; R. Robertson, 1992, 1994, 1995, 2003) as "different worlds are potentially present at a single place" (Beck, 2000d, p. 76) and "[t]he continents of the world may also be experienced and suffered in *one* global place" (p. 75). However, "biographical glocalization" is especially characterized by "the changing and choosing of place" (Beck, 2000d, p. 74), and by "place polygamy," "marriage to several places at once, belonging in different worlds" (p. 73) such as "nations, religions, cultures, skin colours, continents, etc." (Beck, 2000d, p. 75). "Place polygamy" (Beck, 2000d, p. 73) is the simultaneous commitment to multiple geographical locales and their associated cultural spaces, facilitated by circular migration (regular back-and-forth migration) between more than one place of residence. It is similar to transmigration in that it suggests "simultaneous embeddedness" in more than one society through migration (Glick Schiller et al., 1995, p. 48). However, I would not categorize "place polygamy" (Beck, 2000d, p. 73) within the transnational paradigm of migration because when we practice "place polygamy" in its original concept, we do not incorporate places into a transnational space, but connect *to* rather than *across* places.

Although the concept of "place polygamy" (Beck, 2000d, p. 73) originally referred to physical places, it also applies to representations of places in nineteenth-century news (Rantanen, 2003) and the immigrant press (Cheng, 2005), that is, media representations of space (Couldry and McCarthy, 2004), "space in communication" (Jansson, 2009), and "place-in-media" (Adams, 2010).

As we practice "biographical glocalization," we might ask ourselves the following questions:

> To what extent is the place 'my place', and 'my place' my own life? How are the different places related to one another in the imaginary map of 'my world', and in what sense are they 'significant places' in the longitudinal [sic] and cross-section of my own life?
>
> (Beck, 2000d, p. 76)

As we continuously ask and address these questions, we engage in an open-ended construction of "glocalities" in relation to other "glocalities" (Meyrowitz, 2005; R. Robertson, 1992, 1994, 1995, 2003)—a construction we can conceptualize as "relational glocalities."

As we distinguish between "the place," "my place," "different places," and "significant places" "in the imaginary map of "my world," we not only unequally differentiate local places in a "global field" (Glick Schiller and Çağlar, 2009), but also construct our relations to these "glocalities" (Meyrowitz, 2005; R. Robertson, 1992, 1994, 1995, 2003). I would conceptualize these subjective relations to space as another dimension of relational glocalities.

How do we relate to space? In academic research on migration and media, we often focus on relations of belonging.

I have argued that I would not categorize the original concept of "place polygamy" (Beck, 2000d, p. 73) within the transnational paradigm of migration. However, we can develop the transnational paradigm beyond methodological nationalism by integrating it with the concept of "place polygamy" (Beck, 2000d, p. 73). Cheng (2005) does this when she argues that the immigrant press routinely constructs an "imagined community" that expresses a "transnational, multilocal sense of belonging" to two types of local spaces: "place-oriented" and "people-oriented." These types of local spaces are incorporated into the transnational media space of the newspaper.

Identity and community are specific relations of belonging in and across a broad range of interconnected spaces (Georgiou, 2006; Morley, 2000). For example, we constitute "diasporic space" from "the home," "the public," "the city," "the nation," and "the transnational" (Georgiou, 2006).

"Home" is the space we especially associate with belonging and related ideas of familiarity, purity, and security (Morley, 2000). We experience "home" in many ways as we move across diverse spaces: individual, family, private, public, domestic, work, urban, surburban, national, global, and spaces associated with various media technologies (e.g., television, mobile communications, and the Internet) (Morley, 2000). We constitute all these spaces in relation to one another as we manage the boundaries between these spaces through "macro" and "micro" processes, especially processes directly associated with media (Morley, 2000). We construct "home" mainly through "purification," practices that

> expel alterity beyond the boundaries of some ethnically, culturally or civilisationally purified homogenous enclave, at whatever level of social or geographical scale. In these processes the crucial issue in defining who (or what) "belongs" is, of course, also that of defining who (or what) is to be excluded as "matter out of place."
>
> (Morley, 2000, p. 3)

We construct the space of "home" through "purification" (Morley, 2000) because we tend to believe that we are more likely to belong to groups of people who are similar to us. However, spaces of belonging can be heterogeneous and we can construct them through difference (Hall, 2003[1990]; Papastergiadis, 2000).

Having considered the different ways in which we have conceptualized relational space, I would like to propose a tripartite concept that I call "relational spaces." We can use the concept of "relational spaces" to analyze how we construct social spaces in three dimensions: spaces constructed *through* social *relations* (social spaces), *relations between* social spaces, and *relations to* social spaces.

How do we construct spaces through our relationships with others? How do we group and distinguish social relations in and through space? How do relate one social space to another? How do we relate to social spaces?

How can we develop this concept of "relational spaces" to understand our experiences of migration and media?

"Transcultural" Relativity

In developing a new conceptual framework for thinking about migration, media, and social space, I have discussed how we relate the global and the local, and how we relate society and space. Now, I would like to conceptualize how we relate culture to space.

Too often, we differentiate cultural units by "nation" and "state." However, a "transcultural" perspective recognizes that we constitute culture across territories (Hepp, 2009b, p. 7). Andreas Hepp's "transcultural" comparative approach encourages us to study the "*specificity*" and "complex interrelations" of media cultures "in the frame of an increasingly global communicative connectivity" (2009b, p. 8, original emphasis). Instead of predefining cultural units, it is more accurate to observe "cultural patterns" of "thinking," "discourse," and "practices," then analyze how we relate these "cultural thickenings" to various references (e.g., "territorial," "deterritorial," "ethnic," "commercial," "political," and "religious") (Hepp, 2009b). This approach allows us to compare cultures based on how they are distinctive and how they overlap. It also enables us to appreciate the relativity of media cultures in a global space of communication.

Migration tends to imply contact between otherwise distinct national or ethnic cultures. But the concept of "transcultural diversity" (Robins, 2007) broadens our vision to consider how we use migration to constitute spaces that are open-ended, shifting structures of cultural diversity:

> The concept of "transcultural diversity" points to the creation of a European space conceived in terms of a different kind of cultural configuration. It may be characterized in terms of cultural porosity and fluidity operating *across* space(s), rather than in terms of a landscape of boundaries containing sedentary communities living *inside* national jurisdictions. It arises out of ongoing cross-frontier movements of people that continually renew the landscape of cultural diversity in national jurisdictions.
>
> (Robins, 2007, p. 164, original emphasis)

If we view spaces as open-ended structures of cultural diversity that we continuously reshape with cultural flows, we might explore how we experience culture (including cultural diversity and flows), how migration and media are relevant for these experiences, and how these experiences change our perceptions of space.

As open-ended structures of cultural diversity, spaces offer various opportunities for culturally diverse social relations. Through our various social relations, we develop different types of connections with multiple spaces. For example, we might expand our economic connections into diverse industries and markets through international business contacts, as well as cultivate several cultural identities and interests through personal relationships within a culturally diverse extended family. In this way, we construct spaces of "culturally diverse groups and networks" (social spaces), connect different national jurisdictions" and transnational (e.g., regional) spaces (*relations between* social spaces), as well as develop "plural cultural identities and different loyalties" to these social spaces (*relations to* social spaces):

> It [the European space] creates culturally diverse groups and networks linked to a number of different national jurisdictions, through a variety of coexisting vital interests (birth, work, marriage, family, etc.). And it favors sustaining plural cultural identities and different loyalties over the desire to identify and achieve specific equality status as a fixed minority in any particular state.
>
> (Robins, 2007, p. 164)

I use the term "transcultural relativity" to highlight that we construct social spaces as open-ended, shifting structures of cultural diversity that are distinguished and intersecting relative to one another.

This idea of transcultural relativity is especially evident in research on media and cosmopolitanism. Research on media and cosmopolitanism explores how we use media to regard global cultural diversity across local societies.

On the one hand, we can create "new forms of global consciousness" through "media convergence" (Jenkins, 2004, p. 117) and cultivate civic perceptions of "being, or becoming, at home in the world" through the production of foreign news (Hannerz, 2004, p. 23).

On the other hand, we give global relations local meaning (Tomlinson, 1999, p. 196) when we interpret everyday images of "banal globalism" within particular situations (Urry, 2000), continue to consider nation and state important for supranational political discussion and participation (Schlesinger, 2007), and establish national media cultures of cosmopolitanism (A. Robertson, 2010).

Our debates on media and cosmopolitanism are often informed by particular normative and ethical views about developing global cultures of communication in which we respect difference (Stevenson, 2000) and extend "relations of solidarity" across "local, national, and global" spaces (Stevenson, 2003, pp. 118, 124).

In the contemporary "era of ubiquitous media" (Tomlinson, 2011), we are especially interested in how we can use various media and types of professional communication (e.g., journalism and humanitarian communication) to negotiate "proper distance" and create "ethically appropriate" spaces of relations between "self" and "other" (Silverstone, 2003, p. 476; 2007). For example, we can use media to represent relations between "self" and "other" with reference to ideas of "common humanity" and "strangeness" (Chouliaraki and Orgad, 2011). We can use global news of national issues and events to problematize national "frames" of meaning and to perceive "ourselves" as "others" in a process of "estrangement" or "de-familiarization" (Orgad, 2011, p. 402).

"Proper distance" (Silverstone, 2003, 2007) is related to how we represent and interpret geographical and "social distance" through media. Especially through world news and advocacy campaigns, we position ourselves in relation to "distant suffering" (Boltanski, 1999) and translate particular views of war, conflict, and disaster in the developing world (Philo, 2002) into Western, developed world contexts and media cultures. As we continuously structure various configurations of "proximity" and "distance" (including but not limited to "proper distance") (Silverstone, 2003, 2007) between "publics" of "spectatorship" and categories of "sufferer," we establish "hierarchies of geographical place and human life across the globe" (Chouliaraki, 2006; 2008a, p. 845; 2008c, 2011). We use media to map a global society in which local societies and locally situated persons are unequally positioned in relation to one another. These social relations include a "politics of pity" (Boltanski, 1999), "neocolonial" relations and the "world system of socioeconomic relationships" (Philo, 2002, p. 180), forms of "global compassion" (Höijer, 2004), and relations of "solidarity" (such as "pity," "irony," and "agonism") (Chouliaraki, 2011).

We must be aware of how we are unequally related to one another to discern how to justly share resources according to the various needs within local and global societies. But when we are communicating within relations of apathy, condescension, and hostility, it may be more fruitful to use media to facilitate relations of "non-commitment" because:

> it creates a social space...in which people are *sufficiently the same*—sufficiently interchangeable and equivalent—for each person to be able to imagine what it might be like to be in another's shoes.
>
> (Frosh, 2006, p. 281, original emphasis)

In this ethical space, there is not only equal relation between "self" and "other," but also "equidistance" between the "self" and diverse "others" (Dayan, 2007).

These normative approaches to media and cosmopolitanism help us to ethically reflect on how we use media to construct world maps of unequal social relations (social spaces), relations between distant local societies (*relations between* social spaces), as well as relations to local and global societies (*relations to* social spaces).

However, as scholars, a methodological approach to media and cosmopolitanism is useful for problematizing "ordinary" and "other spaces" of communication (Jansson, 2009). For example, when we research migration and media, we can categorize types of social space other than the "nation" (Georgiou, 2007c), analyze social relations beyond traditional concepts of "community" (Robins, 2007), and challenge our expectations that migrants are committed to their countries of origin and settlement (Georgiou, 2007c).

A Cosmopolitan Approach to Relational Spaces

For a concept to be cosmopolitan, it must include diverse definitions, practices, and historical developments, acknowledge its provisional nature, and be open to revision (Breckenridge, Chakrabarty, Bhabha, and Pollock, 2000). As such, I review the main themes and concepts of cosmopolitanism, before considering cosmopolitanism as a methodological approach. My concept of "glocal cosmopolitanism" builds on Ulrich Beck's approach of "methodological cosmopolitanism" (Beck, 2006, 2012; Beck and Grande, 2010; Beck and Sznaider, 2006).

From a longitudinal perspective, we can discern three historical periods of thinking about cosmopolitanism: classical (particularly Stoic), enlightenment, and contemporary cosmopolitanism (see Brown and Held, 2010; Kleingeld and Brown, 2011). Whereas early cosmopolitan philosophy viewed moral and political communities in the context of universal law and human reason, contemporary cosmopolitan ethics relates these ideas of community to practical and institutional conditions (Brown and Held, 2010).

Contemporary cosmopolitanism explores the themes of "global justice," "cultural cosmopolitanism," "legal cosmopolitanism," "political cosmopolitanism," and "civic cosmopolitanism" (Brown and Held, 2010). Concepts of "cultural cosmopolitanism" (Brown and Held, 2010) are most relevant for understanding how we experience migration and media, because they explain how each of us might create personal meaning and identify ourselves in the world.

"Cultural cosmopolitanism" calls for us to recognize that our social relations are translocal as it "argues for moral duties and obligations that supersede or transgress localized obligations based solely on aspects of ethnicity, culture, and nationality" (Brown and Held, 2010, p. 10). We can adopt multiple positions in relation to social spaces and consider local cultures relative to one another, as "cultural cosmopolitanism" is "the ability to stand outside a singular location (the location of one's birth, land, upbringing, conversion) and to mediate traditions" (Held, 2002, p. 58). "Cultural cosmopolitanism" is a "cultural project" that requires:

> recognition of the increasing interconnectedness of political communities in diverse domains including the social, economic and environmental;
>
> development of an understanding of overlapping "collective fortunes" that require collective solutions—locally, nationally, regionally and globally; and
>
> the celebration of difference, diversity and hybridity while learning how to "reason from the point of view of others" and mediate traditions.
>
> (Held, 2002, p. 58)

Through "cultural cosmopolitanism" (Held, 2002, p. 58), we realize that various types of societies are intertwined and we need to cultivate collaborative relations across local, national, regional, and global spaces.

Cosmopolitanism is evident in different domains of social life ("cultural," "legal," "political," and "civic") (Brown and Held, 2010). It can be expressed in various ways, as

> (a) a socio-cultural condition, (b) a kind of philosophy or world-view; (c) a political project towards building transnational institutions; (d) a political project for recognizing multiple identities; (e) an attitudinal or dispositional orientation; and/or (f) a mode of practice or competence.
>
> (Vertovec and Cohen, 2002, p. 9)

If we focus on the cultural dimension of cosmopolitanism, we might view cosmopolitanism as "(a) a socio-cultural condition, ... (e) an attitudinal or dispositional orientation; and/or (f) a mode of practice or competence." Seeing cosmopolitanism as "a socio-cultural condition," we might evaluate how "a socially and culturally interpenetrated planet" (Vertovec and Cohen, 2002, p. 9) can be "celebrated for its vibrant cultural creativity as well as its political challenges to various ethnocentric, racialized, gendered and national narratives" (Vertovec and Cohen, 2002, p. 9). At the same time, we would be concerned not to create a "rootless," homogenized global culture at the expense of local and national identities (Vertovec and Cohen, 2002, pp. 9–10). Thinking about cosmopolitanism as "an attitudinal or dispositional orientation" encourages us to discern our everyday consciousness of the world and the quality of our appreciation of diverse local cultures (Vertovec and Cohen, 2002). Considering cosmopolitanism as "a mode of practice or competence," we would assess our abilities to move between cultures ("systems of meaning" (p. 13)) (Vertovec and Cohen, 2002).

We articulate particular normative positions and agendas when we conceptualize cosmopolitanism as (1) a form of morality, (2) a "cultural project" (Held, 2002), (3) a "socio-cultural" reality that is positive or negative, and (4) cultural appreciation and "competence."

It is "singularly useful" to distinguish between "cosmopolitanization" as a process of global social transformation and "methodological cosmopolitanism" (Glick Schiller, 2010, p. 415). Whereas most concepts of cosmopolitanism focus on social conditions and social actors' perceptions and practices, we become conscious of how we analyze the social through a methodological approach to cosmopolitanism. In contrast to "philosophical and normative cosmopolitanism" and the "outlook" of the "social actor," my work focuses on "analytical-empirical cosmopolitanism" and the "methodological" approach of the social scientist (Beck, 2000a, 2006, 2012; Beck and Grande, 2010; Beck and Sznaider, 2006).

"Methodological cosmopolitanism" is "an approach which takes the varieties of modernity and their global interdependencies as a starting point for theoretical reflection and empirical research" (Beck and Grande, 2010, p. 412). Its theories of society are not generalized from particular national Western societies, but they recognize how different societies experience "reflexive modernization" and how these experiences are increasingly interrelated in "world society" (Beck and Grande, 2010). "Reflexive modernization" is the "modernization" or transformation in the "principles" of "modern society" (Beck et al., 2003, p. 1). "Reflexive modernization" transforms how we experience social spaces—we become aware that the boundaries of social spaces are contingent and perceive that we need to construct and negotiate multiple boundaries (Beck et al., 2003).

If we approach migration and media through "methodological cosmopolitanism" (Beck and Beck-Gernsheim, 2009), we would analyze how we experience diverse local societies developing in relation to one another. How are migration and media relevant for this experience? We would not predefine local society as a particular type of society (such as national society) or a particular society (such as the country of origin or settlement). Instead, we would explore our boundaries of diverse social spaces and types of social spaces.

Through "methodological cosmopolitanism," we conceptualize migration and media in a "global frame of reference" (Beck and Beck-Gernsheim, 2009, p. 26). Since our "observer perspective" is distinct from the "actor's perspective" of the "global frame of reference" (Beck and Beck-Gernsheim, 2009, p. 26), we can conceptualize migration and media in a global context regardless of whether the people we study are conscious that they experience migration and media within global society.

"Methodological cosmopolitanism" broadens our vision to understand how we relate with one another as "*transnational fractions*" of a "global generation" through migration and media (Beck and Beck-Gernsheim, 2009, pp. 33–34, original emphasis). The world's wealth is unequally distributed and our share in global wealth depends on where we live and work. We learn how global wealth is unequally distributed as we compare media representations of richer and poorer societies, and as migration brings us into contact with people we associate with richer or poorer societies. Whereas those of us in poorer parts of the world experience richer parts of the world through media and migrate to obtain a higher proportion of global wealth, those of us in richer parts of the world often resist this migration because we feel that our possession of wealth is insecure (Beck and Beck-Gernsheim, 2009, pp. 33–34). In this way, the experience of migration and media is shared and differentiated within global society.

"Methodological cosmopolitanism" also explores how "global families" negotiate "the tensions... between the centre and the periphery" and "global inequalities" as they develop close personal relationships across geographical distance and cultural difference (Beck, 2012, pp. 9–10).

"Methodological cosmopolitanism" builds on the critique of "methodological nationalism" by developing new concepts and empirical data (Beck, 2006). This book presents new concepts of social space and original data on how Singaporean students in Melbourne, Australia, experience migration and media. In doing so, I show how we can study migration and media without making assumptions about migrants' commitments to particular nations and states.

Earlier, I conceptualized "relational spaces" in three dimensions: spaces constructed *through* social *relations* (social spaces), *relations between* social spaces, and *relations to* social spaces. I now develop Ulrich Beck's approach of "methodological cosmopolitanism" (2006) along these dimensions of "relational spaces."

Spaces of Social Relations: Social Networks across Globalized Cities

We will advance the study of migration and media by developing a cosmopolitan paradigm that is not "nation-centric," but examines

> the multiple spheres of activity—this being political, cultural and social—that unravel in overlapping or coexisting spaces. The transnational and the urban domains, the network and the community, have become increasingly useful framing, interpretative and operational categories.
>
> (Georgiou, 2007c, p. 19)

A cosmopolitan paradigm is not centered on "nation" and "state," but considers them as equally relevant as other types of social spaces, such as "transnational," "urban," "network," and "community" spaces.

Globalization has always been evident in transnational urban networks. In the nineteenth century, we developed news not between nation-states, but in networks of "cosmopolitan" or "world cities" (Rantanen, 2007). Today, "networks of global cities" are new "mixed spatio-temporal assemblages" that are

> partly territorial and partly electronic geographies that cut across borders and the spatio-temporal orders of nation-states yet install themselves or get partly shaped in specific subnational terrains.
>
> (Sassen, 2006, p. 393)

"Global cities" are "subnational places where multiple global circuits intersect and thereby position these cities on several structured cross-border geographies" (Sassen, 2007, p. 91). They are sites where "spatialities" and "temporalities" of today's diverse media, "subnational," "national," and "global" types of "spatio-temporal order" converge and diverge in specific ways (Sassen, 2006, 2007). When we use particular "networks of global cities" (Sassen, 2006) as a starting point for an exploratory study, we can conduct in-depth analysis into patterns of configuring diverse social spaces.

"Global cities" and their "multicultural neighbourhoods" are significant sites where we engage in everyday practices of cosmopolitanism (Georgiou, 2007a, 2007c, 2008). Open to alternative "juxtapositions of difference," they are where we experiment with diverse "positions and positionalities" (Georgiou, 2007c, p. 297) in and across local, national, transnational, and global spaces (Georgiou, 2007a, 2008).

I prefer to use the term "globalized cities" to indicate my openness to the idea that "all cities are now globalising, but are embedded within differential power hierarchies" (Glick Schiller and Çağlar, 2009, p. 182). Concepts of "global cities" tend to focus on major cities (such as New York, London, and Tokyo) that seem to be networked independently from the nation-states where they are geographically located; however, I would like to consider a much wider range of cities and "city-scale" positionings (Glick Schiller and Çağlar, 2009). I also use the term "globalized cities" to emphasize that these spaces open up diverse types of social space, not just the global.

Although "community" is an alternative type of social space to "nation" and "state" (Georgiou, 2007c, p. 19), community is only one type of social relation. Today's "sociality" is "based on social networks", social connections that are "individualized" and open-ended, continuously constructed in view of changing experiences (Robins, 2007, p. 156).

"Methodological cosmopolitanism" encourages us to look beyond "*national–national* relations," and to use "*local*," "*national*," "*trans-national*" (or "*translocal*"), or "*global*" angles to explore "*national–global*[,]... trans-local, local–global, trans-national and global–global patterns of relations" (Beck, 2006, pp. 76–77, 81–82, original emphasis). By focusing on social networks across globalized cities, we can explore how diverse "glocalities" (Meyrowitz, 2005; R. Robertson, 1992, 1994, 1995, 2003) are constructed *through* social *relations*.

My case study focuses on Singaporean students who have experiences of social networks across the globalized cities of Singapore and Melbourne. Since "social networks across the globalized cities of Singapore and Melbourne" is a shared characteristic of all my study participants, it is a category of social space that I can use to research and compare my participants' experiences of migration and media.

Relations between Social Spaces: "Internalization"

In contrast to the view that cultural identity is a fixed "essence" based on "common historical experiences and shared cultural codes," I understand cultural identity as "*positioning*" that refers to a "dialogic relationship" of similarity and difference in historical experience (Hall, 2003[1990], pp. 234–235, 237, original emphasis). We define the ""doubleness" of similarity and difference" in our cultural identities through the "inner expropriation" of "otherness" (Hall, 2003[1990], pp. 236, 238). For example, colonized group A identifies itself by defining its similarity to and difference from colonized group B. It internalizes that both A and B are similarly excluded from colonizing group C, but they differ in their relations of "otherness" to C.

Through "cosmopolitization," "societies are internalizing each other" (Beck and Grande, 2010, p. 417). We create overlaps and interrelations between "ourselves" and "others" such that our distinguishing boundaries are not *between* "us" and "them," but *within* "us."

We define our cultural identities by contextualizing ourselves among diverse interrelated spaces of social relations. For example, Caribbean identities express "positioning" vis-à-vis the "presences" of "Africa" (the "site of the...silenced"), "Europe" (the "power" of discourse), and "America" (the "ground, place, territory...the juncture-point where the many cultural tributaries meet...the space where the creolisations and assimilations and syncretisms were negotiated") (Hall, 2003[1990], pp. 239–243). We unequally relate spaces such as the "Carribbean," "Africa," "Europe," and "America" based on their relative value for flows of global communication.

How do we construct *relations between* social spaces? By showing how "glocalities" (Meyrowitz, 2005; R. Robertson, 1992, 1994, 1995, 2003) overlap. How is each "glocality" both similar to and different from other "glocalities"?

Relations to Social Spaces: "Inclusive Differentiation"

Through migration and media, we have multiple relations to social space. For example, we relate to places where we live, places we represent on media, and places where we produce media:

> Yes, we are connected to the earth—but not to "a" place on it, simple and self-evident as the surroundings we see when we open our eyes. We are connected to all sorts of places, causally if not always consciously, including many that we have never traveled to, that we have perhaps only seen on television—including the place where the television itself was manufactured. It is frightening to think how little progress has been made in turning invisibly determining and often exploitative connections into conscious and self-critical ones, how far we remain from mastering the sorts of allegiance, ethics, and action that might go with our complex and multiple belonging.
>
> (Robbins, 1998, p. 3)

How aware are we of our involvement in establishing unequal social relations? Are we becoming more ethical and competent in managing our commitments and social impact?

The "'territorial either/or'...metatheory of identity, society and politics...assumes that a space defended by (mental) fences is an indispensable precondition for the formation of self-consciousness and for social integration" (Beck, 2006, p. 5). Since social scientists assume that we must distinguish between "ourselves" and the "foreign" to construct "identity, politics, society, community," we often practice "exclusive differentiation," categorizing people into mutually exclusive social groups (Beck, 2006, p. 5). But "methodological cosmopolitanism" advances the "both/and logic of inclusive differentiation," analyzing how we construct our identities by combining incompatible, "globally available identities" (Beck, 2006, pp. 4–5).

Whether we consider ourselves as "locals" or "cosmopolitans," we collaborate to develop global and local spaces of culture. We create "world culture" as "locals" preserve "local culture" and "cosmopolitans" are open to diversity across "local cultures" (Hannerz, 1996, Chapter 9).

We can distinguish "local cultures" into "transnational cultures" and "territorial cultures" (Hannerz, 1996, Chapter 9). Within "transnational cultures," we experience diverse "territorial cultures" through migration; within "territorial cultures," we experience various "transnational cultures" through media (Hannerz, 1996, Chapter 9). As "cosmopolitans," we emulate "locals" by advancing our fluency in different "local cultures" (Hannerz, 1996, Chapter 9). However, "cosmopolitans" and "locals" relate differently to space: whereas "locals" situate ourselves in a single "local" ("transnational" or "territorial") space, "cosmopolitans" position ourselves across one type of "local" space (e.g., "transnational" space), from a different type of "local" base (e.g., "territorial" space).

How do we position ourselves in both global and local societies, by developing a set of *relations to* multiple "glocalities" (Meyrowitz, 2005; R. Robertson, 1992, 1994, 1995, 2003)? Do we follow a "*neither/nor*" logic in relation to particular places by making "a choice neither to display loyalties to the country of origin nor to the country of settlement" (Georgiou, 2007c, p. 18, original emphasis)?

Relational Glocalities and the "Universalism-Particularism Nexus"

We experience "global interdependence" in everyday life, and this experience transforms "national consciousness" "*from within*" (Beck, 2006, p. 73, original emphasis).

> Cosmopolitanization is a non-linear, dialectical process in which the universal and the particular, the similar and the dissimilar, the global and the local are to be conceived, not as cultural polarities, but as interconnected and reciprocally interpenetrating principles.
>
> (Beck, 2006, pp. 72–73)

Through globalization, we establish the "interpenetration" of "universalism" and "particularism" in a worldwide "nexus" (R. Robertson, 1992, Chapter 6). This "universalism-particularism nexus" consists of two processes: the "universalization of particularism" and the "particularization of universalism" (R. Robertson, 1992, Chapter 6). As forms of "particularism" are "universalized" and forms of "universalism" are "particularized," we anticipate universal experiences of the particular and particular experiences of the universal (R. Robertson, 1992, p. 102).

"Universalism and particularism [are] central analytical concepts for understanding diasporic media cultures beyond binaries and oppositions" such as ethnic segregation/integration, national/transnational, and majority/minority (Georgiou, 2005a, p. 482). By contextualizing diasporic media cultures in a "universalism-particularism continuum," we can analyze how they express the relationship between "particularistic" and "universalistic" types of "project" (Georgiou, 2005a).

I propose that we construct social spaces as "relational glocalities," "global fields" (Glick Schiller and Çağlar, 2009; R. Robertson, 1992) that are locally differentiated, through the "universalization of particularism" and the "particularization of universalism" (R. Robertson, 1992, Chapter 6).

"Cosmopolitan Gaze"

Ulrich Beck uses the term "cosmopolitan gaze" to refer to our experience of global communication, global public opinion, and global challenges:

> The cosmopolitan gaze opens wide and focuses... guided and encouraged by the evidence of worldwide communication (often just another word for misunderstanding) on central themes such as science, law, art, fashion, entertainment, and, not least, politics. World-wide public perception and debate of global ecological danger or global risks of a technological and economic nature ("Frankenstein food") have laid open the cosmopolitan significance of fear.
>
> (Beck, 2000a, p. 79)

Since "cosmopolitan gaze" (Beck, 2000a, p. 79) explores the global significance of various interests and issues, I would use the term "cosmopolitan gaze" to analyze how we construct diverse "global fields" through the "universalization of particularism" (Glick Schiller and Çağlar, 2009; R. Robertson, 1992).

"Cosmopolitan gaze" (Beck, 2000a, p. 79) or "cosmopolitan outlook" (Beck, 2006, p. 3) is the perception of a global, transcultural space where we continuously organize our social relations in open-ended arrangements:

> Global sense, a sense of boundarylessness. An everyday, historically alert, reflexive awareness of ambivalences in a milieu of blurring differentiations and cultural contradictions. It reveals not just the 'anguish' but also the possibility of shaping one's life and social relations under conditions of cultural mixture.
>
> (Beck, 2006, p. 3)

As "universalism" and "particularism" are "interpenetrated" in a worldwide "nexus," we experience "the world" as a "global field" with four "reference points": "individual selves," "national societies," "relationships between national societies," and "humankind" (R. Robertson, 1992, pp. 25–28). These four coordinates are "shifting," "interrelated," and given different "emphases" relative to one another (R. Robertson, 1992, p. 28), through

> the universalization of particularism and the particularization of universalism . . . more specifically . . . the interpenetrating processes of societalization, individualization, the consolidation of the international system of societies, and the concretization of the sense of humankind.
>
> (R. Robertson, 1992, p. 104)

Relating Beck's (2006) "cosmopolitan gaze" to Robertson's (1992) "global field," I would like to analyze how we construct continuously changing "global fields" through the open-ended arrangement of social relations. We arrange our social relations in "global fields" by making associations between diverse positions ("selves"), "societies" (dense "clusters" (cf. Papastergiadis, 2000) of social relations), and "humankind" as a type of social relation.

"Cosmopolitan Vision"

Although Ulrich Beck uses the terms "cosmopolitan gaze," "cosmopolitan outlook," and "cosmopolitan vision" interchangeably (Beck, 2006), he uses "cosmopolitan vision" to recognize how we relate with diverse cultures in global society:

> What is enlightenment? To have the courage to make use of one's cosmopolitan vision and to acknowledge one's multiple identities—to

> combine forms of life founded on language, skin colour, nationality or religion with the awareness that, in a radically insecure world, all are equal and everyone is different.
>
> (Beck, 2006, p. ii)

Since "cosmopolitan vision" (Beck, 2006) appreciates our particular relations in global society, I would use the term "cosmopolitan vision" to analyze how we differentiate "global fields" into local spaces through the "particularization of universalism" (Glick Schiller and Çağlar, 2009; R. Robertson, 1992).

Since the "global field" comprizes multiple "societies" and its interrelated coordinates are shifting and given different "emphases" relative to one another (R. Robertson, 1992, pp. 25–28), I would like to examine how we arrange our social relations in "clusters" (Papastergiadis, 2000) that vary in their relative density, positions, and significance.

In this chapter, I have introduced "glocal cosmopolitanism" as a new approach to studying how we experience migration and media. Through this approach, I conceptualize social spaces as "relational glocalities"—"glocal" social spaces that are locally and unequally differentiated in relation to one another within "global fields" (Glick Schiller and Çağlar, 2009; R. Robertson, 1992). Using the parameter of "cosmopolitan gaze," I would like to analyze how we construct "global fields" through the "universalization of particularism" (cf. Beck, 2006; Glick Schiller and Çağlar, 2009; R. Robertson, 1992). Using the parameter of "cosmopolitan vision," I would like to analyze how we construct local spaces through the "particularization of universalism" (cf. Beck, 2006; Glick Schiller and Çağlar, 2009; R. Robertson, 1992).

In chapters 5 and 6, I further develop these concepts based on my empirical research with Singaporean students in Melbourne, Australia.

CHAPTER 3

Singaporean Cultures of Migration and Media

In chapter 2, I encouraged us to develop a cosmopolitan approach to study our experiences of migration and media. I also introduced my approach of "glocal cosmopolitanism." In designing this approach, my thinking has been greatly enriched by our advanced resources on cosmopolitanism. But although we have developed sophisticated concepts of cosmopolitanism, these concepts reflect predominantly Western views of a globalized "interconnected world," views from the "old 'core' of the modern world system" (Calhoun, 2010, p. 597). To further cultivate our cosmopolitan thinking, we need to include a broader diversity of worldviews.

We can distinguish East Asia by its historical and cultural experience of globalization (S.-J. Han and Shim, 2010). In this context, how do East Asians experience migration and media? This chapter focuses on how Singaporeans might experience migration and media. Then in chapters 4 and 5, I refine my approach of "glocal cosmopolitanism" in relation to an East Asian, Singaporean context, as I analyze how Singaporean students in Melbourne, Australia, construct "relational glocalities."

Viewing Global Society from East Asia

Although we develop concepts of cosmopolitanism to inform global progress, these concepts are disproportionately based on Euro-American perspectives (Calhoun, 2010). Our view of the world is biased toward the experiences of rich, mobile Westerners who live in the historical centres of global society:

> First,...cosmopolitan theories reflect the perspective of the rich. Second,...cosmopolitan theories are rooted in the West. Third, the

> way in which most cosmopolitan theories try to escape cultural bias is by imagining an escape from culture into a realm of the universal (as though those who travel aren't still shaped by their previous cultural contexts and as though the global circuits themselves don't provide new cultural contexts). Fourth,...because cosmopolitan theories are rooted in the (declining) core of the modern world system, they tend to imagine the world as more systematically and uniformly interconnected than it is.
>
> (Calhoun, 2010, pp. 597–598)

Our relations with others in the world are wilder and more unequal than we imagine. We will understand global society more when we deepen our insight into a wider range of experiences of the world, when we shift our focus from "the singular "cosmopolitanism" to "cosmopolitanisms" in the plural" (Krossa, 2012, p. 8).

How might we map these diverse "cosmopolitanisms" (Krossa, 2012, p. 8)? We can distinguish types of "society" by how we have collectively experienced "reflexive modernization":

> - the *Western* path or model as the project of an unintended, temporally stretched and (more or less) successful modernization of modern societies;
> - the project of an active, '*compressed*' modernization driven by a developmental state (Korea, China);
> - *post-colonialism* as the project of a reactive, enforced modernization;
> - and the path of a '*failed*' modernization—where the establishment of the institutions of the First Modernity (like the nation-state) or the transformation into the Second Modernity ends in failure
>
> (Beck and Grande, 2010, p. 416, original emphasis)

This typology is an example of a Western-centric cosmopolitan view of globalization. It is cosmopolitan in that it recognizes that there are different types of societies and it contextualizes how societies might develop with reference to one another ("reflexive modernization"). However, it evaluates types of societies within a hierarchy that is based on a Western "model" of "success." By incorporating diverse cultures of globalization into a hierarchy of "success" and "failure," this typology unintentionally promotes "exclusionary normativism" (Krossa, 2012, p. 10). The people we study are likely to rank different types of social spaces within a normative hierarchy according to their personal values. However, as a social scientist who seeks to be open to social actors' normative hierarchies, I would be careful about proposing my own normative hierarchies as a concept.

"Reflexive modernization" is a global but culturally distinctive experience (S.-J. Han and Shim, 2010). In East Asia, we have been experiencing "compressed modernization" (Beck and Grande, 2010; Chang, 2010). Immersed in this rapid development, our publics perceive that risks are especially relevant, proliferating, and diverse (S.-J. Han and Shim, 2010). We also engage with a "highly bureaucratic, state-centered, authoritarian pattern of development" and East Asian cultural values of "dynamic balance between individualization and community networks" (S.-J. Han and Shim, 2010, p. 481).

It is worth studying how East Asian media cultures relate to globalization (Chitty, 2010; Choi, 2010; Iwabuchi, 2010) since we have been consolidating an "East Asian Cultural Sphere" through the "cultural regionalization" (Choi, 2010) of media representation, production, distribution, and consumption. For example, Singapore's national Chinese language newspaper *Lianhe Zaobao* routinely represents a decentered "Pop Culture China" through its coverage of entertainment celebrities and events in and across the People's Republic of China, Taiwan, Hong Kong, and Singapore (Chua, 2006). Other major organizations in the Singapore media industry coproduce with regional partners in order to lower costs, increase quality and guarantee distribution, as well as export to regional markets such as the Chinese markets, India and Malaysia (Curtin, 2007). Singaporean audiences are receptive to media that allows them to experience "mixed spatio-temporal assemblages" (Sassen, 2006, Chapter 8) of distance and proximity, global and local:

> Foreign productions are . . . acceptable if they are culturally distant, and Chinese productions can win over audiences if they are historically distant. Contemporary drama is more complicated, requiring a deft mix of local relevance and overseas allure.
>
> (Curtin, 2007, p. 183)

Singapore is distinctive because it is a sovereign city-state that engages with both the East and the West. There are only two other sovereign city-states in the world (Monaco and the Vatican City), and both are in Europe.

On the one hand, Singapore exemplifies "global cities as subnational places where multiple global circuits intersect and thereby position these cities on several structured cross-border geographies" (cf. Sassen, 2007, p. 91). Singapore is eighth out of 65 "Global Cities" in terms of its contribution to globalization across multiple domains: economic, human capital, information, culture, and politics (A. T. Kearney, 2010, p. 2). We used to be only one of two "primary" world cities not situated in a "core" country (an industrial market economy) (Friedmann, 1986, pp. 71–72) and we are today the fifth most "integrated" into the "world city network" (GaWC Research Network, 2010).

On the other hand, Singapore is known for its "highly bureaucratic, state-centered, authoritarian pattern of development" (S.-J. Han and Shim, 2010, p. 481). Singapore is a "model" of a society based on economic neoliberalism and political authoritarianism (Zolo, 2001). Within Asia, Singapore and its geographical neighbor Malaysia

> are concrete examples of the assemblages of neoliberal reasoning, authoritarian rule, and governmentality that have created distinct regimes of human worth.
>
> (Ong, 2008, p. 351)

Here as well as in the rest of the world, we have institutionalized "distinct regimes of human worth" (Ong, 2008, p. 351) through our management of migration. As contemporary Singapore focuses on economic development through knowledge, innovation, and R&D (Singapore Economic Development Board, 2014), we refine an evolving "ecology of expertise" (Ong, 2005) as we manage migrants based on the economic value of their skills (B. Yeoh and Lin, 2012).

Although there are some similarities between Singapore and Malaysia (e.g., geographical location, ethnic composition, political history), we position ourselves differently between the Asian region and the world. Singapore positions itself as a global leader in Asia, whereas Malaysia positions itself as a regional hub that facilitates exchange between sites in Asia and more major centers in global networks (Ong, 2005).

As Singapore and Malaysia have opened ourselves up to global competition and migration, we have developed different "ecologies of expertise" and redefined citizenship in different ways (Ong, 2005). Malaysia experiences a tension between Western modernization and local cultures of citizenship that are based on race and religion (Ong, 2005). In contrast, Singaporeans are sensitive to the public presence and expressions of foreign workers from the West and the Asian region, many of whom are highly skilled co-ethnics (Ong, 2005; B. Yeoh and Lin, 2012).

When we tell the story of Singapore, we officially begin at Singapore's independence in 1965 (SG50 Programme Office, 2015). However, when we include Singapore's colonial history in our public memory, we recognize even more how Singapore has been defined through relations among diverse cultures. When the British developed Singapore as their colony in the early 1800s, they were concerned to construct diplomatic relations with the indigenous Malays and the Dutch who had already established their empire in Southeast Asia (Luscombe, 2015). As the British designed Singapore primarily to be a strategic center of commerce, they encouraged the migration of European and Asian traders, as well as the organization of different religious and ethnic advocacy groups (Luscombe, 2015).

Singapore is a young nation that celebrates 50 years of independence in 2015. However, we are connected to European and Asian civilizations through a long history of migration. Since Singapore actively positions itself in global and regional networks, it is

> a prime site for the contemporary rearticulation of the Orientalist master-narrative of West versus East, where an empowered East, having appropriated and reconstituted Western modernity, now unsettles the established hegemony of the West... Both "West" and "East" here are imaginary entities constructed through a mutual symbolic mirroring, in a battle of overlapping, interested self/other (mis)representations.
>
> (Ang and Stratton, 1995, pp. 66–67)

Multiculturalism in Singapore is based on

> the concept of cultural democracy, which accords separate but equal status to the diversity of races, cultures, languages and religions in Singapore.... Singapore's multicultural policy... aims at harmonious coexistence and integration, rather than assimilation.
>
> (Singh, 2008, p. 418)

Whereas we have researched how Chinese, Japanese, and Koreans experience migration and media (e.g., Fujita, 2004; Kim, 2011; W.-Y. Lin, Song, et al., 2010; Qiu, 2003; Shi, 2009; Zhou and Cai, 2002), I contribute a Singaporean perspective to our understanding of East Asian cultures of migration and media.

Singaporean University Students in Melbourne, Australia

In our research, we rarely consider how international students experience migration and media. Perhaps we believe that international students are more likely to be physically and culturally mobile, so we focus on how other types of migrants "challenge established (and manufactured) canons of national identity by preserving their cultures, languages and religions" (cf. King, 2010, p. 1355).

However, if we view migration and media through a "knowledge perspective," we can understand how we use migration and media to access, develop, translate, and transfer knowledge (Williams and Baláž, 2008, pp. 37–46). Although we cannot fully transfer "embedded" and "encultured knowledge," we can advance "embedded and encultured knowledge in more than one place" through "circulatory migration" (Williams and Baláž, 2008, pp. 43, 45) and the sharing of experiences through intercultural communication. Through education and training, networking, exchange, and extracurricular activities, universities nurture "communities of practice" that connect "those with diverse knowledge within particular parameters of shared ideas and values" (cf. Williams and Baláž, 2008, p. 76). Through knowledge migration (academic and especially student migration), many people around the world join "localized CoPs" and link multiple "localized CoPs" (Williams and Baláž, 2008, pp. 76–77).

Like the rest of us, international students often choose to build on shared culture and language when expanding knowledge and social relations. For example, Chinese international students create a "knowledge diaspora" by publishing magazines that engage with relevant information and events in China (e.g., news on China's advances in science and technology, as well as career opportunities in China) (Qiu, 2003). In their personal time, Chinese students in the United States prefer to use Chinese-language news and entertainment because it is familiar, comfortable, and easy to understand (Shi, 2005).

Like the rest of us, international students use media to expand knowledge and social relations in the societies they live in. Using social networking sites has helped international students to broaden their social relations and ease into a new social environment (J.-H. Lin, Peng, Kim, Kim, and LaRose, 2012). During the 2008 US presidential elections, international students in the United States used American mass media to encourage their interests, opinions, and participation in US politics (Kononova, Alhabash, and Cropp, 2011).

As Singapore aims to function well through globalization, we manage the challenge of mobility (including student mobility) by relating with the diaspora of Overseas Singaporeans (Koh, 2012).

How have we talked about the relations between Singapore, Singaporeans, and Overseas Singaporeans?

As Singapore moved from the twentieth century to the twenty-first century, we aspired "to strengthen the 'heartware' of Singapore in the 21st century—the intangibles of society like social cohesion, political stability and the collective will, values and attitudes of Singaporeans" ("'What is Singapore 21'"). Singapore 21 conceptualized "Singapore heartbeat" and "heartware," prioritizing emotional attachment among Singaporeans, new Singaporeans, and Overseas Singaporeans (Singapore 21 Committee). Contemporary Singaporeans are distinguished by our perception of wellbeing as we reside in Singapore and the world, as well as our ongoing commitment to Singapore:

> The Singaporean of the 21st century is a cosmopolitan Singaporean, one who . . . feels comfortable working and living in Singapore as well as overseas. At the same time, he retains strong ties with Singapore and has an active interest in developments at home.
>
> (Singapore 21 Committee, p. 45)

Singaporeans do not necessarily reside in Singapore, but we are willing to reside in Singapore:

> Whether we live in Singapore or overseas, we must embrace a common vision of the country as a place worth coming home to and if need be, fighting and dying for.
>
> (Singapore 21 Committee, p. 13)

Being Singaporean is not about where we reside; Singaporeans are distinguished by our ownership of Singapore and our alignment with its development:

> We need to feel passionately that Singapore is where we identify with, where our roots are and where we feel is home, wherever we may be around the world.
>
> (Singapore 21 Committee, p. 13)

> Regardless of where we live . . . , we must have a strong sense of belonging to this country. Wherever we might venture, our hearts should be emotionally rooted to Singapore. We should have an instinctive sense of shared values, shared history and shared destiny, simply because we are Singaporean.
>
> (Singapore 21 Committee, p. 42)

Are these relations exclusive? Can we sustain commitments to multiple societies? Can we grow our "roots" deeply and broadly across multiple lands? Can we own multiple "homes"? Can we position ourselves along the journeys of multiple societies?

In 1999 when we proposed Singapore 21, we believed that being Singaporean is more about how we feel than where we live. However, seven years later, we were concerned that where we live is significant for how we feel. Migration and residence are both valuable for cultivating "Singapore heartbeat" and "heartware."

"The Singaporean of the 21st century…feels comfortable working…overseas" (Singapore 21 Committee, p. 45). This statement became real for a significant proportion of Singaporeans. In 2006, the Prime Minister's National Day Rally Speech recognized that some Singaporeans were preferring employment outside Singapore: "We respect the choice of those who work overseas" (H. L. Lee, 2006).

Through emigration and residence outside Singapore, we can immerse ourselves in learning how to function in the global system:

> We encourage Singaporeans to go abroad, spend time abroad, gain experience, understand how the world operates and then come back to Singapore.
>
> (H. L. Lee, 2006)

However, Singaporeans would prefer to limit our period of residence outside Singapore:

> But of course, while it's good to have people abroad, we also hope that they don't spend all their life there and at some stage, they will decide to come back to Singapore.
>
> (H. L. Lee, 2006)

Singapore society and "Singapore heartware" (Singapore 21 Committee) can only be sustained if Singaporeans use what we have learned to work in Singapore:

> We also worry, we worry because if every trained and skilled Singaporean is abroad, then who is going to be here in Singapore, *jaga rumah*, looking after the home, keeping Singapore dynamic, vibrant, beating? If we have so many people overseas but not many in Singapore, where will the next generation of Singaporeans come from?
>
> (H. L. Lee, 2006)

Why must Singaporeans reside in Singapore to invest our talents in Singapore?

We have constructed the Singaporean diaspora as a pragmatic solution to "brain drain":

> We have to maintain strong links with the Singaporeans who are abroad, with our overseas network so that they become a strength for us and not a loss.
>
> (H. L. Lee, 2006)

In a strategy for building loyalty to the Singapore brand, the Singaporean diaspora is a core segment of the global target audience:

> First, we must deal with our diaspora to make them part of the family and treat them as part of the family. Secondly, we must continue to promote immigration into Singapore because just as we accept that Singaporeans have the world as their oyster, so too we must promote immigration here and let this be one of the options which talent from around the world will look for when they are considering where to go and live.
>
> (H. L. Lee, 2006)

In the same year, the government founded the Overseas Singaporean Unit (OSU). The OSU is situated within the National Population and Talent Division of the Singapore Public Service. It manages public relations with Overseas Singaporeans to sustain Overseas Singaporeans' "Singapore heartbeat" (Singapore 21 Committee):

> The Overseas Singaporean Unit (OSU) plans and coordinates a whole-of-government effort to engage overseas Singaporeans to keep them emotionally connected to Singapore.
>
> (Overseas Singaporean Unit, 2015)

In Singapore, we discuss immigration more than emigration because we experience much more immigration than emigration. Of Singapore's total population of 5.5 million, 29 percent are non-Singaporean temporary residents whereas less than 4 percent are "Overseas Singaporeans," "Singapore citizens with a registered foreign address or who are away for a cumulative period of at least six months in the past 12 months to the reference date (i.e. June each year)" (National Population and Talent Division, 2015). Singapore's population has increased mainly because of migration. In the latest year of population statistics, Singaporean citizens gave birth to 31,000 children but Singapore permitted 45,000 new temporary residents, granted permanent residency to 30,000 immigrants, and granted citizenship to 20,000 immigrants (National Population and Talent Division, 2015).

There are 212,000 Overseas Singaporeans (National Population and Talent Division, 2015), and 65 percent of us are concentrated in four countries (Table 3.1).

Table 3.1 Where do Overseas Singaporeans live?

Location	*Number (T. Tan, 2012)*	*Percentage*
Australia	50,000	24
Britain	40,000	19
United States	27,000	13
China	20,000	9
Other	75,000	35
Total	212,000	100

> Singaporeans are also valued in emerging markets such as in the Middle East, Vietnam and Indonesia, in a wide range of industries.
>
> (T. Tan, 2012)

Like other Overseas Singaporeans, most Singaporean international students live in Australia, the United Kingdom, and the United States (UNESCO Institute for Statistics, 2014). More than 40 percent of Singaporean international students live in Australia (Table 3.2).

Singaporeans are the seventh largest group of international students in Australia (UNESCO Institute for Statistics, 2014). Australia hosts 250,000 international students (UNESCO Institute for Statistics, 2014). Approximately one-third of these students are from China, one-third from other countries in Southeast Asia, and one-third from various countries in the world (Table 3.3).

> Southeast Asian (including Singaporean) international students in Australia may best be described as "cosmopolitan locals" for their mix of agency as (upwardly) mobile, educated citizens and liminality in inherently temporary, subject positions, clearly identified with a nation-state in which they choose not to reside presently.
>
> (Weiss and Ford, 2011, p. 231)

However, Singaporean international students in Australia are likely to experience migration and media differently. Unlike other Southeast Asian international students, Singaporeans come from an environment where English is the primary language of communication. International students from the other top ten nationalities tend to complete an English language intensive course in Australia before commencing higher education; in contrast, most Singaporeans and Malaysians directly enter Australian higher education (Australian Education International, 2011).

Table 3.2 Where do Singaporean international students live?

Location	*Number (UNESCO Institute for Statistics, 2014)*	*Percentage*
Australia	9,379	43
United Kingdom	5,253	24
United States	4,365	20
Other	2,780	13
Total	21,777	100

Table 3.3 Where do international students in Australia come from?

Rank	*Origin*	*Number (UNESCO Institute for Statistics, 2014)*	*Percentage*
1	Mainland China	87,497	35.1
2	Malaysia	17,001	6.8
3	India	11,684	4.7
4	Vietnam	11,081	4.4
5	Hong Kong	9,781	3.9
6	Indonesia	9,431	3.8
7	Singapore	9,379	3.8
	Other	93,734	37.6
	Total	249,588	100.1

One in four Singaporeans have thought about emigrating and 15 percent of Singaporeans think emigration is realistic (E. S. Tan, 2005). Why would Singaporeans emigrate? The answer is related to how they perceive their social relations, which depends on where they locate themselves. For example, Singaporeans in Singapore believe that ethnic and local-foreigner relations are weak in Singapore (E. S. Tan, 2005). In contrast, Singaporeans permanently resettled in Australia in the 1990s because of family reasons: their relatives in Australia sponsored their migration and they migrated to improve the wellbeing of their families (Khoo and Mak, 2003). Whereas these Singaporeans did not prioritize their careers (Khoo and Mak, 2003), Singaporean expatriates in China "define their relationship with China primarily in terms of career, business and economic motivations, or secondarily in terms of heritage and a 'return to roots'" (B. S. A. Yeoh and Willis, 2005, p. 273).

Once Singaporeans have migrated, how do they experience their new places of residence? Singaporean migrants in the 1990s have experienced greater success in the Australian labor market compared to other Asian migrants: they are more likely to use their qualifications and to express job satisfaction, perhaps because they are highly proficient in English, the local language (Khoo and Mak, 2003). In contrast, although Singaporeans in China are ethnically similar to the local Chinese, they perceive that the local culture of business communication is significantly different (Chan, 2005). The Singaporean businessman may experience discomfort with this difference, but he creates a "zone of comfort for himself and the other" by expressing the similarity between them (Chan, 2005, p. 167). When interacting with the local Chinese, the Singaporean businessman uses his ethnic similarity and national difference to offer the Chinese a meaningful view of Western economy:

> The Singaporean provides the Chinese with a window to the west, to the world. To a Singaporean, his greatest asset lies in his ability to strategise on his ethnic identity (of being Chinese) and his national identity (of being Singaporean) in his presentation of self. He invokes his identities in context.
>
> (Chan, 2005, pp. 167–168)

The Media Environment of Singapore

In the mid-1990s, the Singapore government significantly transformed the Singapore media environment through corporatization and globalization (Curtin, 2007, p. 178). Singapore moved beyond a domestic public media environment and positioned ourselves as a global center of finance and information based on "a state-of-the-art communication infrastructure that was open to services from around the world" (Curtin, 2007, p. 178). A new private organization, Singapore Cable Vision (SCV), constructed a national fiber optic network, enabling us to watch domestic and international commercial channels (Curtin, 2007, pp. 178–179).

Both Singaporeans and non-Singaporeans often emphasize the Singaporean government's role in media and communications, as we contrast the development communication model of Singapore to "the Fourth Estate model of Western liberal democracies" (Singh, 2008, p. 434). However, the roles of government, business, and public have been changing as public relations in Singapore have developed over different phases, from "nation-building," through "market development," to "regional interdependence" (Van Leuven, 1996). Furthermore, we are developing newer media such as mobile television between the spheres of "policy," "industry/market," and "technology" (T. T. C. Lin and Liu, 2011).

Singapore's cultures of public communication have been significantly shaped through governance. Singapore's media and communication law grants the Singapore government significant discretion, and there is little room for review and appeal (Cenite, 2006). Through the Singapore government's long-term management of Singapore's domestic and foreign press, we have established a culture of "self-censorship" and "mutual-censorship" in journalism, and citizens are careful about expressing public opinion through mainstream media (Tey, 2008, p. 896).

The Singapore government manages its public image through "gestural politics," which

> occurs or operates when "liberal gestures" in the forms of rehearsed rhetoric, public statements, press releases and, indeed, the propagation of buzzwords by the regime are bestowed with greater discursive powers in shaping perceptions as compared to actual substances or power symmetries.
>
> (T. Lee, 2008, p. 173)

We need to train ourselves in critical media literacy to discern and constructively respond to "gestural politics" (cf. T. Lee, 2005, 2008). However, in Singapore's legally restricted environment of public communication, mainstream political discourse is uncritical by international standards, and civil society and political opposition are relatively fragile (Kenyon, 2010). Singaporeans are insecure about "out-of-bounds markers" which implicitly circumscribe what can and cannot be publicly discussed; so we appear to be politically disengaged and there is little public debate (T. Lee, 2008, p. 171). Singaporean junior college students do not critically understand, deeply engage, and question news' claims to truth because they perceive that the newspaper is a "'schoolie' text" (Koh, 2004, p. 54) and their news consumption is "guided by a purposeful and pragmatic logic that aims to uncover (*not* 'discover') as much information as possible" in order to meet academic requirements (p. 52, original emphasis). Moreover, Singaporean junior college students value "cultural proximity" and are interested in familiar topics such as news on Singapore and lifestyle news (Koh, 2004, p. 52).

However, the structure of Singapore's online public sphere reveals some opportunities for marginalized people and collectives to bypass Singapore's restricted offline media environment and generate an alternative space for political expression (C. Soon and Cho, 2011). Singapore's online public sphere is dominated by densely interconnected political blogs and political parties that are interlinked apart from the governing party; issue-based advocacy groups and media organizations are disconnected and peripheral (C. Soon and Cho, 2011). Interestingly, almost two-thirds (17 out of 27) of the news media agencies in Singapore's online public sphere are foreign, as bloggers and political organizations value foreign information sources (C. Soon and Cho, 2011, pp. 101–102).

Across East Asia, youth who are interested in politics use the Internet for civic engagement (W.-Y. Lin, Cheong, et al., 2010). In the East Asian cities of Hong Kong, Seoul, Singapore, Taipei, and Tokyo, youth are starting to use the computer at a younger age; they are increasingly using digital and convergent media (e.g., mobile Internet); and they are engaging more and more in online civic activities such as news reading and civic discourse (W.-Y. Lin, Cheong, et al., 2010).

However, East Asian media cultures differ in their political and civic contexts, media practices, and forms of civic engagement (W.-Y. Lin, Cheong, et al., 2010). Compared with other East Asian youth, Singaporean youth discuss international events more (W.-Y. Lin, Cheong, et al., 2010). Singaporeans engage more in online civic discourse and petitions, using the Internet to create an "alternate civic space" in a highly controlled environment where political discourse and participation are repressed through media, political and legal restrictions (W.-Y. Lin, Cheong, et al., 2010, p. 14).

Similar to Western youth, East Asian youth use the Internet primarily for entertainment and to relate with one another (W.-Y. Lin, Cheong, et al., 2010). Singaporeans spend more time playing video games than Americans, but the level of pathological gaming in Singapore is similar to other places in the region and the world (e.g., South Korea, China, and Spain) (Choo et al., 2010). Singaporeans view Internet gaming as a personal choice, an activity that is personally significant and compatible with other areas of life (Wang, Liu, Chye, and Chatzisarantis, 2011).

According to the 2015 World Economic Forum Global Information Technology Report of 143 countries, Singapore is most capable of using Information and Communication Technologies effectively (World Economic Forum, 2015). However, there are "post-adoption digital divides" among 15–29-year-old Singaporean citizens studying at higher education institutions in Singapore (Cheong, 2008). Singaporean students differ in their experiences of computer and Internet use, according to their "technological proficiency" (p. 788) and the extent to which they depend on others to solve their technological problems (Cheong, 2008).

Having lived in the Singapore media environment, Singaporean university students in Melbourne are likely to be high media users who are up to date with new technologies. They will probably prefer commercial entertainment, and will possibly consume a mix of global and regional media from both the West and the East, in both English and Asian languages. We might expect that Singaporean university students in Melbourne will have mixed views about migration, cultural difference, and politics. They may be careful about expressing their opinions, especially on Singaporean politics and sensitive issues. However, Singaporean university students in Melbourne can be adaptable to new contexts of residence, education, media, communication, and cultural diversity. How do Singaporean university students in Melbourne actually experience migration and media? How do they actually view the world and its social spaces? I address these questions in the next two chapters.

CHAPTER 4

Geographies

In this chapter, I draw on a comparative interpretation of interviews with 21 Singaporeans in Melbourne, Australia, to analyze constructions of "relational glocalities" in experiences of media and migration. This chapter reveals constructions of the self across interrelated spatial contexts (cf. Appadurai, 1996) of social relations. In particular, it identifies diverse configurations of the local in the global (Giulianotti and Robertson, 2007; Meyrowitz, 2005; R. Robertson, 1994, 1995, 2003) and the global in the local (de Block and Buckingham, 2007; Sassen, 2006).

As discussed in chapter 2, Robertson considers "universalism" and "particularism" as "interpenetrating" in a "nexus" (R. Robertson, 1992, pp. 100–105). This conception is echoed in Beck's cosmopolitan approach in which he argues that "the global and the local are to be conceived, not as cultural polarities, but as interconnected and reciprocally interpenetrating principles" (Beck, 2006, pp. 72–73). In the (European) context of media and migration, Georgiou builds on Robertson's notion of the "universalism-particularism nexus" (R. Robertson, 1992, pp. 100–105), viewing a "universalism-particularism continuum" in which "[u]niversalism and particularism become central analytical concepts for understanding diasporic media cultures beyond binaries and oppositions" (Georgiou, 2005a, p. 482).

Informed by these ideas, I understand global and local sociospatial dimensions of "glocality" (Meyrowitz, 2005; R. Robertson, 1994) as coordinates along a continuum, corresponding not to particular scales, but relevant for constructions of spaces at and across various scales. Multiple global and local coordinates are viewed as appearing with greater or lesser prominence relative to one another, contributing to the definition and "differential positioning" (Glick Schiller and Çağlar, 2009, p. 188) of various "relational glocalities."

I use the terms "geographies" and "cartographies" for the comparative interpretation of macrostructural and microstructural constructions of social spaces respectively. I view macrostructural "geographies" as juxtapositions of relatively fixed and bounded "absolute space[s]"[1] (cf. Harvey, 2009, pp. 134–135) such as countries and cities of residence. In contrast, I view microstructural "cartographies" as associations of social spaces that emerge as subjective "contexts" of meaning (cf. Appadurai, 1996, p. 184).

During the recruitment process, I requested personal information about subjective (previous and current) places of residence and the amount of time of residence in each place. This information suggests that biographies often include places of migration other than current places of presumed origin and residence (e.g., Singapore and Melbourne/Australia). In addition, the interviews reveal that a much wider diversity of places are perceived as meaningful, associated, for example, with experiences of media and second-hand experiences of migration in the biographies of significant personal relations.

In this chapter, I provide a brief overview of the subjective "geographies" of social relations. This approach will also identify perceptions of the transforming media environment in contexts of public communities and public issues/events.

"Glocal Biographies": Between Family Relationships and Individual Aspirations

As Appendix 1 shows, migration[2] trajectories often reflect notions of biographical history, life, and aspiration in relation to three or more places. Although this outcome is influenced by my selection criteria (I selected to interview participants who had lived in a greater number of places), it highlights the relevance of places of migration other than presumed places of origin (e.g., Singapore) and residence (e.g., Melbourne/Australia), even for respondents who identify as Singaporean and whose migration biographies are relatively short given their age of young adulthood (20–26 years old).

In the following subsections, I distinguish patterns of migration experience according to the biographical life stage at which migration is perceived (childhood and young adulthood), the relevance of particular types of social relations (familial and peer relations) for experiences of migration, and the mode of experience (first hand and second hand) (Figure 4.1).

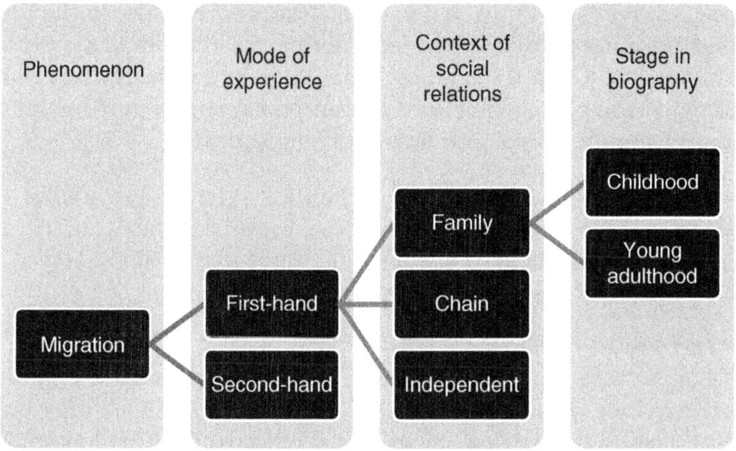

Figure 4.1 Geographies

Family Migration in Childhood: Exclusive Identification with the Country of Settlement or Cosmopolitan Lives

Approaches to media and migration rarely account for childhood experiences, with the exception of studies exploring experiences of refugee children in Europe (de Block and Buckingham, 2007; de Leeuw and Rydin, 2007a, 2007e). In contrast to previous studies of media and migration (including the few studies of children's experiences), my study reveals young adult perceptions of media and migration in childhood, as well as the relevance (or not) of childhood experiences for postchildhood experiences of media, migration, and social spaces.

Of the four respondents who have migrated as children, two have migrated to Singapore from their birthplaces in Chengdu, China (Will, Male) and Hong Kong under pre-1997 British rule (Natasha, Female). The other two have been born in Singapore and migrated to Malaysia (KoT, Male) and Perth, Australia (Jamie, Female). Will, Natasha, and Jamie have migrated when they were six to seven years old[3] and this similarity in age at migration could facilitate, to some extent, comparison across their otherwise quite diverse childhood migration trajectories and experiences.

Although perceptions of birthplace can be significant for mediated postmigration experiences of community space (Hiller and Franz, 2004), for Will and Natasha, awareness of birth in Chengdu/China and Hong Kong/United Kingdom, respectively, does not contribute to a sense of identification with these places and their associated societies. Will lists China as one of the places of residence in the personal information details provided during the recruitment process; however, he does not mention China in the interview. Natasha only refers to Hong Kong once, and this reference is made in the context of justifying the central significance of Singapore:

> I didn't really grow up in Singapore, I spent the first six years in Hong Kong, then after that I went to Singapore. But the main bulk of my life was spent in Singapore. And that was the place I would consider home. And that is the place where you've grown up.
>
> (Natasha, Female)

For Natasha, residence in Hong Kong during childhood means that her biography is longitudinally divided between Hong Kong ("the first six years") and Singapore ("after that"). This longitudinal division of life between two places is a slight issue that restrains Natasha from unproblematic identification of Singapore as "home" in the singular: her association with Singapore as "home" cannot be exclusive (related to either growing up or not in Singapore), but it has to be qualified ("I didn't *really* grow up in Singapore," emphasis mine). Contrary to this "concession," however, Natasha concludes that Singapore "is *the* place where you've grown up" (emphasis mine), pointing to the significance of exclusive association with Singapore as "home." To justify this conclusion, Natasha emphasizes the proportion of her divided biography ("the main bulk of my life") spent in Singapore relative to other places.[4] (I discuss the relevance of significant life events such as birth and development ("growing up") for notions of "home" in experiences of media and migration later.)

Strikingly, both Will's and Natasha's interviews reflect little or no mention of birthplace, coupled with narratives that highlight the central significance of Singapore. For example, Will identifies exclusively with Singapore and, in view of this identification, assumes ("naturally") that it is of high value to keep continuously updated on news of Singapore:

> that's where my home country is, so naturally I would want to find out what's happening there.... as a Singaporean, it's pretty important to know what is happening back home.
>
> (Will, Male)

Will makes this statement as he explains why he uses *Channel NewsAsia* online while in Australia. His use of *Channel NewsAsia* reflects the high, sustained, and almost exclusive[5] relevance of

Singaporean mainstream news media sources for news: in Singapore, Will reads the *Straits Times* and *Lianhe Zaobao*[6] national broadsheets, and he watches *Channel NewsAsia*[7] on television; in Australia, he reads *Channel NewsAsia* online twice a day and the Saturday print edition of the *Straits Times*[8] on a weekly basis. Will trusts Singaporean mainstream news media sources for news about Singapore and the world, hinting at "the refraction of even 'world events' into a specific [Singaporean] imagined world" (cf. Anderson, 1991, p. 63) (even) in a media environment characterized by easy access to and awareness of a wider diversity of (global and national) sources.

Given the negligible relevance of birthplace coupled with the central significance of Singapore as a cultural space, it could be tempting to describe Will's and Natasha's perceptions of migration in childhood in terms of assimilation, defined as "the narrowing of differences between immigrants and the native-born majority population in certain aspects of social life" (Bloemraad et al., 2008, p. 163). However, Will and Natasha do not express any sense of cultural differences, let alone the "narrowing" of these differences. Rather than assimilation, their perceptions of migration in childhood highlight the irrelevance or marginal relevance of birthplace for identification in the context of conscious commitment to the country of settlement. These associations to places of birth and settlement also differ from the conscious negation of commitment that Georgiou seems to suggest in her conception of "neither/nor" forms of noncommitment—"a choice neither to display loyalties to the country of origin nor to the country of settlement" (Georgiou, 2007c, p. 18). Drawing on Natasha's and Will's interviews, perceptions of migration in childhood point not to a (conscious or unconscious) turn away from countries of origin, but to the irrelevance of countries of origin.

Comparative interpretation of perceptions of migration in childhood reveals a clear difference in place relations, between the two respondents who have migrated to Singapore (Will and Natasha), on the one hand, and the two respondents who have migrated from Singapore (KoT and Jamie), on the other hand. Whereas Will and Natasha perceive the negligible relevance of birthplace coupled with exclusive identification with the country of settlement, KoT and Jamie articulate sustained experiences of, and active relations to, both the birthplace (Singapore) and the place of relocation (Malaysia and Perth, respectively). Although the period of relocation can be extensive (for most of KoT's lifetime and at least three years for Jamie), KoT and Jamie do not perceive the place/country of relocation as a place/country of permanent settlement.

Together with a Singaporean parent and a Malaysian parent,[9] KoT has resided on the Malaysian side of the Singapore-Malaysia border for most of his life. The geographical proximity of his place of residence to Singapore, schooling in Singapore, visa restrictions, as well as the presence of relatives in Singapore present multiple strong justifications for routine cross-border mobility to Singapore. The Singapore-Malaysia border on which KoT lives has also mediated (and not just geographical) dimensions. KoT's subjective media environment can be described as positioned on the border of the Singaporean and Malaysian media environments—it reflects the presence of the mainstream print newspapers and terrestrial television channels of both countries, and, as such, offers "opposing view[s] to every issue":

> There are different views in the media, in the Singapore *Straits Times* or the Malaysian *New Straits Times*.... they would be pro-government, but pro for their own government. I grew up reading two sides, I grew up having an opposing view to every issue, I was brought up... having many views and forming an opinion for myself.... I could receive every free-to-air Singapore channel. So that's where I got my views from. And I tend to watch Singapore channels rather than Malaysian channel [sic] when I was growing up.
>
> (KoT, Male)

KoT's childhood experience of media and migration reveals the development of a transnational life defined by "simultaneous embeddedness" in two societies and transnational connections across these societies (Glick Schiller et al., 1995, p. 48). It shows the construction of a transnational life through routine and sustained "grass-roots" practices enabled by mass transport and communications technologies (Portes et al., 1999). More specifically, KoT's account shows how experiences of dual nationality in immediate and extended families, extensive cross-border mobility for what could be considered basic activities (e.g., schooling, visa logistics, and family visits), as well as everyday, critical consumption of mediated discourses from two countries can interplay to contribute to the establishment of a transnational life. Anecdotal evidence and another interview (Zack, Male) suggests that KoT's experience of everyday transnational life and mobility between the geographical neighbours of Singapore and Malaysia is common.

KoT's experience of media and migration in childhood contexts of family life corresponds to Beck's characterization of "global families" as negotiating "the tensions between two countries" in experiences of dual nationality and migration (Beck, 2012, p. 9). In addition, KoT's experience shows how growing up in a dual-national family on a territorial border can facilitate familiarity with opposing perspectives, as well as learning to work through these perspectives to develop personal positions on public issues.

Held conceptualizes "cultural cosmopolitanism" as "the ability to stand outside a singular location (the location of one's birth, land, upbringing, conversion) and to mediate traditions," as well as a "cultural project" of "learning how to 'reason from the point of view of others' and mediate traditions" (Held, 2002, p. 58). KoT's experience reveals how "cultural cosmopolitanism" can be developed from a young age through the routine renegotiation of cultural borders in an environment that is culturally demarcated in its geographical, mediated, and family dimensions.

Although only Singapore and Malaysia as countries of birth and relocation emerge in KoT's narrative of media and migration in childhood, KoT initiates this narrative in the context of explaining why, years later in Australia, he values keeping informed of "what's going on in the world." KoT's interest in what he views as current world events includes news across different types of political contexts: global political centers such as Australia and America, as well as "countries with repressive government" such as Myanmar, Afghanistan, and Iraq. For KoT, being "connected to the world" means keeping up to date with world events and the strategies of multiple heads of state for national and global politics:

> Connections would include... Presidents and Prime Ministers of countries. So I read what they have to say on the news and I do follow them on Twitter.... I learn more about what plans they have for the nation and what plans they have for the world.
>
> (KoT, Male)

Relating KoT's childhood and young adulthood experiences of media and migration in a biographical context discloses that the "motives" (Schutz, 1966) for "cultural cosmopolitanism" (Held, 2002) can be established in developmental experiences of "border-living." Core "motives" for subjective positioning in a transnational context of "cultural cosmopolitanism" that extends globally later in life can precede contemporary experiences of networked media as well as current experiences of transmigration (e.g., between Singapore and Australia).

Family Migration in Young Adulthood: Transnational Personal Relations

Besides the four respondents whose biographies reflect family migration in childhood, another two respondents (Naomi, Female;

Timothy, Male) have resettled in young adulthood as legal permanent residents with immediate family in Australia. Naomi has resettled at 18 years old[10] with her parents and siblings, and Timothy has resettled at 20 years old with his mother.

In these two cases of family migration in young adulthood, the presence of immediate family in Australia is cited as the main justification for attachment to Australia and vision of a future in Australia. For example, Naomi perceives that the daily corporeal presence of family contributes to a distinctive sense of relational security that encourages her to move on from life in Singapore to anticipate life in Australia:

> I'm here, I'd better be 100% here. Not having my heart in Singapore and always wanting to go back, but looking forward to what this new journey is, the rest of my journey. And my family is here too, so different.... every day is family day.... More comfortable. More stable, being at home with family.... they're people who love you and accept you no matter what you do.... compared to my housemate, this friend.
>
> (Naomi, Female)

Naomi's experience suggests that the corporeal copresence of family not only facilitates affective relations to the country of settlement, but it is also a core consideration in decisions regarding migration and (short-term) mobility to other countries, including the country of origin. Despite having applied to, and been accepted by a university in the United States, she cites being with family as the first reason for finally deciding not to study in the United States, but to study in Australia instead. In addition, although Naomi perceives that it is both the norm and a social expectation to return to Singapore "every holiday" (at least twice a year), she has been using the presence of family in Australia as an acceptable "excuse" for "only [going] back twice... in four years."

In both cases of family migration in young adulthood, strong attachment to the country of settlement is compatible with strong, ongoing identification with the country of origin: Naomi expresses intense love, pride, and commitment in relation to Singapore as "my country," and Timothy refers to both Singapore and Australia as "(my) home."

In both cases, attachment to the country of settlement is based on the corporeal copresence of immediate family in the country of settlement, and identification with the country of origin is based on the corporeal presence of friends and (extended) family in the country of origin. Elaborating on her concern and effort to "keep in touch" with Singapore, Naomi remarks that "[t]he country is the people." This statement suggests that subjective transnational connections to country-scale societies are grounded on the corporeal presence of significant personal relations in associated territorial places.

When migration is experienced in young adulthood, significant familial and friendship relations have already been established in the country of origin. At the same time, in contexts of family migration, the corporeal copresence of immediate family in the country of settlement is a core, even distinctive factor encouraging plans for resettlement. The distribution of significant personal networks across countries of origin and settlement, (bidirectional[11]) practices of transnational mobility to (re)create situations of corporeal copresence, as well as shared discourse of private and national public issues through personal (email) conversations and news sustain constructions of "transnational social fields" (Levitt and Glick Schiller, 2004).

Chain Migration in Young Adulthood: Corporeal Copresence with Intimate Personal Relations

In addition to the above patterns of simultaneous migration as a family, patterns of concurrent chain migration are evident in familial and close friendship contexts.

Research on what could be called aspiration to migrate associates trans-state chain migration with the "diasporic function" (Mai, 2005, p. 552) of transnational media based in the place of settlement. In particular, chain migration is related to transnational mainstream media representations of postmigration (Mai, 2004) and exilic media productions which represent the place of settlement as an idealized version of the place of origin (Johnson, 2010).

Whereas these studies focus on mass-mediated institutional aspects of chain migration, the work of Hiller and Franz (2004)[12] offers analytical resources for understanding the networked mediated connectivity aspects of chain migration. In the context of transborder chain migration within country (rather than across countries), chain migration can be facilitated by the informational and emotional support of local community relations developed online across pre- and postmigration settings (see Hiller and Franz, 2004). Hiller and Franz claim that "the pre-migration experience online is purely instrumental" and that the community relations relevant in premigration settings are dominated by "weak ties" (Granovetter, 1973) such as otherwise anonymous, distant familial, and indirect friendship[13] relations (Hiller and Franz, 2004, pp. 738–740).

In contrast to these studies, in my study, patterns of chain migration are motivated by perceptions of intimate personal relations corporeally located in or near the potential place of settlement. Three respondents (Thornton, Male; Jamie, Female; Clara, Female) have selected to migrate to Melbourne instead of another overseas[14] location, primarily because of the presence—and potential copresence—of immediate (Thornton) or extended (Jamie) family members, or a significant other (Clara) in Melbourne. In addition, Clara has migrated to Brisbane prior to her migration to Melbourne, motivated by the proximity of close friends residing in other major (compared to Brisbane) cities in Australia.

Thornton's statement below suggests that, at a microlevel, chain migration can be primarily motivated by intimate personal relations with "post-migrant" or "settled migrant" (Hiller and Franz, 2004) subjects. Explaining his decision to migrate to Melbourne, Thornton says:

> My sister's here. She chose it, not me. She was here studying already, so that's why I came here, to join her.
>
> (Thornton, Male)

Interpreting the above statement, Thornton's selection of Melbourne as the migration destination has been centered on his sister's prior selection of Melbourne as the migration destination ("she chose it"), her corporeal presence at the migration destination ("my sister's here"), and the value of corporeal copresence achieved through migration to the particular destination ("I came here, to join her").

The significance of intimate personal relations for chain migration is also echoed in shorter-term trans-state mobility experiences. Sally (Female) has spent 5 of the past 12 months visiting her sister and brother-in-law in London, traveling between Melbourne and London via Singapore every semester break. This practice of frequent mobility is motivated by her perception of the corporeal location of her sister in London, intimate family relations, and the value of corporeal copresence:

> London is where my sister is, and I'm very close to my sister, so go there and visit her.
>
> (Sally, Female)

As in contexts of simultaneous migration as a family, in contexts of chain migration, the corporeal copresence of intimate personal relations encourages not only migration, but also settlement. Having met her Australian-born Malaysian Chinese boyfriend in Melbourne and having obtained permanent residency,[15] Nicole (Female) is planning to set up a family in Melbourne.

Similar to Mai's study in the context of Albanian migration to Italy (Mai, 2004, 2005), my study reveals premigration experiences of subjective trans-state chain migration across particular places (Singapore-Melbourne, Vancouver-Brisbane, Melbourne-Singapore-London). However, echoing to some extent Johnson's study in the context of Cuban migration to Miami, the United States (Johnson, 2010), Nicole's discussion of her sponsorship of her parents' permanent residency applications shows postmigration contribution to the chain migration of intimate personal relations. Although Nicole's parents, who are planning to migrate to Australia, have lodged an application for migration,[16] Nicole perceives that the recent[17] lowering of immigration quotas could make migration more difficult. With this concern in mind, she keeps as a backup plan sponsorship of her parents' permanent residency applications to Australia, leveraging on her permanent residency status.

Whereas parents are perceived as the central actors in experiences of family migration (see previous subsections), there is a greater sense of the agency of close peers within and outside the family in experiences of chain migration.

Independent Migration in Young Adulthood: Transnational Cross-institutional Linkages across Globalized Cities

In contrast to experiences of family and chain migration, experiences of independent migration reflect greater subjective agency in migration planning.

Five respondents (Clara, Female; Rachel, Female; Stryker, Male; Natasha, Female; Lisa, Female) have engaged in independent migration to destinations other than Singapore and Melbourne, for (a combination of) study- and work-related purposes.

The "geographies" of Clara, Rachel, Stryker, and Natasha reflect one to three places of independent migration before migration to Melbourne. Clara completed three and a half years of undergraduate study in Vancouver, Canada, followed by one year of study exchange in Brisbane, Australia. She then returned to Singapore for half a year of work before returning to Vancouver for another half a year to finish her undergraduate studies. Rachel has spent two to three years in London (reason not given) and has worked for one year in Shanghai. Stryker has spent two years in Brunei on an overseas work posting. Combining study and work, Natasha has spent six months in

Shanghai completing an internship as part of a polytechnic (postsecondary) course.

Whereas the above migration experiences have taken place before migration to Melbourne, Lisa has spent a year in the United States in between her time in Melbourne. As part of her undergraduate degree in Melbourne, she has gone on a six-month study exchange to Texas. Considering that her US visa allowed her to work in the country for the same length of time that she had spent on exchange, she applied for employment in the United States and moved to Washington, DC for six months of work before returning to Melbourne for further study.

The above examples of migration in contexts of study exchange, course-related internship, and overseas work posting suggest that independent migration follows transnational cross-institutional linkages in globalized contexts of education and work.

From the above experiences of independent migration, I would argue that subjective trajectories are highly individualized. To elaborate, there is very little overlap between the five trajectories in terms of their places of migration[18]: with the exception of Shanghai (Rachel; Natasha), places of migration differ between subjective trajectories.

Considering that the five experiences of independent migration reflect globalized migration across cities, enabled by transnational linkages between education and work institutions, it could be tempting to understand these experiences as elite experiences of (hyper)mobility in global networked "space[s] of flows" (cf. Castells, 2010). Such an understanding is reflected in Ong's critical description of neoliberal cosmopolitanism in the context of second-generation migration from Hong Kong:

> Even more cosmopolitan than their parents, the children—mainly educated in Great Britain and the United States, now worked for global companies throughout European and Asian capitals. These "yompies" (young, outwardly mobile professionals) in their late twenties and thirties, armed with degrees from Oxford, Cambridge, Harvard, and other Ivy League universities, consider themselves "global citizens." They maintain a loose network with other Asian, mainly ethnic Chinese yompies from Singapore, China, Malaysia, and India, formed through the global networks of higher education, corporate employment, and favourite vacation destinations....they are free-floating corporate-borne individuals who may dip periodically into these cities for cultural "brain food" in between bouts of global dealing.
>
> (Ong, 2008, pp. 153–154)

In Ong's description, the "geographies" of neoliberal "global citizens" are structured as global networks of elite social relations based on centers of power (regional capitals and elite education institutions). Free mobility is enabled by global networks of global corporations ("free-floating corporate-borne"). Ong's depiction of neoliberal "global citizens" corresponds to de Blij's categorization of "globals" as subjects characterized by the power to engage freely in mobility (de Blij, 2009).

Perceptions of independent migration in my study challenge the neoliberal cosmopolitan view of "global citizens" engaged in elite networking and (hyper)mobility in global networks.

Across all 21 respondents, plans for the future after the completion of studies in Melbourne include life in Melbourne, return to Singapore, and/or migration for work or further study to countries such as Japan (Andrew, Male; Isabel, Female), Germany (Jamie, Female; Wendy, Female), and Canada (Nicole, Female). Whereas some respondents are seriously planning to migrate to a destination other than Melbourne or Singapore, from as soon as in the next six months (Isabel) to as late as in the next ten years (Nicole), others are keeping their options open.

Second-Hand Experiences of Migration

Three respondents have one or two (step-)parents from countries other than Singapore, namely, Malaysia (KoT, Male), China (Mark, Male), and Myanmar (Timothy, Male).

In addition, having migrated and/or having friends who have migrated, a close network of friends who currently reside in places such as the United States, the United Kingdom, Sweden, France, India, China, Japan, Brunei, and Perth constitute their core segment of social relations:

> I've got friends all over the world. US, UK. It's everywhere, places where I have went [sic] to and friends that I have acquainted and they have gone back to their home country.... Save for Antarctic, I haven't reached that continent yet.
>
> (Stryker, Male)

> I lived in Shanghai, I met a lot of people who are overseas. So they've all returned to their own countries.... Most of my friends I met when I was overseas were from UK and Sweden.
>
> (Rachel, Female)

Media Environment, Public Communities, and Public Issues/Events

Media Environment

Media and migration studies often focus on the sociospatial aspects of a particular type of media technology, for example, the development of global and local ethnic communities around diasporic audiovisual media (Sinclair and Cunningham, 2001), the everyday relevance of transnational satellite television for perceptions of and relations to the country of origin (Aksoy and Robins, 2003a), transnationalism in ethnic newspaper production (W.-Y. Lin, Song, et al., 2010), as well as the construction of "cyber-place" (Parham, 2004, pp. 205, 209) and "online territories" (Christensen et al., 2011).

In contrast, my study shows that social spaces are constructed in "transmedial" (Hepp, 2009a, p. 330) environments in which a wide range of media technologies are relevant. Relevant media technologies include the Internet, the mobile phone, cable and broadcast television, the newspaper, radio, the video game console (e.g., PlayStation and Wii), the portable music device (e.g., iPod), DVDs, books, magazines, advertisement posters, and pamphlets.

Within such a variety of media technologies, however, almost all the respondents perceive that the Internet is their favorite medium. The Internet is seen as a multifunctional platform for work and leisure, news and entertainment, personal interest and social networking, as well as logistical functions such as banking and geographical navigation.

The Internet is thought to be distinctively capable of spatially relevant technological convergence, in contrast to other media technologies. Whereas the respondents previously accessed content through a combination of multiple media technologies,[19] similar and additional content can now be accessed through the convergent multimedia Internet as it selectively but significantly incorporates and replaces previous media technologies of accessibility.[20] Studies of online diasporic networks have focused on the relationships between media and geographical spatial dynamics of connectivity and territorialization (Christensen et al., 2011; Hanafi, 2005; Kim, 2011; Parham, 2004). However, online multimedia convergence also means the reconfiguration of multiple media technological networks through online networking (see chapter 5 for a discussion of multiple media technological networks of social relations).

Timothy considers the Internet as a technology of accessibility ("an avenue where I can get everything") that is personally significant ("to me it's the most important"). His appreciation of the Internet is associated not only with its replacement of other technologies ("it cancels out the need for the TV or the radio"), but also with its convergent incorporation of these technologies (e.g., via Internet TV):

> It's an avenue where I can get everything easily and efficiently. It cancels out the need for the TV or the radio, when I can actually get it all on one platform. So to me it's the most important currently....I enjoy watching the English Premier League, it's not shown on local TV, Australian TV, and it's usually pay-per-view, so I managed to watch it online....I watch it on this player called TVU Player. It's a [sic] Internet TV application which allows you to watch many channels from overseas.
>
> (Timothy, Male)

For Timothy, online multimedia convergence means the opening up of geographical and financial access to "everything," that is, content that contributes to his sense of wellbeing, meeting personal needs for routine enjoyment and satisfaction. Online multimedia convergence enables access to content beyond the place of residence and its territorial media environment: Timothy can "watch many channels from overseas," including content that is "not shown on local TV, Australian TV." Timothy can also bypass financial (e.g., "pay-per-view") constraints, accessing broadcasts of the English Premier League which are not available on free-to-air television or which can only be accessed offline through paid subscription to cable television.

However, although the respondents articulate many instances of access to content through online multimedia convergence, Zach's statement below indicates that online access to content can be limited to selected modes of representation:

> Soccernet.com. Which is the world largest soccer news website. So whenever there is news, there will very up-to-date [sic]. For example, last weekend, there's match. So after the match end, I just refresh the page. There are reviews, reports on the match.
>
> **Do you watch the match as well?**
>
> No, because they only telecast on Foxtel [cable television], which I doesn't [sic] have.
>
> (Zach, Male)

The mobile phone is also one of the key platforms, considered to be a portable medium through which the respondents can enjoy two-way access with others wherever they are at all times.

Public Communities

Although the respondents situate themselves in a variety of mediated symbolic environments, when asked about public communities, "friends" were sometimes given as an initial answer. Friends are perceived not only as significant personal relations, but also as core public relations. Their dual role as personal and public relations means that they can be viewed as bridges to public communities, essential for the respondents' initial and sustained participation in public communities.

Some respondents join public communities friends participate in, such as fan clubs, university student groups, and church.[21] The active participation of friends in what Isabel describes as "fandom communities" is the reason for her initial participation in these communities:

> Fandom communities . . . I'm quite active on those . . . 'cos quite a few of my friends are quite active in these, so I ended up taking part in it as well.
>
> (Isabel, Female)

Although Japanese anime fandom is transnationally popular, news about it is not available in Isabel's countries of origin and settlement. As such, Isabel and her friends rely heavily on the Internet for (translated) news, merchandise, and fan production (fanfiction and fanart):

> I'm into Japanese stuff. The anime fandom is really big. And since there's not much news about Japanese stuff both in Singapore or here [Melbourne], you only can use the Internet to find out more about the news. Some people will translate Japanese articles about what's coming out and merchandise. And people taking orders for new merchandise and acting like middlemen to buy things like the new series that are coming out. . . . there's also the fanworks community where they write stories based on the TV series, or they draw.
>
> (Isabel, Female)

In the "fandom communities," other subjects are relevant as cultural and economic brokers who provide linguistic translation of news, facilitate the purchase of (new) merchandise, and create secondary content based on the primary television content. Isabel not only is a beneficiary of this brokerage, but also contributes as a broker by opening up possibilities for the transnational distribution of "raw material" (e.g., primary or official products) to current and potential fans:

> If I were to order a photo book of an actor, I might sacrifice the book a bit and scan it and share the scans with people. Because they might

> not be able to buy it in their country. And if I buy a special edition dvd, the original one, I might rip it and put the whole thing or part of it for loan.... spreading the raw material around so people on the Internet would find the post you did, the thing you made, shared. And they might be interested in it and the series would have more fans.... I've scanned articles and I've ripped a cd... if you haven't heard of a certain artiste or series you might not be sure if it's worth investing. We use it more like a preview and hope that people who like it will still buy it.
>
> (Isabel, Female)

Although the fandom communities are based on online sharing of symbolic resources, these resources are based on a particular television series, such as "Tenipuri" ("Prince of Tennis"). In addition, some of these resources have originally been made available through non-Internet technologies. As such, they need to be processed for online distribution, for example, through the scanning of a print photobook or the ripping of CD and DVD. In this sense, "fandom communities" can be characterized not only as "transmedial" (Hepp, 2009a, p. 330), but also as based on brokerage in "transmedial" networks.

Isabel's participation in transnational Japanese anime fandom communities centers on the online circulation and brokerage of symbolic resources in "transmedial" networks. In contrast, KoT's sense of participation in the community of the Liverpool soccer fan club is based on the collective viewing of mass mediated events in national (Singapore) and local (the official fan club) settings of corporeal copresence and interaction:

> I support Liverpool, so if I'm in Singapore... whenever I have time, I try to visit the official fan club. You catch screenings with them, you have a drink with them. Makes me feel part of a community.
>
> (KoT, Male)

When corporeal copresence is not possible, communication with "friends from the community" through instant messaging and social networking platforms becomes more relevant for KoT to sustain relations to the community ("catch up with my community"):

> I don't know everyone at the fan club. There're hundreds of people. But I do have personal contacts with a few of them, around five of them. I do have them on my MSN, I do have them on Facebook. We still talk a lot. I can't meet them face-to-face, but I still discuss stuff with them, so I do catch up with my community in that sense.... without the Internet, I don't think I'll be as connected to them.... I have handphone, I can call them, but again, call charges would be expensive. The

> Internet has made things really easy for me to get in touch with friends from the community…I wouldn't send someone a snail mail.
>
> (KoT, Male)

The respondents appreciate public communities that resonate with their values, for example, national, regional, religious, and cultural ways of life and work, academic experiences, migration experiences, and/or leisure interests.[22] Some respondents not only participate actively, but also serve in leadership within these communities. Public communities are also perceived as important, especially during particular events.[23]

When information about and within communities is shared through online group pages and forums, online spaces not only encourage relationships developed in corporeal copresence, but also enable outreach to potential members. Interest in particular communities is initiated and developed through websites, video streaming, blogging and instant messaging, and social networking platforms.[24]

Most respondents use online forums and blogs to develop knowledge in "communities of practice" (CoP), defined by Williams and Baláž as networks that "link together those with diverse knowledge within particular parameters of shared ideas and values" (Williams and Baláž, 2008, p. 76). Results of my study support Williams and Baláž's suggestion that "migration may be critical for gaining entry to a localized CoP" (Williams and Baláž, 2008, p. 77). However, results also show the relevance of migration for experiences of media(ted) "communities of practice."

The respondents appreciate the sharing and exchange of information, opinion, advice, and resources in these communities. Some communities discuss leisure topics ranging from celebrity fashion and gossip, photography, and climbing, to a particular band (e.g., Blur), computer game, or fanfiction of a particular anime series (e.g., "Tenipuri"). Other communities discuss politics or professional interests such as the arts and information technology. These communities have been established through the accumulation of interactive discourse on a topic of common interest.

In local communities, the exchange of ideas in interactive discursive spaces is oriented toward what Lisa phrases as "relationship building." The respondents get to know "locals"[25] within specific collective spaces on online social networking platforms.[26] They also network and meet with people one on one at prearranged corporeal meetings such as a conference, a social event, as well as over lunch and coffee. In contrast, they access global or worldwide communities for knowledge rather than networking and friendship. Global communities are also characterized by transient connections in social media spaces such as forums, blogs, and Twitter groups.

Friends are also the main social relations with whom the respondents discuss public issues and participate in public events. For Andrew, the discussion of public issues is unplanned, emerging naturally as conversations with friends shift from light-hearted topics to "serious" themes such as news events:

> At home talking to friends, get together, just discuss. Sometimes every Friday we'll just get together. We can talk a lot of nonsense, that's for sure, but we can also talk a lot of serious stuff like what's going on in the recent news.... MSN. To me it works like interaction at home with my friends, just that we don't go onto group conversation, so it's just one-to-one. If it just happens, sometimes we'll talk about a social issue or political issue online.... Facebook, I don't think I've left any academic comments before. It's usually just the everyday life interaction.
>
> (Andrew, Male)

For Andrew, the discussion of public issues in contexts of friendship varies depending on the discursive environment. Group discussion of public issues unfolds face to face in routine domestic situations of corporeal copresence. Public issues are also discussed one on one through instant messaging. However, public issues are not discussed in a social networking setting.

In direct contrast to Andrew, Strkyer (Male) intentionally advocates regarding public issues (especially environmental issues) in social networking settings of friendship. In the cases of Natasha (Female) and Mark (Male), public issues also become relevant in domestic environments, in communication among housemates. I discuss later the relevance of (different) communication technological forms for the construction of different spaces of social relations.

In the next subsection, I discuss perceptions of specific, significant public issues/events.

Public Issues/Events[27]

A variety of global, transnational, and national events[28] are perceived as important. Important global events include the US presidential election contended by Barack Obama and John McCain, as well as the global financial crisis. Important transnational events include the swine flu pandemic, the terrorist bombings in Mumbai, the violence against Indian international students in Melbourne, as well as the

Black Saturday bushfires in rural Victoria. Important national events include the AWARE controversy in Singapore, the Singapore National Day Parade, and the Singapore general elections. All these events are mediated. In addition, these events were recent at the time of interview: interviews were conducted in 2009 and most of these events had occurred in 2008–2009.[29]

Issues/events are considered to be significant because they are important to a worldwide public, they could have direct personal impact, or they draw attention to a compelling need for action.

The respondents consider significant public issues/events to be those that interest and impact the global public that they are part of. In explaining why these issues/events are important, they say that "we all" or "everyone everywhere" are "affected." For example, although Lisa names issues such as the Iran election protests and Michael Jackson's death in association with a central political society (Iran) or figure (Michael Jackson), she defines them as key global issues because of their significance for a globally distributed public:

> For the Iran election and Michael Jackson, all that, these are big issues, global issues that we all have a shared memory. Those are important issues to everyone everywhere.
>
> (Lisa, Female)

Global events can be categorized as geographically noncentered (e.g., global warming and Michael Jackson's death), centered on a particular national society (e.g., the Iran election protests and nuclear developments in North Korea), or centered on multiple societies (e.g., "the state of the world's markets"). In multicentered events, geographical centers are viewed as more or less significant relative to one another. For example, Zack (Male) focuses on news on the US markets considering that "most markets are tied to their performance."

Issues associated with forms of marginalization, such as oppression, poverty, and illness/disability, are significant as particular groups are recognized as situated in (human[30] or particular societal[31]) conditions of suffering and need (Nicole, Female), evoking emotional responses of pity (Jamie, Female) and "human compassion" (Nicole, Female). Lisa perceives that an overarching interest in issues of "victimization" motivates her concern for particular marginalized populations, expressed in an interest in specific issues such as the "wellbeing of the Aboriginal communities in Australia," "the wellbeing of international students, especially the attacks on Indian students" in Melbourne, as well as the abuse of migrant workers in Singapore.

A number of respondents express strong commitment regarding public issues such as gender- (Clara, Female; Lisa, Female) and sexuality-related issues (Sally, Female). Strong commitment to acting on public issues can be seen, for example, in the choice of areas of study/research, employment in an issue-related organization, participation in issue-related events (such as the AWARE and pink dot events, see below), as well as in discussions with personal relations.

In contrast, others (e.g., Ivan, Male; Jamie, Female) downplay the significance of particular social/political movements, considering these movements to be trivial in contrast to issues in which lives are perceived to be at stake:

> [Global warming] affects everyone. No matter if you are rich or poor, we're all going to get burnt to death. So that's the only one which I think it's worth championing for: recycling, green cars, for example. Other political events like gay liberation or women's rights or labour union strikes are not really important. They are just things that people do to try and make noise to get attention to themselves...it'll sort itself out....Whereas with global warming, its effects can be felt on a global scale, and it's not something that will sort itself out, it's something that we are continually perpetuating, exacerbating the problem.
>
> (Ivan, Male)

As the above statement shows, Ivan considers sexuality-, gender-, and class-related social movements as merely ("just") self-interested expressions by vocal minorities. For Ivan, these social movements only concern particular segments of (global) society and they will be naturally resolved in time. In contrast, Ivan regards global warming as an important issue/event because its consequences are global ("affects everyone") and globally experienced ("its effects can be felt on a global scale"). He regards the problem of global warming as deserving of advocacy, given that it is ongoing and worsening.

Ivan's perception that global warming is a worsening, translocally experienced problem is related to his experience of circular migration. As Ivan is engaged in circular migration, he senses and compares longitudinal trends in local weather across two places, which he interprets as a translocal phenomenon of global warming:

> In Singapore, it wasn't so hot. I do remember being able to walk around my house and feel normal, feel cool...ever since 2004 onwards, the average temperature in Singapore has gone up a couple of degrees, and even just standing around and doing nothing, you'll start to perspire....Whereas in Melbourne...in 2006 I can't remember more than

> any two or three days having rained in the whole year, but whereas for 2009 it has rained quite a lot.
>
> (Ivan, Male)

Some issues, such as environmental and economic issues, become important when they are personally experienced in both global/translocal and local terms. In explaining why the issue of global warming is of great personal significance ("I'm very concerned"), Nicole repeats her personal observation ("seeing") of what she interprets as the impact of global warming at global, national, and local (domestic) levels ("I'm seeing the effects on earth," "seeing the situation here [in Australia], the trees and everything burning up," "seeing the grass under my apartment turning brown and disappearing"):

> Environmentally, climate change is interesting to me because I'm very concerned about global warming.... I'm seeing the effects on earth...it's something that touches me directly, with the drought in Australia, seeing the situation here, the trees and everything burning up. And reading that it's global warming that's causing all these things got me quite a bit, because it's the world I'm living in, it's so day-to-day. Seeing the grass under my apartment turning brown and disappearing—it's quite scary. So on an emotional level it touches me. Aesthetically it touches me as well. And just it being so close to home.
>
> (Nicole, Female)

Nicole personally senses and feels global warming in mediated and corporeal experience ("reading...got me quite a bit," "it's quite scary. So on an emotional level it touches me. Aesthetically it touches me as well"). As such, she considers global warming as a proximate phenomenon ("touches me directly," "so close to home"), associated with the experience of everyday life in the global ("it's the world I'm living in, it's so day-to-day").

Drawing on corporeal experience of the local environment and mediated interpretation of public discourses that relate local environmental phenomena to global warming, global warming is perceived as important because it is a "glocal" (Meyrowitz, 2005; R. Robertson, 1994, 1995, 2003) issue—experienced simultaneously locally and globally.

In his conception of cosmopolitanism as "ethical glocalism," Tomlinson builds on his view of the "local constitution of the human lifeworld" to argue that

> wider global commitments need to be concretised in terms relevant to this lifeworld. We cannot expect people to live their lives within a moral

> horizon that is so distant as to become abstract: the cosmopolitan ethic may have to be, in a rather literal, but positive, sense, 'self-centred'.
> (Tomlinson, 1999, p. 196)

Tomlinson's idea of the self-centered relevance of global commitments to local lifeworlds is supported by the respondents' associations between the importance of an issue and personal glocal experiences of the issue.

A variety of significant global, transnational, and national events[32] are experienced live online (through streaming or social media) or through television. Live events are coincidentally or intentionally experienced. This distinction is most clearly illustrated through a comparison between Timothy's experiences of the September 11, 2001 terrorist attacks, on the one hand, and his experiences of the Champions League final soccer match and the US presidential debate, on the other hand.

Timothy associates a situation of "sudden news or emergency news" (such as the September 11, 2001 terrorist attacks) with coincidental location "there at the current time, at the current place," in front of the television when the program is "cut" by a "news flash" that announces the event.

In contrast, Timothy locates live television broadcasting of the US presidential debate within a "series of events." The televised debate is first announced, described, and its outcome predicted through newspaper and word of mouth. Timothy perceives that the televized debate can be viewed "live, wherever, everywhere." For Timothy, this worldwide broadcasting indicates the importance of the debate for global politics and, in turn, the global audience of which he is a part: "because it's so important to the world's affairs, so everyone's going to watch it. So I decided I'll watch it too." After the debate, "critics" and "scholars" offer "educated" analyses of the debate online. Where a major event has been expected within a "chain of events," Timothy intentionally positions himself to experience it live. This intentional positioning is reflected in Timothy's experience of not only the US presidential debate, but also the Champions League final soccer match. He stays up at 4 am to watch the match through the Special Broadcasting Service (Australian public broadcasting), adapting to the time difference between his corporeal location in Australia and the geographical center of the match (Europe).

Whether the live experience is coincidental or intentional, it is characterized by strong feelings of involvement. In Timothy's case of intentional positioning, for example, although he is conscious of the geographical distance of the event as he explicitly locates the event "in

Europe," in the mediated timespace of the event he expresses a strong sense of collective time, that "every moment is ongoing" and that he "live[s] the moment with the team." This perception of shared time is foundational for developing solidarity as he "want[s] to be there in the moment to support them in the little way I can."

Similarly, Lisa, who has been "on Twitter long enough" to discover first-hand accounts of the Iran election protests through the hashtag #iran election, articulates strong feelings of involvement across geographical distance, in a global public:

> to read real time updates about what was happening over there [in Iran], which the news can never capture, is exciting. 'cos you're really into it, and people just update every few minutes.... [The Iran election protests] would be a worldwide movement. 'cos everyone was tweeting, everyone from everywhere. And they were retweeting. If an Iran blogger tweeted about something that happened, people around the world will retweet it and [it] will spread around the world very quickly through the rhizome, through the network.
>
> (Lisa, Female)

Moving from a global, transnational level to a global, diasporic national level, experiences of the Singapore elections reveal that whereas interest in the event "wherever I am" can be met through the Internet, corporeal and mediated experiences of the event are distinguished from one another:

> Wherever I am, I will probably be interested in the Singapore elections. Except that obviously you wouldn't get the full atmosphere and feeling the pseudo patriotism that goes around the air during the election period...everyone is so into the whole election during that period of time, then even when you take taxi [sic], everybody will be talking about how反政府[fan zheng fu, anti-government] everything [sic]...it's just interesting that people would be so united over their disdain for the government.
>
> (Wendy, Female)

On the one hand, the "full atmosphere" of the event can only be corporeally experienced through attendance at campaign rallies and through everyday conversations with fellow citizens (e.g., a taxi driver). This atmosphere is related to a temporary, intense feeling of civic, anti-state nationalism, characterized by "the pseudo patriotism that goes around the air during the election period" as "everyone...would be so united over their disdain for the government."

On the other hand, even without corporeal experience, multifaceted experience of the event is facilitated through the Internet, in particular blogs where corporeal experiences or feelings of rallies are shared, as well as YouTube videos such as 'Singapore Rebel" and political satire where opinions are communicated sometimes in humorous ways:

> I'll find out events that are happening through the Internet, that's pre-event.... During the event, I can't really know what's happening because it's not streamed on radio. It's not streamed on TV. But post-event is when the most information is being stored online. You have pictures of public rallies, you have transcripts of speeches, you have photographs of the massive amounts of people who cram into stadiums just to listen to one opposition speaker speak, or you have all the people cramming just to listen to the PAP [People's Action Party, the ruling party] speak.
>
> (KoT, Male)

As the respondents could be affected by issues/events, they need to be aware of these issues/events through news: "You gotta know what's going on and prepare yourself, 'cos ultimately it's your world" (Thornton, Male). The respondents seek online news, blogs, video, social networking, and email to become better informed about a particular issue/event, to experience the event live, as well as to discuss and act on the issues with others.

"Biographical Glocalization" and "Place Polygamy"

The comparative overview of subjective "geographies" reveals quantitative[33] and qualitative insights regarding the places that are relevant in experiences of migration.

In terms of the number of relevant places in experiences of migration, results show that apparently obvious[34] places of origin and settlement (such as Singapore and Melbourne/Australia) are not the only relevant places in experiences of migration. Rather, a multiplicity of places emerge as relevant, at different points in biography, related to one another within various patterns of migration that reflect both family and individual considerations. In addition, places that are prominent in the global media environment (such as the United States) often become significant during globalized events. The multiplicity of places in biography echoes Beck's concept of "place polygamy" as a feature of "biographical glocalization" (Beck, 2000d, p. 74) (see chapter 2).

The respondents' experiences of migration are dominated by Asian and world cities, paralleling conceptions of an Asian region of media (Choi, 2010; Curtin, 2007; Iwabuchi, 2010) and migration (Chitty, 2010), as well as "networks of global cities" (Sassen, 2006, p. 393).

(Media and) migration studies focus on either the country of settlement or the country of origin, or both these countries (see Ho, 2008a). Studies of experiences of media and migration—which favor ethnographic methods—tend to reflect ethnographic traditions in delving into local contexts of community residence (e.g., Gillespie, 1995; Ogan, 2001), although multisited ethnographic approaches are emerging (e.g., Georgiou, 2006). However, my study indicates that experiences of media and migration are often characterized by a multiplicity and diversity of relevant places.

CHAPTER 5

Cartographies

In the comparative overview of subjective "geographies" in the previous chapter, I have mapped constructions of social spaces based on relatively objective macrostructural phenomena such as countries and cities of (first- and second-hand) migration experience, as well as perceptions of media environment, public communities, and public issues/events.

In the following comparative interpretation of "cartographies," I compare subjective notions of microstructural phenomena in relation to the three dimensions of "relational spaces" outlined in chapter 2: spaces as constructed *through* social *relations* (social spaces), *relations between* social spaces, and *relations to* social spaces.

Relational Spaces

Social Spaces

Relational configurations of communication spatialities, networks, and modes (CSNM)

Online sociospatial experience is commonly described in terms of communication with social relations of "everybody" and "anyone," in spaces of "everywhere" and "anywhere." The prefixes "every" and "any" do not refer to undifferentiated notions of universal society or space; rather they define the outermost boundaries of a specific set of social relations—social relations that are, to some extent, "interchangeable and equivalent" (Dayan, 2007; Frosh, 2006, p. 281). In this sense, "every" and any" can be interpreted in a similar way to Gillespie's view of specific[1] "[d]igital diasporas" constructed around access to the BBC "anytime, anyplace, anywhere" (Gillespie, 2009).

The following quotes by Sally (Female) and Stryker (Male) show two contrasting perspectives of the (outermost) sociospatial boundaries of online discourse.

Sally imagines a blogosphere that is characterized by personal discourses of everyday life and differentiated based on types of social relations—sisterhood, friendship, nation ("Singaporean"), and non-acquaintance ("strangers"):

> The blogs that I go to is usually everybody's blog. My sister's blog, friends' blogs, strangers' blogs. It's about people talking about their own lives, the boring stuff. Occasionally it's the usual Singaporean blog like 'Mr Brown' or 'Popagandhi'.
>
> (Sally, Female)

Within the blogosphere as a social context, Sally distinguishes between categories of social relations based on the extent to which she perceives that she has a personal (e.g., friendship) or societal (e.g., national) relationship with others associated with the category. In addition, she views others not only as individuals engaged in self-expression about "their own lives," but also as representatives of their associated category (as friends, strangers, Singaporeans). Different categories of social relations are viewed relative to the self and to one another in a personalized, shared blogospheric network.

Stryker also distinguishes between a friend and a stranger, based on the extent to which he perceives the existence of a "social bond," that is, a form of social relation based on a sense of reciprocal interpersonal knowledge ("you know each other"):

> I wouldn't go to a stranger and start telling him, "ok, you must reduce, you must recycle." I don't think the message would go across as effective as a friend to a friend.... if a stranger suddenly comes and approaches me and starts saying something, I will feel a bit defensive about it, like "hey, I don't even know you, why are you talking to me?" Whereas on a friend-to-friend basis, there's a sense of you know each other, so there's... a social bond, so it's easier to talk [sic] certain issues.
>
> (Stryker, Male)

Whereas Sally distinguishes between groups of social relations in the personal discourse ("people talking about their own lives") context of the blogospheric social space, Strkyer differentiates levels of social relation in a public discourse context, for example, in relation to discourse about environmental public issues (advocacy for reduction in consumption and recycling). He locates public discourse (and its potential for social change) in communication among personal relations, articulating a view that is common among the respondents. It is in this specific context—public discourse among personal relations—that Stryker appreciates online connectivity:

> I would think that Internet is [sic] the greatest impact, because I think the Internet has the greatest reach. The reach of the Internet is there's no limit. What you say over here can actually be felt by someone in [the] UK, someone reads your message. So I would say the Internet has the greatest reach, greatest impact.
>
> (Stryker, Male)

The above quote constitutes Stryker's justification for prioritizing the Internet as a medium for public discourse in what he describes as his "immediate surroundings, immediate friends." Stryker values online communication as having the spatial potential to extend infinitely across geographical, rather than social, distance. Whereas "everybody" demarcates the outer boundaries of a socially differentiated blogospheric space in Sally's case, for Stryker, "someone"[2] indicates the outer boundaries of online public discourse in a geographically differentiated, friendship network.

Although online connectivity extends across geographical distance, online communication partners are often explicitly located not only in particular geographical locations, but also in their geographical proximity and distance. For example, Natasha (Female) uses the terms "everywhere" and "anywhere" to delineate an online, personalized sphere of friendship that incorporates multiple geographical locations without diminishing her sense of geographical location and proximity/distance:

> Everywhere. Like here, back home as well. There's no one place where they're located. Actually sometimes I even talk to my housemate when I'm lazy to get out of my room. So it really could be anywhere. They could be right next to you, they could be very far away.
>
> (Natasha, Female)

In Natasha's online friendship sphere, the self and others are situated in their respective geographical locations in territorial societies (in the places of "here" and home") and different sections (rooms) of a domestic place unit. These geographical locations are meaningful in terms of their relative proximity/distance to the self ("here," "back," "next to you," "very far away").

This discourse of geographical location and proximity/distance illustrates that online communication is sociospatially relevant not for the elimination of a sense of geographical distance between communication partners, but for the extension of communication across geographical distance.

Rachel also considers the extension of communication across geographical distance as important; however, she prioritizes mobile connectivity for both its spatial and temporal characteristics. For her, mobile connectivity means immediate (or close to immediate) access to (geographically distant) communication partners at any time.

The following quote illustrates not only the sense of geographical location and proximity/distance in experiences of mobile connectivity, but also the interplay between experiences of mobile connectivity and multiple (types of) migration experience (see chapter 4 for my analysis of different types of migration experience):

> I text [through the mobile phone] my parents quite a lot because they're not in the same place.... friends that are still in Singapore and friends who are living in Melbourne with me now. And I text to the UK and Sweden quite a lot. Europe. Most of my friends I met when I was overseas [in Shanghai] were from [the] UK and Sweden.
>
> (Rachel, Female)

For Rachel, mobile connectivity is highly significant for everyday communication with geographically distributed personal relations (family and friends). Mobile connectivity is significant for geographically distributed communication because first-hand experiences of migration (from Singapore to Shanghai and Singapore to Melbourne) mean that a particular category of relations (friendship) is established in multiple, distinct territorial societies (Singapore, Melbourne, and Shanghai). In addition, mobile connectivity means continuity of communication when there is transformation of the geographical distribution of Rachel's personal network. The geographical distribution of Rachel's mobile-mediated personal network has transformed to include additional territorial societies (United Kingdom and Sweden), in the process of interplay between first-hand (Singapore-Shanghai) and second-hand experiences of migration (the migration of friends from Shanghai to the United Kingdom and Sweden).

Research on mediated networking in media and migration contexts focuses on the relevance of "internet genres" (Siapera, 2007)—for example, discussion lists, bulletin board systems, and chatrooms—of interactive communication for the development of (imagined) territorially associated community networks (Hanafi, 2005; Hiller and Franz, 2004). These studies focus on examples of "internet genres" that are specific to a territorially associated community: for example, the Palestinian Scientists and Technologists Abroad (PALESTA) discussion list (Hanafi, 2005) and "bulletin boards created specifically for Newfoundland expatriates" (Hiller and Franz, 2004, p. 737).

In contrast, my study shows that mediated networking in media and migration contexts is usually not specific to a territorially associated community. In addition, it is facilitated through mobile, social networking, instant messaging, and email platforms. Moreover, it is characterized by personalized networking through global media platforms such as MSN (subsequently renamed as Windows Live Messenger), Facebook, and Hotmail.

The respondents organize permanent connections with personalized contacts through the above-mentioned platforms. The selection of specific shared platforms reflects and reinforces peer networks for two reasons. First, the respondents tend to streamline all their friend ship connections through platforms that are used or suggested by their friends. Second, as they converge all their friendship connections through these platforms, they lose contact with friends who do not share these platforms and who thereby become inaccessible:

> I have a friend who doesn't have a phone and Facebook...she's out of this world, she's living somewhere else. It's impossible to contact her.
>
> (Rachel, Female)

As more and more contacts are made accessible through particular mobile, instant messaging, social networking, and email platforms, these platforms become essential for the respondents to be constantly accessible to their contacts. The respondents imagine the possibility that others want to contact them and find no avenue of access. They take steps to avoid this possibility by keeping themselves constantly accessible.

The social pressure and social consequences associated with connectivity through a particular shared platform are highlighted by Wendy's (Female) statement that she "feels obliged" to keep her mobile phone on and that switching it off would mean "becoming a social recluse." The embeddedness of constant mobile connectivity in everyday life is further supported by Rachel's (Female) narrative of not missing a mobile phone call for two months.

Naomi's (Female) response that "you can check in but you can't check out" points to the capacity for connection to a platform-specific social network, coupled with the lack of capacity for disconnection from this network. Quoted from the lyrics of the song "Hotel

California" in the context of a discussion on Facebook-related social networking, Naomi's (Female) response refers to the need to sustain connectivity in a personalized social network.

Although many connections on a particular platform are latent and invisible, it is precisely this latency and invisibility that practically restricts or discourages the respondents from disconnecting from a particular platform or migrating to a newer and personally preferred platform. KoT perceives that the importance of maintaining two-way accessibility with others, coupled with the sheer quantity of contacts he has established over time through a particular email platform (Hotmail), practically limits his ability to shift to a newer, technically preferred email platform (Gmail):

> The reason it's so hard for me to change from Hotmail to Gmail, even though I like the Gmail interface better, is because many of my friends know me by my Hotmail address.... job searches, university application, or subscription to magazines online. My Hotmail account is tied down to too many companies. So to switch to Gmail, I can't just send a mass email out to all the companies that are connected to my Hotmail. Because I do not know how many companies are connected to my Hotmail anymore. I don't keep a list 'cos it would have overflowed anyway.
>
> (KoT, Male)

Although the respondents tend to value a particular platform primarily based on its social value among their friends, they also appreciate it for its features such as its interface or games. For example, Naomi describes Facebook as a "glorified address book." She means that it is more appealing than other contact lists because it organizes and displays her contacts through search function, event notification, and visual representation:

> It's a glorified address book.... if you ever want to talk to them you can just search for them.... it tells you when their birthdays are, it shows you their faces and their photos.
>
> (Naomi, Female)

I would argue that distinct sets of social relations are constructed around particular configurations of communication spatialities, networks, and modes (CSNM).[3] The selection of different CSNM for communication with different sets of social relations is based on considerations of the relative financial cost of the CSNM and the extent to which the time difference between communication partners must be negotiated in order for the CSNM to be shared. Migration is relevant for the construction of CSNM because these considerations involve taking into account the geographical location and distribution of the communication partners, as well as the geographical distance between the communication partners.

On the one hand, corporeal experiences can be visually represented across spacetimes through CSNM enabled, for example, by mobile phone multimedia messaging service (MMS) and voice-over-Internet Protocol service:

> Before it was $3 a month for unlimited MMS to people in the same network. That was really exciting, because now you can communicate with a picture, like where I am, or I saw this interesting thing, and attach.... For friends who ... don't really have time to check their email, we just communicate by messaging MMS. And even friends who are overseas, 'cos it's live, they get it immediately.
>
> (Naomi, Female)

On the other hand, different CSNM-associated communication spaces are influenced by social factors such as the type of social relation (e.g., familial relations) and the preferences of social relations. Different CSNM-associated communication spaces are also shaped by geographical factors such as the geographical locations and distribution of the communication partners, as well as the geographical distance between communication partners. These geographical factors inform temporal considerations (e.g., time difference) and the cost of a particular means of mediated communication.

The following statement shows how different CSNM-associated communication spaces are distinguished in relation to perceptions of the type of social relation, geographical distribution and distance, and associated cost considerations:

> Mobile phone is for people here in Melbourne.... MSN is usually for friends who are around the world, 'cos some of my classmates have been studying in [sic] US, UK... I do call my parents back home [in Singapore] by mobile, but it's quite costly so I try to do it over the Internet by Skype.
>
> (Zack, Male)

Zack identifies three spheres of mediated interpersonal communication, labeled as the sphere of the mobile phone, MSN, and Skype. The mobile phone sphere is distinguished by its spatiality, specifically its local geographical reach, the local being defined relative to the geographical location of the self ("people here in Melbourne").

The MSN sphere is associated with a particular type of social relation (friendship) and its spatiality, specifically a global geographical reach that incorporates particular territories ("around the world," "in US, UK").

The online Skype sphere is relevant for a particular type of social relation (familial), which expresses preference for a particular (audio) mode of communication. Although both the mobile phone and online Skype spheres permit audio communication across geographical distance, they are situated in different economic geographies. The creation of the online Skype sphere for familial communication is informed by Zack's perception of the high cost of the mobile phone sphere, considered against the relatively lower cost of the online Skype sphere.

Tomlinson argues that "telemediated intimacy" and "embodied intimacy" are different orders of proximity that are "integrated with [each other] in everyday lived experience" (Tomlinson, 1999, p. 165). Different CSNM-associated communication spaces are often characterized by different levels of intimacy. On the one hand, as Zack's statement above illustrates, the respondents communicate with the same significant personal relations through multiple CSNM.

On the other hand, different CSNM are associated with different groups of personal relations, distinguished by their levels of intimacy. Although it is unclear whether "online friends"[4] (Natasha, Female) are considered friends, they are distinguished from close friends with whom the respondents communicate in person, as Wendy suggests:

> Your friend's friends, you are close enough to talk to them on MSN word format a lot, but when you see them, video, it's a bit awkward, you have reservations. And if *you are so close to them online* already, when *you meet them in person, when you're not actually so close* to them, it's quite awkward.
>
> (Wendy, Female, emphasis mine)

Silverstone's concept of "proper distance" (Silverstone, 2003, 2007) has been developed in a context of societal distance: it focuses on the relations between the self and anonymous, culturally distant others in mediated spaces. However, the negotiation of "proper distance" characterizes many respondents' experiences of personal networks constructed around the Facebook social networking platform.

For these respondents, the negotiation of "proper distance" is associated with experiences of what Castells describes as "mass self-communication" (Castells, 2007). "Mass self-communication" is especially experienced when the 'self' views personal photographs which the other uploads for a specific "mass" audience—the other's personal network. The combination of "mass" and "self-communication" is viewed as a form of indirect communication: through the sharing of recent personal photographs, the respondents keep up to date with the life events of their personal relations without having to contact them directly and regularly.

Sally's experience of her mediated personal network involves the adoption of a "voyeur" subject position, characterized by the observation of others without direct contact:

> I'm just a voyeur. I like to just see what people are doing without having to ask them straight in their faces. Probably the next time if you see them, you can say, "Oh, I saw this picture in your Facebook! So, tell me more about the stuff that you did." It's like a conversation starter.
>
> (Sally, Female)

Sally associates direct contact with confrontation ("ask them straight in their faces"). She is open to initiating direct contact. However, she eases the sense of confrontation by building on existing shared resources of personal knowledge developed through indirect communication.

As media spaces characterized by "mass self-communication" (Castells, 2007), the personal networks constructed around the Facebook social networking platform are one example of CSNM. Different CSNM are associated with different spatiotemporal dynamics of communication: for example, the speed at which meaning can be expressed and exchanged in particular spaces, as well as the extent to which the respondent's corporeal position is limited within particular spacetimes (e.g., in an prearranged face-to-face meeting).

Lisa's statement below illustrates the relevance of different CSNM for different purposes in the maintenance and development of personal relations:

> In Facebook, when you have status updates, you comment on that, it might take two hours before you see the status and you comment on it. And the person takes a while longer to respond. So it's a long, drawn out conversation in the public sphere, it's not as private as it would be if I was chatting one-on-one with the person.... the level of hierarchy, MSN would be to build relationships one-on-one on a closer level, Facebook would just be to poke your nose as and when.
>
> (Lisa, Female)

Lisa distinguishes between the CSNM enabled by social networking and instant messaging platforms. Both CSNM are similarly characterized by interactive forms of interpersonal communication, but they differ in their associated experiences of privacy, temporality, and intimacy. Sally (above) experiences her personal Facebook network as a media space of "mass self-communication" (Castells, 2007) and indirect communication. In contrast, Lisa experiences it quite differently, as a space of interpersonal, direct, public, and asynchronous communication. Lisa contrasts this public and asynchronous CSNM with the private and synchronous CSNM enabled by instant messaging. She associates the former CSNM with the development of intimate personal relations, and the latter CSNM with occasional contact.

CSNM also vary in their integration of "presence" and "absence" (cf. Sheller and Urry, 2006, p. 222). For example, Wendy contrasts the full presence of face-to-face communication with the simulated ("artificial") presence of mediated communication:

> Video acts as an enhancer, artificial presence when the person is not around.... face-to-face is the most personal you can get, whereas video act as a buffer.
>
> (Wendy, Female)

Wendy correlates presence with intimacy ("personal"). For Wendy, the distinction between corporeal and mediated configurations of "presence and absence" corresponds to the distinction between "embodied intimacy" and "telemediated intimacy" (Tomlinson, 1999, p. 165). Although mediated communication facilitates continuity of personal relations in experiences of migration, it is of limited relevance in sustaining intimacy among geographically distributed personal relations.

"Transcultural" spaces of "glocal" subjectivity

Research on media representation in contexts of media and migration focuses on problems of minority representation in national media cultures (see chapter 1). In addition, cosmopolitan approaches emphasize problems in Western media representation of the developing world (see chapter 2).

My study reveals problems in media representations of youth as a "Global Media Generation[ ]" (Beck and Beck-Gernsheim, 2009; Volkmer, 2006). Although the following example is the only one across the interviews, it shows how a very negative impression of a particular worldwide population is developed through comparison of news and online video representations of associated local populations. As Mark sees example after example of youth in different countries worldwide engaging in deviant behavior,[5] he concludes that "their mindset is totally different":

> You see pretty appalling things that's going on in the world, that's being done by the youth today.... this German guy or some Caucasian guy who's only 12, who has a baby with his girlfriend, who was 13.... this guy who was into Satanism and one day when his cat ran away, he went so berserk, or he saw that as a sign, he murdered both his parents... my housemate, he showed me this video on the Net, somebody had this collection of school fights. Elementary school kids in China. And they fight in gangs, they bully one kid in a corner, throwing chairs and desks, literally burying him in a sea of tables.... this case of murder in Australia... a kid got killed over some lunchtime table debate by a group of kids or by [an] individual.
>
> (Mark, Male)

However, my study reveals that migration is important for the development of cross-cultural personal relations that facilitate nuanced interpretation of global media representation of distant territorial societies.

When the respondents lack experience of a place, they especially appreciate learning from the personal experiences and opinions of others. On the one hand, "locals with foreign experience" offer insight for interpreting news media representations of foreign places:

> I wouldn't know [about the Iran elections], 'cos it's on the other side of the world to me, Iran. But good thing I had this friend who explained to me how the political system in Iran works, how there's this supreme leader who's mostly above the law, and how bad the current president is.... I have this Italian neighbour... he did comment that unless the politicians really behave really badly, such 'minor' [behaviour] in inverted commas, such as spending money with entertainment, is overseen [overlooked] by the people. [The people] don't really bother unless [the politicians] are corrupt or they come out with a policy that adversely affects a large proportion of the population.
>
> (Mark, Male)

On the other hand, in contrast to the state and locals, "foreigners with local experience" offer "particular and relevant" information about "what to be aware of, or what you should do, or what you shouldn't do" in places such as Shanghai, Japan, Australia, and

Singapore. "Somebody who is foreign to the place but has been there" is a helpful information source because he/she has developed local experience from a similar foreign situation, being "the same as you" but familiar with the experience of "going there as you." For example, unlike locals, foreigners with local experience have engaged in and are aware of specific foreign practices that need to be locally adapted. They offer cross-territorial comparisons of practical, professional, and personal issues such as finances (starting salary, living expenses, and income tax), domestic helpers, "networks of friends and seniors," as well as marriage prospects ("to meet someone that's here, meet someone who's from here, or meet someone from another country…where your future will be"). Thus, the respondents value dialogue on expatriate forums organically developed in online space or organized in geographical space.

Whereas Hannerz distinguishes between "locals" and "cosmopolitans" (Hannerz, 1996, Chapter 9), I view "locals with foreign experience" and "foreigners with local experience" as two types of "cosmopolitan" subjects. I would describe these "cosmopolitan" subjects as "glocal" (Meyrowitz, 2005; R. Robertson, 1994, 1995, 2003) subjects rather than as "global subjects" (Bayart, 2007).

Multiethnic places are perceived at various geographical scales such as the neighborhood, the city (e.g., Melbourne and Shanghai), and the country (e.g., Singapore). It is interesting how differently respondents perceive globally open, multiethnic places. For example, Lisa (Female) associates these places with relations to "people from all over the world," whereas Nicole (Female) describes being a "citizen of the world… bringing your own culture into the place."

At an individual level, Nicole suggests that she enjoys individual uniqueness in a multiethnic place: "Where you can feel very cardboard copy in Singapore," in Melbourne "no one is the same as you. You take another Singaporean [in Melbourne], they've had different experiences from you."

At an intercultural level, social lives can be characterized by "transcultural" equality in a local society where diverse (communication) cultures coexist. Zach (Male) suggests that "the society here [in Melbourne] is more vibrant because there are more than 200 nationalities and languages, which means that the racist problem here is lower than in other cities." In Melbourne, he mixes with an entirely different group of Singaporeans that "I don't have a chance to meet" in Singapore: elite educated, "very English so they don't speak Hokkien, they don't speak Chinese," and "all Christian." Andrew's statement below indicates that one also better understands cultures in relation to one another through collaboration with culturally diverse others in corporeal copresence, and through alternative media from various territories:

> The most knowledge I've learned from is the film festival, 'cos you meet a lot of different people from different backgrounds...Asian people, European people, American people working together...exposed to films of different countries. [The films] are usually not mainstream and it's good 'cos they are able to portray a lot of social, political meanings.
>
> (Andrew, Male)

Notwithstanding these experiences of local cultural diversity, some respondents construct culturally homogeneous forms of local collective identity. Culturally homogeneous local community develops when similarities[6] enable "natural understanding" and relational comfort, encouraging strong bonding or "cliquing." In addition, culturally homogeneous local community results when differences[7] are intentionally minimized as the respondents adjust to suit the culture of the community.

Sense of comfort in a local environment depends on the extent to which the foreign subject and the local other perceive similarity of appearance between them. Given its associated phenotypic aspects, ethnicity is a more significant dimension of similarity/difference than nationality in constructing a basic space of relational comfort relevant for community building. A local space of comfort can be constructed among ethnically similar but nationally different subjects. For example, Rachel (Female) says that "being a Singaporean in Shanghai, I somehow just felt more at home [than in Melbourne], because I don't feel like they look at me any different." However, a local space of comfort cannot be constructed among nationally similar but ethnically different subjects:

> Being in an unfamiliar place, having to adapt to a lifestyle that you feel doesn't embrace you as much as you try to embrace it...I always feel like the other here, I'm Asian, I *was* an international [sic], and there's always a difference when you're standing outside the International Office and when you're a domestic student. There is always a difference, and that bothers me....it shouldn't, but there is always a sense of being an alien, and foreign.
>
> (Nicole, Female, original emphasis)

State and civic spaces of societal representation

Based on the results of my study, I have argued above that migration is important for the development of cross-cultural personal relations that facilitate nuanced interpretation of global media representation of distant territorial societies. The following account of Lisa's changing perception of America does not directly address the relevance of media, but it shows the relevance of migration for developing more nuanced understanding of territorial societies, specifically by encouraging differentiation between state and civic segments of territorial societies.

Prior to her migration to the United States, Lisa had a strong negative perception of the United States, influenced by her opposition to US state action regarding the war in Iraq:

> That time it was the height of the Iraq war. And to me, when an American comes abroad and I talk to him or her, the first thing not only me but people in general were thinking then, they were hating American [sic]. They didn't respect Americans because of what the government did.
>
> (Lisa, Female)

Lisa's opposition to US state action resulted in a negative preconception of Americans, including corporeally copresent Americans living outside America. She equated the United States with its state representative, reflecting, to some extent, a "national outlook" (Beck, 2006) on global politics.

Lisa had interacted with Americans in a situation of corporeal copresence prior to her migration to the United States. However, a different context of corporeal copresence was created through migration to Texas. Being corporeally situated in Texas meant that Lisa observed American society more holistically and discovered that American society is not only diverse in political orientation, but it (in particular the youth demographic) also reflects similarities with the global public and differences from the American state. Informed by this discovery, proximity is encouraged instead of distance. Whereas Americans tended to be disliked and despised in the past, they are now more likely to be valued:

> Texas is where George Bush came from. So I saw how conservative people could be, but I also saw how liberal the youth can be, how idealistic they can be.... going there I realised that the government represents only one part of the country. The people are really what matters. The people can share collective disappointment with the rest of the world, as a lot of them did with their government.
>
> (Lisa, Female)

In this way, Lisa's perception of local society has been confirmed but also problematized and transformed through corporeal experience.

Corporeal experience has encouraged greater awareness of local complexity and diversity. Although a section of global society is negatively viewed, it is understood more holistically (both positively and negatively) through "meeting people on the ground" and establishing relationships with them.

Being a Singaporean means keeping up to date with news and information "on the ground": events, issues, and perspectives that Singaporean citizens[8] are concerned about. Such news and information is intentionally accessed online through an "unofficial channel" (Stryker, Male), such as the "Mr Brown" blog, "Hardware Zone" (described by Zach (Male) as "the largest forum in Singapore"), and the complete, uncensored version of a Singaporean film on YouTube. Building on Stryker's remarks, an "unofficial channel" can be understood as a citizen media source that Singaporeans recognize to reveal the "dirty laundry" of Singapore society. In contrast, the respondents think that an "official channel" (Stryker) such as a Singapore-related news organization covers up or downplays issues and events, thereby projecting a public image of Singapore that lacks transparency. An "unofficial channel" is accessed after an "official channel" as it offers claims to truth for "questioning the authenticity of the official publications" (Stryker). It offers information about an issue or an event that encourages moral agency: "You will start…start to reason as to what or why it happened…start to speak up about it and act upon it. Try to right the wrong" (Stryker). It publicizes "culturally intimate aspects of Singapore society": "things that only you would know if you've lived in Singapore long enough or if you are Singaporean" (Ivan, Male). An "unofficial channel" offers Singapore society a true representation of itself, whereas an "official channel" such as *Channel NewsAsia* is oriented toward a non-Singaporean audience in Asia and the world:

> Usually when something big happens in Singapore…And you just get a short report on the *Channel NewsAsia* website. And then you go over to the "Mr Brown" website and you see that there's a lot more criticisms from people on the ground about that particular event that wasn't reported….the things that are reported on *Channel NewsAsia* are more for a regional or global audience…we're hosting the F1 event, we're opening the new Singapore flyer, we're building something new on Sentosa….Whereas for the Mr Brown website, it's more issues of people being inconsiderate, putting their tissue packets to book seats, the education system being too rigid and based on rote learning rather than creativity, criticising or supporting National Service, or criticising the nationalist propaganda that the government keeps portraying.
>
> (Ivan, Male)

Relations Between Social Spaces

Relations between local media environments and global spaces

The respondents favor the Internet's "all on one" capability[9] together with its accessible and personal qualities. These features encourage the respondents to routinely access the global from individual private domestic space. This cross-spatial pattern of access is evident especially when the respondents corporeally reside in Melbourne, outside the family residence in Singapore. Although the Internet can be accessed from anywhere (including Singapore and Melbourne), in Singapore, the respondents tend to also routinely access the global from individual or family private domestic space through broadcast and subscription-based cable television as well as home-delivered print newspapers. However, these technologies are relatively inaccessible or shared in Melbourne. They are either too costly outside the family domestic space or affordable only when the respondent corporeally moves to public (domestic) spaces such as those in share accommodation and at university.[10] In contrast, the Internet is convergent, accessible, and personal, offering more convenient and comfortable access to global content associated with other technologies, from individual private domestic space.

Through the Internet, the respondents eliminate geographical distance between them and local points of access to the global. Local Internet access points partially remove the need for corporeal travel to centers where worldwide content is physically located, such as DVD shops and libraries. As Andrew states:

> majority of my research is based on the Internet, very minimal at the libraries.
>
> (Andrew, Male)

The online space is a highly valued source of information in the workplace. When Wendy needed technical knowledge to solve a work-related problem, she consulted a corporeally proximate expert but was instead redirected to the online information space:

> When I used to work for a advertising agency, I would ask my account director...could you tell me what's up with the HTML? Then she'll come to me and she'll "Google.com, there, you have all your answers." That's when I realised that everything is on the Internet, you really really don't have to ask anyone anything.
>
> (Wendy, Female)

Translocal access is broadened as the distinctive convergent technology of the Internet transcends not just corporeal distance, but also disconnection between geocultural territories. Although the relationship between online convergence and geocultural transcendence is implied in a number of interviews, its specific dynamics can be especially explored through an in-depth analysis of the following statement:

> I use a lot of Internet because I use it for a lot of online radio, I listen to it very much 'cos I really don't like Australian radio.... I watch a lot of TV shows on Internet, which I can't get in Australia. Especially Asian programs like from Singapore, Hong Kong dramas, Taiwan variety shows.
>
> (Andrew, Male)

Andrew's statement suggests that access to preferred content is geoculturally closed when radio and television are used apart from the Internet. Radio space is closed around the homogeneous national culture of the country of corporeal residence ("Australian radio"), whereas television space is closed to the culturally diverse transnational beyond the country of corporeal residence. Specifically, television in Australia is closed to the geographically proximate but culturally different Asian region and its national (Singapore and Taiwan) and subnational (Hong Kong) constituents. Thus, tuning into offline radio and television has two implications. First, it means only being able to access unwanted content. Second, it means being unable to access preferred content: content he has enjoyed in a different country of residence (Singapore) and content he has not yet come across but may enjoy.[11] In contrast, access to preferred content is geoculturally open when radio and television are used through the Internet. As such, Andrew uses the Internet highly for its convergence: "a lot of Internet... a lot of online radio... a lot of TV shows on Internet."

Relations between networked digital spaces

Corporeal location is of limited relevance for access to particular spaces as the respondents consistently access these spaces through the Internet.

> once I'm on the Internet... I will check out the sites.
>
> (Andrew, Male)

The respondents follow connections from one site to another within the online space as they trust general and academic search engines such as Google, Google Scholar, and the University of Melbourne Supersearch database. They assume that these directories would bring up relevant texts. After reviewing selected texts, however, the respondents do not conclude their search for information. Rather, they follow the hyperlinks in these texts to other texts:

> I just searched for 'atheism' or 'secularism'. I saw the word somewhere, [a] long time ago when I was a kid. I wondered what it was and I just keyed it in and found out about it. One thing led to another, one website links to another website and [I] slowly build [sic] up this knowledge of atheism.
>
> (Ivan, Male)

Official community spaces such as The Fashion Spot and Blur forums are located at a permanent corporate address. In contrast, a grassroots community space temporarily emerges around a global event such as the 2009 Iran election protests, in the form of a hashtag group on the Twitter microblogging social networking service. The respondents directly access an official forum, sometimes from its affiliated offline space. For example, Ivan vertically connects ("come up") from the computer game to its official forum:

> There was a link to the website from the game and they pop up a window where you come up to this forum where you can discuss. So that's how you got into it.
>
> (Ivan, Male)

The respondents also discover numerous grassroots community spaces by searching through Google or within Twitter. They choose to participate in a space where the flow of information is seen to be fast:

> For the climbing one, you just do a Google search. And there are hundreds of websites, you just pick one that you see is very active. Then you sign up with the forum.
>
> (Ivan, Male)

The respondents' attention is naturally drawn to news not only through a news organizational website, but also through hyperlinks within other websites[12] accessed for other purposes such as email:

> Whenever you want to check your Student Portal email or go on LMS [Learning Management System], naturally you'll see this box that contains news headlines. Since it's already there and sometimes you may

> just see a piece of news that will interest you somehow, therefore it's a convenient way for you to find out more about it.
>
> (Will, Male)

On weblogs and social networking sites in particular, the respondents share personal information with a mass group of significant personal relations "any time of the day." However, within this larger group, subgroups that differ in their levels of intimacy access these spaces and communicate with one another. As such open access and communication could expose problematic acts, one respondent disciplines herself to act appropriately through "self-surveillance." Alternatively, the respondents separate meaning spaces from the larger information space such that information that is open to all is only understood by some. The respondents phrase information in an abstract way or conceal particular connections, for example, between their Facebook profile and a friend's photo album:

> It's easier for them [her parents] to know what I'm talking about: when I'm saying "you know that person," "yeahyeahyeah, I saw her picture already"...[but] if for example, I bought a really expensive bag then I cannot let my parents know, my friend tag me in a picture that there's the bag, then I'll quickly untag!
>
> (Wendy, Female)

As a local community leader, one respondent has represented the community simultaneously on two social networking platforms (Facebook and LinkedIn), to build networks around members' existing presence on these platforms. The respondents also develop relationships within a local community across corporeal and online spaces. On the one hand, relationships are initiated in online spaces since it can be impossible or difficult for members to "suddenly...get to know each other" at corporeal meetings. On the other hand, where the community has been created at a once-off corporeal gathering, it is sustained online through the exchange of personal opinions and corporeally situated personal experiences:

> I went for a Christian conference in January, so that [sic] was a lot of young leaders from all around Australia. And after the conference, even during the conference, they already created the group. And they still talk about issues there. So I read a book on queer forums, what do they think about it. Even about the bushfires, some of you are in those places, right? So how are you doing?
>
> (Naomi, Female)

Cross-territorial spaces of mobility

Migration between Singapore and Melbourne can be viewed as cross-territorial mobility rather than resettlement, as "going to school and going home from after school." In this everyday context of ontological security, cross-territorial communication is not necessary:

> day to day things, you don't have to call. Like mum, I'm still alive, I'm feeding myself!...you're not living in the Gaza Strip where you could be killed anytime.
>
> (Jamie, Female)

However, during a crisis event such as the swine flu pandemic,[13] cross-territorial mobility is blocked in state responses to contain the spread of the virus. In this situation, official statistics from both the Singapore and Australian states are frequently checked for "first-hand information," "accuracy and the reliability of the news":

> I was visiting the Department of Health Service [Australia] website quite often to see how the figures were jumping. And of course, I also went to the MOH [Ministry of Health, Singapore] website pretty often to see how things have changed, what level of alert are they on and what measures are being taken...I was going home, so I wanted to know if I was going to be quarantined once I touched down at Changi [Airport, Singapore] or what was going to happen, and what were the potential complications, what if I'm quarantined back home in Singapore and cannot come back for this semester.
>
> (Peter, Male)

This perception of a cross-territorial space of mobility is especially relevant if Clare (Female) migrates between geographically proximate territories such as Singapore, Melbourne, India, and territories within the Asian region such as Vietnam. In contrast, when she migrates across geographically distant territories such as Singapore and Canada, she experiences the lack of "stay[ing] somewhere" and instead perceives a nomadic experience of "having two houses here and there" and "living in a box": leaving a part of herself in one territory while locating another part of herself in another territory. The ease and attraction of cross-territorial mobility is influenced by two factors: first, how the territories are related in terms of geographical proximity, cultural familiarity, and economic differential; and second, the logistics of mobility, such as political and legal requirements:

> Melbourne's a lot closer to home so I won't mind staying around here, but with Canada being so far away...I wouldn't let go of an

> opportunity to go back to Canada for a year or two.... other places may be fine... but I don't know if I could live in a third world country. Vietnam, that's Asia, I could understand it a little bit more, but to live in a country [sic] like Africa? I don't know if I could actually face that utter poverty.... Just in an Asian context, it's [Vietnam] a lot closer to home, it's not hard to fly back and forth. Whereas with Africa... Too much bend around the political processes, or visas... India is fine, but Africa is far.
>
> (Clara, Female)

Hierarchies of places in media representation and reception

Some respondents perceive that current knowledge about world politics is important as territories are interrelated:

> from the war in Afghanistan to the first Black president being elected, politics all over Europe, anywhere, war in Georgia. It's just understanding how countries are relating to each other.
>
> (Ivan, Male)

The respondents significantly trust news organizations to bring to their awareness "the most important things that are happening around the world." One respondent suggests that it is an industry trend for news organizations to offer "instant news, you don't have to spend so much time cooking it, you put it in a pot, two minutes, it's out." In other words, the world events that the respondents consider to be important depend less on their evaluation and more on what the news organizations report as important. Every news event that the newspaper reports is important: "If it's important, it's important, there's no one over the other." Crises[14] in different territories are viewed as important for the world as a whole:

> the Australian bushfires, which was top of the world [section]. The plane that crashed into the Hudson river. The Zimbabwe situation[15]. And, obviously, Israel and the Gaza Strip. All these are big news.
>
> (Jamie, Female)

The respondents construct global worldviews through not just private but also professional development. Through university modules such as "Women in Global Health" and "Genesis of a Nation," they learn (how) to compare societies as they conceptualize social phenomena such as gender relations and development within interrelated local and global hierarchies. One respondent speaks of "women living in patriarchal societies like Bangladesh" and another respondent traces the history of China in relation to the West: "China was actually more developed than Caucasian countries in the 1600s... China has been put back in terms of its development compared to other countries." Where a professional field is less developed in Singapore, the respondents plan to grow in more developed and even world-class professional fields such as in North America (speech pathology), Japan (media), and Australia (management of nonprofit organizations). For example, despite "few speech pathologists and no local research" in Singapore, "the world of speech pathology" has been opened up through "e-journals from overseas and Australia and everywhere" and "PhD possibilities" are discussed through email with university representatives in "different parts of the world." Outside the university, professional worldviews are broadened and challenged as the respondents relate mediated representations of different local cultures. For example, one respondent has gained awareness of everyday "speech pathology experiences" through the blogs of speech pathologists, biographies, and *The Diving Bell and the Butterfly*, "a French movie about someone who went through a major stroke." Another respondent understands the film industry as he identifies unique and alternative cinematic approaches reflected in films produced by different local industries:

> Hollywood, Hong Kong, French, German, whatever, they have a very significant style. Or the way they explain their films is very different. And their script is different. And there are concepts where [sic] you will not find in other film industries. For example in French movies you will always find weird sex scenes... sex scenes it's always there in Hollywood films. But they are portrayed in [a] socially acceptable way... in French films you watch you just, Orh! [sic] What are they doing, man? Is this even possible? Or why are you doing [this] in the first place?... cinematographies of the way they hold the camera. It's just different. It's just interesting to see how they do different things, even though it's the same industry.
>
> (Andrew, Male)

Territories reported in the news are primarily ranked according to a personal hierarchy of news and secondarily ranked according to a global hierarchy of news:

> news which is closer to home. That would be the main priority.... after that, the second priority would go to global powers... [thus] Singapore would be first. Australia would be second. Burma, third. The United States, fourth. And EU, fifth.
>
> (Timothy, Male)

As personal relations are corporeally concentrated in "home," "home territories" (cf. Morley, 2000)[16] are ranked at the top of a personal hierarchy of news. However, territories including but not limited to "home" become more important than territories of global influence when the respondents' personal relations are corporeally present or proximate to the geographical centre of the news event, especially during crisis events:

> I have friends in India, not in Mumbai. But just immediately [I smsed] "Are you ok"... I started to hear that my friend's brother was there in one of the hotels that was being bombed! So they ask you to pray and you are watching, hoping he wouldn't be on the death toll.... sitting there, watching the whole news report, watching those little banner things that go by with the latest updates. That really reminded me of 9/11...9/11 was a very surreal, Hollywood type thing...America has such international significance that it was of viewing value. But Mumbai there's so much more human contact, simply because of the people I knew there....[9/11] was more entertainment...Whereas Mumbai I really hope things are fine.
>
> (Nicole, Female)

Relations to Social Spaces

Interactive engagement in spaces of public discourse

Online space is often the first destination for information of personal interest. The Internet is perceived as a hub without limit to searching for "everything and anything." Within this perceived limitless, uncharted space, the respondents create personalized information pathways by entering their specific requests for information into interactive directories:

> just Google what I want to know and the things come out.
>
> (Andrew, Male)

The perceived distinctive openness of online space to interactive discourse also allows the respondents to relate to others who have experienced, interpreted, and responded to a common issue or event. The respondents need information that others are in the position to provide, or they are interested to compare others' perspectives with their own, to see if others' comments "mirror my views." However, the respondents perceive that print news is closed to public opinion because it is regulated, in particular by the Singapore state. Print news is also thought to be noninteractive. In contrast, the respondents consider online discourse to be a source of reliable and updated content because it is characterized by the "free flow of information." Online information space is not only personally valued. It is also viewed to have broader social significance because it enables free expression and it exposes rumors of secrets to be assessed by the public:

> To society it's important because it's a place where people can express their ideas freely. A lot of conspiracy theories come out there. Whether it's true or not, at least it's out there for people to evaluate.
>
> (Ivan, Male)

Although online forums are open to interactive discourse, how the respondents engage in the discourse depends on how much time they have spent in the forum. The respondents value the perspectives of those who have spent enough time in the forum to develop familiarity with its topic and culture. They sense that newcomers to the forum are new to its topic and culture. It is thus conventional for newcomers to ask questions, at most, but not to express views. Knowledge of the topic is seen to be passed down within the forum:

> You normally would find this group of experienced people or experts who you can turn to for questions. And after you've been in the forums for enough time and you know enough about the topic, someone else who is new joins in and you teach them whatever other people have taught you. Exact same thing, so it's a transfer of knowledge.
>
> (Ivan, Male)

Cultural spatial differentiation in, and relativization of, news constellations

The respondents keep up to date with current events around the world, positioning themselves in a global news space. However, they view the global news space through many sources and platforms. News organizations are an important source of news. The respondents go to the organizations' websites, receive news through the organisations' email alerts, or use a program that downloads the online newspaper daily. They create routine connections to the organizations' websites by making them their home pages or adding them to their "Favorites." Although sources such as the *BBC*, *Channel NewsAsia*, and *The Age* are important for a number of respondents, news preferences vary from respondent to respondent. The respondents access a combination of global, regional, and local news from organizations such as the *BBC*, the *Guardian*, *CNN*, *CNBC*, the *New York Times*, *Reuters*,

Bloomberg, *Yahoo! News*, *Sky News*, the *Japan Times*, *The Age*, *Channel NewsAsia*, *The Straits Times*, and *Today Online*:

> What papers do I read? The two papers from Singapore—*The Straits Times*, *ChannelNewsAsia*. All these are online, obviously. I subscribe to *CNN*, *BBC*, *New York Times*. I do not read any Australian newspapers.
>
> (Jamie, Female)

The respondents also access local and global content through local news organizations. A number of respondents mention that Australian news organizations have a narrow focus on Australia. One respondent only reads the Business section of *The Age* because he is interested in IT news but not Australian news. In contrast, the respondents express that Singapore news organizations such as the *Straits Times* cover much world news. Peter relates the local coverage of Australian organizations to his experience of the global coverage of Singaporean organizations:

> *The Age* talks a lot about local news, which is understandable. But having used the *Straits Times*, I also need updates on what's going on around the world, and I think the *Straits Times* does that better.
>
> (Peter, Male)

The respondents view news organizational spaces as combinations of geographical spaces of production, content, and audience. For example, Timothy views a news organization as a local (American) producer that reports on local (Iraq) content for a global audience:

> with coverage of the Iraq war, I have lesser faith in the American broadcasters.
>
> (Timothy, Male)

The respondents select global news organizations that are reputable for neutral perspective and content, and local news organizations for local and otherwise unavailable content:

> Singaporean news would only feature on websites such as *Channel NewsAsia*, not on *BBC* or *The Age*...you'll have to make an effort to find media about Singapore. Likewise for Burma. Whereas for countries like Australia, United States and EU, you don't have to make so much of an effort. Most agencies will have news about these three countries [sic] because they're so big and they have such a presence in the world today.
>
> (Timothy, Male)

News on Singapore is accessed through local, regional, and/or global news organizations. For example, during the global financial crisis, one respondent searched for Singapore news on *Bloomberg* and Yahoo.com.sg, disappointed by the lack of financial news on *Channel NewsAsia*.

However, the respondents access global and local (regional) content through global news organizations:

> *BBC* would be worldwide news....they have different categories, for example World news, Asia-Pacific, South America. And the one that I go to most of the time will be World and Asia-Pacific. Places closer to home, closer to me....home would be Australia, so closer to Australia.
>
> (Timothy, Male)

In addition to news organizations, the respondents access global news directly from primary sources such as friends, states, and citizens of authoritarian states, through social media such as Facebook and Twitter.

> The social group I have on Facebook...would be my primary connection. Whereas other connections I have would include people like Kevin Rudd or Barack Obama. Presidents and Prime Ministers of countries. So I read what they have to say on the news and I follow them on Twitter....I learn more about what plans they have for the nation and what plans they have for the world....I want to know what's going on in the world. What my friends are doing...or what's going on in countries with repressive government...like Myanmar, Afghanistan, Iraq.
>
> (KoT, Male)

As news organizations are biased, alternative views of the world are sought through various news organizations. Bias is related both to the organization and to the geographical focus of the content:

> *CNN, CNBC, Channel NewsAsia, Today Online.* It's a different perspective, different part of the world has different news...I just like to be informed about what's happening in the world, get a different perspective. Because sometimes it's very one-sided, and I just don't want to have that kind of thinking this is wrong, this is right, but see a different view.
>
> (Thornton, Male)

Continuity toward places of migration

It is quite interesting to note how current events of places within the space of circular migration are perceived. Attention to news is related to the imagination of past, present, and future[17] residence in these places. News builds on and builds up emotional attachment to a place of past residence and its current residents. For example, where the respondent has departed a place, she can experience a local event with local friends through news: "*The Age* in Singapore online kept me connected to what was happening here [in Melbourne] and I could share so many of the experiences that my friends here had been feeling." Being corporeally absent, the respondents are unfamiliar with aspects of a place of future residence: "[Melbourne] is the place where I study, and I wasn't sure what was going to happen when I came back." Through news, however, the respondents acquire and accumulate information on changes to the place since their departure. Such intellectual preparation prior to return eases ontological transition upon return. As one respondent says, "After being physically away [from Singapore] for a number of years, you don't want to go back and be ignorant of what's been going on."

For this reason, where the respondents engage in circular migration, they follow the local news of more than one place:

> Keep myself updated with Singapore...so that I won't be so lost when I go back...keep myself updated with the Melbourne side 'cos I'm currently in Melbourne. Cannot be my mind is in Singapore, but my physical body is here. I need to know both sides of the story, what's happening here and back home.
>
> (Wendy, Female)

Outside the space of circular migration, however, the respondents are less interested in the news of places of noncircular migration (such as places of permanent emigration):

> I'm more interested in Singapore news, because after Melbourne, I wouldn't go back to Malaysia. I would either choose to stay here or go back to Singapore....I would know the big issues in Malaysia, but not the small issues. I understand more about Singapore than Malaysia.
>
> (KoT, Male)

The respondents distinguish between countries of pragmatic sojourn and countries of permanent settlement. Some respondents experience Australia as "hi, bye...the transition station," "a place that I go to just to study," where "everything you want that you can get here is tangible, material." In contrast, they perceive Singapore as "the final destination," distinctively associated with the "intangible...whole feeling of being in Singapore."[18] Similar to how these Singaporean international students in Australia view Australia, Chinese international students in Singapore are considered (albeit in a more negative light) to view Singapore as a temporary stop en route to other countries such as the United States:

> They're just using Singapore as a springboard . . . to other places like the US. For example, if a China student comes to Singapore, he wouldn't be so naïve to take up Singapore citizenship and tie himself down. . . . Singapore's not permanent for them. They've no ties with Singapore.
>
> (KoT, Male)

In Melbourne, some respondents long for places where they have temporarily resided, in some cases with family and friends, such as London and Canada. They sustain their memories of places they have left through news and drama associated with these places. For example, a respondent who has spent five of the past twelve months with her London-based sister describes Law & Order: United Kingdom as her favourite show on Australian TV because "I miss London" and the program represents London visually through "a lot of London shots and scenes." However, in contrast to "home" as the respondents experience it, a place of temporary residence may only exist in memory and cannot be recovered through news or even through corporeal return. Clara[19] stopped reading the Canadian national newspaper online after her first few months in Melbourne because

> it [reading the newspaper] creates this almost sickly nostalgia, 'cos you know that you aren't going back [to Canada] . . . if it happens I would, but I wouldn't want to keep living for that life that happened there. . . . if I ever go back, I'll keep missing that part of me. It's different already because I'm not going to live in the same house, those friends have left school . . . over time I started accepting that life isn't going to be the same and there's no point pining for what isn't there.
>
> (Clara, Female)

"Exclusive" and "inclusive differentiation" between cultural spaces

The respondents divide the world into Asian and Western cultural geographies. On the one hand, Asia and the West are "exclusive[ly] differentiat[ed]" (Beck, 2006, p. 5) such that cultural location in Asia excludes cultural location in the West: "it's just two. Either you're in an Asian culture or you're [sic] Western culture." The relations between Asia and the West are fixed such that cultural position is unrelated to places of corporeal residence and migration. For example, "if a Westerner is born and bred in Singapore...even if he speaks in a Singaporean accent, you can't look past it, he's just White" and the Overseas Christian Fellowship is described as "a whole bunch of Asian...international students."

On the other hand, Asia and the West are "inclusive[ly] differentiat[ed]" (Beck, 2006, pp. 4–5) such that local cultural geographies emerge from their intersection. One respondent describes Singapore, Hong Kong, and Shanghai as different configurations of "East meets West," where Singapore reflects "more of West" and Hong Kong reflects "more East 'cos it's tied to China a lot." The relations between Asia and the West are fluid such that cultural position is related to places of corporeal residence and migration as well as the personalities of individual respondents. For example, whereas "Hong Kong would be more East 'cos...it's slightly more conservative than Singapore," "the Hong Kong people that I meet here [in Melbourne], some of them are really very havoc[20] whereas some of them are really, really, very, very, very, very, very conservative."

Asia and the West are hierarchically related such that Asia is viewed as inferior to the West. Where this hierarchy is fixed in migration, the respondent experiences favor or discrimination depending on whether her place of origin is Asian or Western compared to her place of residence: "When I was in China, if you came from a Western background, they look up to you. But over here [in Melbourne], because they're from a Western background, they don't look up to you. If anything, they look down on you." Where this hierarchy is fluid in migration, the respondent develops greater appreciation of Asian culture vis-à-vis Western culture, as she attends to and selects to view its associated media:

> When I'm here [in Melbourne], when I see or hear anything Asian even in the media, my attention is picked up immediately, and I'm not so attuned to the White culture as I used to be. In terms of cultural appreciation of different Asian countries like Hong Kong or Korea, just a different series that I've been watching, especially when I went home [to Singapore] over the holidays in December. I realised that I've changed in that there isn't that idea that White is supreme anymore. But now I'm starting to see a lot that I'm starting to appreciate in the Asian culture as well.
>
> (Nicole, Female)

Beyond these perceptions, multiple local perspectives are developed through experiences of migration and residence in various local societies. The respondents' experiences of society may vary depending on the country where they reside: "in Australia or in Singapore or in UK or whatever, I'm a different person in different social contexts, and I think differently in different social contexts." As the experiences of various local societies are viewed as alternative or "different viewpoints," they "broaden my mindset" beyond a single local society. The respondents appreciate this wider perspective as indicating the maturity of a person and/or a society. Personal and societal maturity complement each other: a society grows as its citizens grow. Citizens grow as they view the global through alternative local lenses, instead of through a single local lens that is prescribed by the state:

> Singapore is a very young society. It's only about 49 years old. It's some postcolonial hangover. And that's why we all have very strong nationalist sentiment. But in order for Singapore to mature as a society, to become more aware of global issues and for citizens to be more active in the political scene, there needs to be movement away from government propaganda. So people need to stop being repressed and taken care of so well. People need to go out more and see the world differently. See the world and then when they come back to Singapore, they realise how different it is. Over in Melbourne, there're tons of protests all the time.
>
> (Ivan, Male)

The respondents become aware of and compare alternative perspectives not only through migration, but also through media. On the one hand, Andrew (Male) is surprised to discover similarities across cultures reflected in different territorially situated views, for example, as he finds his opinions supported by a territorially different other through YouTube:

> This guy said *exactly* the things that I want to say. So through the media we are able to have common understanding despite physically we are not able to be in the same place . . . he's a Taiwanese and I'm Singaporean, so although there might be similarities, but ultimately his background is different from mine . . . to have someone that is not from your country makes your cultural background even more diverse from yourself. So [what are] the chances, to have something that's said on television, like what the person said and I said? It's a good thing to have this consensus of culture through the media.
>
> (Andrew, Male, original emphasis)

On the other hand, differences between territorially situated views are also relevant. As the respondents become aware of and critically evaluate one view in relation to another, they support one view against another view. One respondent, Peter (Male), rejects a particular view because he believes that the scenario it presents is not suitable for another context. For example, he says that whereas "in Malaysia, there's this Muslim court that recently, they're going to cane this woman for drinking beer," reflecting "where a religious belief has become a political policy," "Singapore cannot have that." With this scenario in mind, he agrees with the view put forward by the Singapore government that "there must be a clear stand dividing religion and public policy." However, supporting one view can also be compatible with understanding and recognizing the legitimacy of another view. As Peter phrases it, through the news "I can see both points of view and both are valid." As territorial societies directly represent, interpret, and respond to one another, one set of bilateral relations is evaluated in relation to another:

> When Singapore made Melbourne a "do not travel unless necessary," Melbourne responded Singapore is overreacting. It was quite amusing to me. You can say that way. Obviously they have an interest because they don't want tourists to stop coming. But the fact [is] that [swine flu] cases are increasing here and it's only fair that Singapore protect her own interest by issuing travellers' advice. It's the same: when the bombings in the Marriott and the Ritz Carlton in Jakarta [occurred], Australia also issued warning its people to not go to Jakarta. That's perfectly natural. I would think that it's very amusing if Jakarta issued to say that no, you're overreacting.
>
> (Peter, Male)

Through the experience of migration, more than one territory is relevant for identity; however, territories vary in their particular relevance for identity. Identifying themselves as Singaporeans residing in an overseas territory, many respondents associate their identities primarily with Singapore and secondarily with the territory of residence. When identity is constructed in relation to more than one territory, it partially reflects more than one territorial identity and fully reflects none. As identity fully reflects no territorial identity, it is distinguished from the latter:

> I am a Singaporean who is an international student studying in Melbourne....I am not a Singaporean in Singapore. I am not a local Australian....I can relate to both sides, but I will never truly be totally on one side or the other.
>
> (Peter, Male)

Awareness of distant places
Worldwide exotic places are viewed as accessible and attractive through documentaries, photographs, and as respondents know of family and friends who have traveled there. Some respondents want to "travel and see the world" for "new knowledge and new experiences." They perceive that staying or being "rooted down in any one place" limits the extent to which they experience what is different and "out of your comfort zone." In addition, they believe that they are only able to travel for a season, especially during their youth, "being in your 20s." Jamie illustrates the extent to which worldwide travel is a personal lifestyle and a realistic aspiration:

> I've never been to Europe, and I have friends who have parents staying there, they go there all the time to visit them. They go like [sic] France, Germany, Italy. I just had a friend who just came back from Venice, I see the photo and it's so nice and I just want to see it before it's all gone! . . . In Australia I've been to Perth, Cairns . . . I've seen a lot of the East Coast. I went to Tasmania a couple of years ago. Went up to Broome . . . I haven't been to Darwin. I want to go to Alice Springs and Adelaide. . . . When I was in Singapore, I went to Bali a few times to dive, went up to Thailand to backpack, went to Vietnam to do the same thing, budget travel. I go to Batam quite often to water-ski . . . I really want to go Cambodia and backpack through there as well. I want to go Nepal and backpack, 'cos my cousin did that, and so cool [sic]. I want to go to China, 'cos everyone I know has been to some part of China and I've never stepped into the country.
>
> (Jamie, Female)

Current knowledge is also important as the respondents relate with other societies in the world through mobility. On the one hand, "to go from one place to the next," one needs to be worldly: "knowing what is happening beyond where you're staying" rather than having the narrow perspective of "a frog in the well." As territories differ, for example, in political stability and in cultures of communication, one needs to adapt to avoid danger to the self and offence to others:

> Political upheaval in Thailand, at least you know that now is not a good period to travel . . . Makes you more aware, more sensitive to what's going on so you don't say things. Like if you read about Thailand, you know about their law against insulting the king. So if you went there and you didn't know about it and you just made a remark about the king, you get thrown into jail, and you wonder, oh crap, what happened?
>
> (Ivan, Male)

On the other hand, global worldview and self-perception as a global citizen are developed through mobility across "different worlds" or societies within the global society.

The respondents become familiar with a country through five interrelated modes of experience. First, the respondents come across representations of the country in the media of another country: Zack (Male), for example, is aware of the United States as "Singapore papers...focus on the US markets." Second, the respondents experience the country as it is represented in its media. Jamie (Female) learns what she "never knew" about American "geography, where places are, what places exist, how the whole system works" through the "drive up to this place, go to there, and take a trip down" journey in American films. Third, the respondents relate with others who have had corporeal experiences of the country. Having developed an impression of America through mediated experience, this impression is clarified as Jamie discusses it with "people who've been to [and] lived in America." Fourth, the respondents relate with others who have had mediated experiences of the country. Mark (Male), for example, compares his mediated experience with his experience relating with others who have been heavily influenced by media of the country: "Hong Kong dramas, you see that it's a lot of love and the music, strongly sentimental. So it's probably why Hong Kong girls are dreamy." Fifth, the respondents corporeally experience the country, for example, through mobility. Andrew (Male), for example, knows Taiwan through a combination of corporeal and mediated experience:

> Most of my understanding [of] Taiwan [sic] culture comes from my visit there on holidays and from what I see on TV. And how the audience, when they go on shows, they interview them and their reaction. So I try to decipher their understanding of their culture.
>
> (Andrew, Male)

Although the respondents suggest that there is a limit to understanding distant societies entirely through media, media is essential and effective in promoting fandom in relation to a global fan base oriented toward a geographically distant center.[21] While collective fan interest is facilitated in a corporeally copresent group, the respondent is more convinced of the value of the fandom when it is represented in media:

> Manchester United, it's a football club in another continent, it's far away. If there was no media about it, I would have never known about

it. If there's no advertisements, if there's no football matches about the club, I would never have been able to watch them play, I would never have been able to know their members, their team, their style. . . . it can't be someone goes to the UK, comes back to Singapore and says, oh, I watched this soccer team play and they were so awesome, they were called Manchester United, and I'll be like oh, I like them too. But if another guy comes back and says, oh, I watched Liverpool play, then what's the difference between Liverpool and Manchester United when both people said they're both so awesome? So it has to be the media which has garnered my interest.

(Timothy, Male)

"Home" as a Relational Glocality

"Home" as a Territorial Society based on Personal Relations

Many respondents perceive Singapore as their territorial home. The respondents usually refer to "home" rather than "my home," suggesting that they experience it as a natural place of "being" rather than as an intentional place of "belonging" (cf. Levitt and Glick Schiller, 2004, p. 1010). The respondents position themselves in both past and present relations to Singapore as "home." In the past, Singapore/"home" was the respondent's place of birth and/or development: "I was born and raised there," "I grew up there." In the present, Singapore/"home" is the place where significant personal relations are corporeally located: "I have family there," "I have friends there." As the place of birth, development, and family, Singapore has not been chosen as "home," but it is "home":

It's home not necessarily because I was born there, but because I spent most of my years there, my growing years there. And your family's there, your close-knit circle of friends are there. Everything is there.

(Natasha, Female)

"Home" is seen not only as a place where the respondent resides with family and friends, but also as a broader territorial society of concern. The respondents not only communicate directly with significant personal relations "back home," but they also seek "home news, news back at home." "To feel a little bit closer to home, to know what's happening, when I'm not there," the respondents seek news on Singapore through sources such as *Channel NewsAsia* online, the Saturday edition of the *Straits Times* on campus, and #singapore on Twitter. Media that are irrelevant when one is in Singapore become very significant when one is away from Singapore. For example, one respondent visits *Channel NewsAsia* only when she is not in Singapore, because she feels homesick at least once a week. Singapore is felt more as "home" the longer the respondent is away from it:

> Sometimes because I'm such a homesick patriot, I search for [the] Singapore hash tag [#singapore on Twitter], just to get in touch with what's happening on the ground.
>
> **Why is it that you're specially interested in what's going on in Singapore?**
>
> In Singapore? 'cos it's my home. It's home. It's home. It will always be home.... The longer I am away from Singapore, the stronger I feel for Singapore.
>
> (Lisa, Female)

The respondents address concerns for family and friends at "home" by keeping aware and informed of major Singapore news events that affect these personal relations. Major Singapore news events include the global financial crisis in its local relevance and the escape of the terrorist Mas Selamat from a Singapore detention center. To keep up with "news back home in Singapore" means "you want to know if everyone's doing fine at home." Conversely, not doing so demonstrates that "you don't care" about significant personal relations at "home." Being "home" with family in Singapore is "very, very important" during festive seasons such as Christmas and Chinese New Year. However, even if Singapore is not a central place, it is still considered "home" if it is where family and friends reside:

> Even for people who don't intend to go back, if you apply for PR [permanent residency], or if you change citizenship, if you have friends and family there, I still think it's important to find out what's happening at home.
>
> (Jamie, Female)

Relations between "Home" and "Overseas"

Some respondents define "home" in relation to "overseas." They view "home" and "overseas" as two mutually exclusive and separated contexts of residence. Whereas Singapore is described as "home," places of residence outside Singapore are considered as "overseas." Residence in different places outside Singapore (such as Melbourne and Brunei) is experienced as being "based overseas, just that it's a change of location."

"Being away from home," "being overseas," and "being an international student," the respondents feel the need to actively develop relationships with family and friends "back home." Experiencing the concern of and for significant personal relations, relationship expectations, and loneliness, the respondents want to sustain their presence in their significant personal relations' awareness through online communication (particularly instant messaging and Skype platforms) and mobile communication. In the respondents' words, "instead of Singapore when you are in a safe haven, suddenly you are transported into this alien place. You want the world to have updates on your life," "to let people know that you're still alive." In contrast, when the respondents reside "at home" in Singapore, they not only meet corporeally with friends rather than communicate through media, but they also sense more greatly the presence of family and friends, even when the latter are not corporeally copresent:

> MSN, I'm never online when I'm at home, but when I'm overseas, I'm on a lot more.
>
> **Why is that?**
>
> To keep in touch with people. If you don't, you feel like you've cut off this entire connection with what you've once considered home.
>
> **How do you "feel connected" when you're not overseas?**
>
> When I'm not overseas, so when I'm back home in Singapore? I don't know. And I don't think that there is a need to feel connected because you are home already. The physical presence of being at home makes me feel connected even though I might just be in my room.
>
> (Natasha, Female)

Besides news, programs on Singapore television are accessed through a trial subscription to the video on demand service MediaCorp Online Broadband Television (MOBTV). One respondent "catch[es] all the local shows...when I'm here" through MOBTV streamed from "back home." However, free-to-air television in Singapore is also expected to be free online. One respondent says "if it's free, I'll watch," but "I don't want to pay a single cent for...free TV." Having "use[d] up all the trials" and being unwilling to watch MOBTV through paid subscription, she watches Taiwanese dramas instead because the Chinese language in the program "remind[s] me of home, my roots." As Taiwanese dramas are among the many imported shows on Singapore television, they are considered "Singaporeanish." "Being in contact with anything Singaporeanish" enables her to feel secure rather than "diasporic," "lost," "you don't belong here, you don't belong there."

Singapore is perceived as "home" which is justified as a context of familiarity, the location of "everything that I have thought of as normal" and "everything you're familiar with." The respondents make sense of unfamiliar experiences outside "home" by comparing them with familiar experiences in "home," such that "home" is the "benchmark for everything else." The ontological boundaries of "home" that distinguish the familiar from the unfamiliar correspond to the territorial borders of Singapore. As Singapore is the context of familiarity, one respondent is unconscious of it, its value, and her residence in it, when she experiences it from within. However, she becomes conscious of these aspects of Singapore from a postmigration vantage point outside Singapore. As she says, "I never think much about my presence in Singapore" and "I took it [Singapore] for granted." "But when you come out of your comfort zone, you can see everything from outside." "You realised that your life is really there" and you now "notice the good stuff." Awareness, appreciation, and action in relation to Singapore society increase when one is outside Singapore, even when one has been "patriotic at heart" in Singapore:

> I was from a local advertising agency, so they would always support local stuff...we'll watch local films at cinema.sg, which is quite indie in Singapore. But after you come over here, then all the more you appreciate everything that we have in Singapore and all the efforts that people put in making Singapore unique. Then you would want to support them. Most of my friends here also became more patriotic.
>
> (Wendy, Female)

The respondents naturally and deliberately contact "Overseas Singaporeans" (see chapter 3) in their relations with Singapore as "home." One respondent naturally got to know an Overseas Singaporean, having been introduced by a Singaporean friend. He also deliberately initiated relationships: he started a thread on the Hardware Zone "studying overseas" subforum calling for Singaporeans who would be studying in his cohort in Melbourne, corporeally met with those who responded, and "knew them," all before migrating to Melbourne. Another respondent says that "being close to Singaporeans in Australia is very important to me now simply because it keeps me connected to home." Especially during major news events "back home in Singapore" such as the global financial crisis and the AWARE controversy, the respondents contact "friends who are from Singapore, either here or back home in Singapore," or in other places outside Singapore. Whereas Singaporeans in Singapore reside at "home," Overseas Singaporeans are considered to share the same "home" while residing outside "home." Compared to Singaporeans in Singapore, Overseas Singaporeans are not similarly aware of events at "home," but they are similarly interested in and impacted by them. Thus, when the respondents establish discursive connections around an event at home, they make a greater distinction between Singaporeans and non-Singaporeans, than between Singaporeans in Singapore and Overseas Singaporeans:

> I only forwarded it [the email my father sent me about the AWARE controversy] to *Singaporeans*. Not so much people who were *overseas* [non-Singaporeans] 'cos I didn't think it would affect them, and it happened at home... I just didn't think that anyone else *outside of Singapore* [non-Singaporeans] would be interested in what's going on in Singapore.... those that I sent to were all *overseas* [Singaporeans residing overseas].... they're not in Singapore *itself*. 'cos if they were, they would have heard about it.... those in Melbourne or studying in US or something.
>
> (Rachel, Female, emphasis mine)

Some respondents seek to experience the annual Singapore National Day Parade and National Day rally live through online streaming and through #ndrsg on Twitter. As the respondents follow the event in real time, they feel shared experience "with everyone else back home" and shared identity as "part of the... Singapore collective." At the same time, however, the respondents consciously distinguish between being "at home" and being "not physically there" but "overseas." In contrast to the experience of the event at "home," the overseas experience is voluntary,[22] second hand, and even impossible as a result of difficulties with the Internet technology:

> I was trying to stream the National Day Parade online but my Internet just failed terribly. And the National Day Rally speech as well, I also couldn't stream it... I wanted to catch it online and say the pledge together... the pledge moment was the most important thing for me for the National Day Parade...
>
> (Peter, Male)

Emotional Investment in "Home"

The respondents are emotionally invested in the future success of "home."[23] As such, they interpret current "home" events in relation to their imagination of "home" in the future. As the respondents observe negative current events, they may orient themselves toward a positive future. For example, Myanmar is viewed as being "under wrong leadership," a "third world" and "renegade country…like North Korea," yet one respondent sees "a lot of potential" for the country and expresses "still a hope that things would work out for the country, because I would still be happy to see the country prosper." As a negative current event presents a negative future scenario, it offers practical suggestions for how the "home" society can avoid the latter. It shows what "nobody hopes will happen in the future," "how things can go wrong," and "how we can do things in future."

Where the respondent does not orient herself toward a positive future but perceives that a negative current event will lead to a negative future, she wants to observe the event in the process of grieving for home:

> It's where I'm going home to, I need to be aware. I don't want to go home and realise all this has happened and I don't even know anything about it. Maybe there is no need to be aware, but I want to be aware. And also because Singapore's home, so this happens, you feel sad, whereas if it happened here [in Melbourne]…I won't give a shit….it's where you feel for more.
>
> (Natasha, Female)

In contrast, the respondents rejoice when a current event indicates that "home" is advancing toward a positive future. As one respondent responds to the AWARE controversy, "I am really happy that things are progressing in Singapore because you don't see very passionate or heated debates in Singapore." The respondents want to pay attention to current home events when they witness the speed and magnitude of transformation in home:

> Singapore is changing. It's going through a renaissance especially in the arts. I've seen it change in the last five years I've been away. It's grown phenomenally. There's so much room for creative industries to flourish now, a lot more space than before. The queer community has really come into being as well, but IndigNation is utilising the Internet a lot to bring people together. It's another community that's really been given the chance to grow. So I find that home is changing so fast and I don't want to be out of the loop.
>
> (Lisa, Female)

Although the term "heartland" was only mentioned in one interview, it is viewed as a uniquely significant space of belonging that is constructed through long-term reciprocal relation between the domestic environment and the broader neighborhood. On the one hand, the neighborhood is sensed from the otherwise private space of the domestic as neighbors come around to visit, contributing to a feeling of "kampong[24] in a HDB flat." On the other hand, informal neighborhood communities are also developed in public spaces such as a food center, through the extensive, everyday corporeal interaction among residents. Experiencing "the feeling of where you're staying," one respondent feels unique affection in relation to a familiar residential community:

> We'll always eat at the hawker centre. So everybody knows everybody. You will also know the stallholders 'cos you stayed there for many years. It's like friends but it's not really friends....a sense of belonging or homeliness, something that you cannot replicate in societies that are different from yours. You don't get this feeling anywhere else except in Singapore or, to be more specific, except where you stay....If you were to go to another hawker centre in Bedok, you can't possibly talk to people like that.
>
> (Wendy, Female)

Although Andrew is an exception, his experience of Japan reveals how a country one has never resided in can become the most important, through the everyday presence of Japanese media. Andrew reflects very high levels of engagement and literacy in relation to a wide range of media cultures: music, cinema and television, and online news. He listens to online radio, accesses news through the *BBC*, *Japan Times*, *Yahoo! News* and *Sky News*, and used to rent ten DVDs of films a week, including Hong Kong, German, French, and Hollywood films. He especially likes watching Taiwanese variety shows through cable television in Singapore and through rental DVDs and later YouTube in Melbourne. Every night in Singapore, he watches hours of Taiwanese variety shows to "keep myself company." However, Andrew singles out Japan from these cultures in ways similar to how other respondents describe Singapore as "home"[25]: "Japan was where, what I grew up with," and "I've always had a very strong passion for the Japanese culture," and he reads the *Japan Times* from between daily to every three or four days to "stay in touch." The primary reason why Japan is most important is that as a result of the J-pop wave in the 1990s, "their fashion, their dramas, their movies, their music" have been "embedded into my everyday life since young, that's why I like to follow closely to their news and what's going on." The strong presence of Japanese media in Andrew's early teenage years has been central in motivating Andrew's subsequent interrelated connections to Japan through media, education, work, and migration. Andrew has taken and failed the Japanese language examination three times, has enrolled in "a lot of Japanese electives" in undergraduate Arts and Commerce, and has volunteered at the Japan festival in Melbourne. He has unsuccessfully applied for undergraduate exchange to Japan, has visited Japan (in particular, the NHK building) as a tourist, has applied for graduate exchange to Japan, and dreams to "happily live the rest of my life there." Despite obstacles to connecting to Japan through language and migration, Andrew's commitment to accessing Japan is impressively high: "I told myself and my parents this is the place I really want to go. So I went there."

CHAPTER 6

Glocal Cosmopolitanism

How do we experience migration and media? How do we view the world and its people? How do we create our own maps of the world, its spaces, and its people? How are migration and media relevant for our personal maps of the world?

In this book, I have offered some conceptual resources and real life examples to encourage us to reflect on these questions. Much of our opinions, discussion, and research on migration and media revolve around particular countries, cultures, and communities (e.g., Georgiou, 2006; Ogan, 2001; Sinclair and Cunningham, 2001). However, my interviews with Singaporean university students in Melbourne, Australia have confirmed that we construct a much wider diversity of social spaces and social relations as we experience the world through migration and media.

We have learned a lot about how we experience migration and media through long-term, in-depth research into specific types of migrant social relations (e.g., minority, transnational, and diaspora) and social spaces (such as spaces associated with particular states, nations, and/or media). However, I have invited us to explore more general "cartographies" of the social and to understand migration as an experience we are all familiar with (first hand and/or second hand), rather than to evaluate the "migrant" as a particular type of social actor.

In chapter 2, I introduced my conceptual approach of "glocal cosmopolitanism," including my concept of "relational glocalities." I conceptualized how we might configure the social and space as we experience migration and media in contemporary globalization. In this concluding chapter, I bring together the key issues and ideas of this book. I elaborate on how we can use "glocal cosmopolitanism" and my research with Singaporean students in Melbourne to cultivate a more cosmopolitan understanding of migration and media.

Conceptualizing Social Spaces through Glocal Cosmopolitanism

When studying how we experience migration and media today, I would consider:

- how we develop personal maps of our social/societal relations;
- how we experience social relations and space between the global and the local;
- our diverse combinations of "state," "nation," and "society" (recognizing that the "nation-state" is only one possible combination).

Subjective "Cartographies" of the Social

Migrant, minority, diaspora, nationality, ethnicity, and religion are categories that we often use to distinguish sets of social relations. My interviewees address what these categories mean to them and explain how these categories are relevant to how they experience migration and media. However, through migration and media, a single respondent may perceive diverse minorities, nationalities, and ethnicities in multiple places. For example, Lisa (Female) is concerned about "victimization" and cares about Aboriginal communities in Australia, Indian students in Melbourne, and migrant workers in Singapore.

Rather than deciding what subject positions, social spaces (e.g., national or media spaces), and social relations (e.g., parent-child relations) I will focus on prior to conducting the research, I prefer to explore subject positions, social spaces, and social relations as open empirical questions.

My interviewees express subject positions that are not specifically related to migrant identities. They reflect on their roles within the family (as children and siblings), other personal relations (as friends, housemates, and neighbors), and interest-based groups (as fans, as well as leaders and members of clubs/societies). They position themselves as students in general and international students in particular, as professionals, as media users, as citizens, as migrants/mobile subjects, and as members of global publics.

We tend to consider how these subject positions are relevant for an overarching migrant subject position (see among the wealth of literature Brah, 1996; Georgiou, 2006; Gillespie, 1995; Hafez, 2007; Ogan, 2001). We also emphasize the migrant subject position when we differentiate immigrant and nonimmigrant groups (cf. Bonfadelli, Bucher, and Piga, 2007). However, we are starting to move beyond the paradigms of "methodological nationalism" (A. Wimmer and Glick Schiller, 2003) and "residentialism" (Kleinschmidt, 2006) by identifying variations in how migrants experience social spaces (Bruneau, 2010; Dahinden, 2010; Glick Schiller et al., 1995; Portes, Fernández-Kelly, et al., 2009; Slade, 2010).

My interviews reveal that migrants and nonmigrants share a variety of subject positions. Although my interviewees sometimes interpret their experiences of migration in the context of these subject positions, these positions are not always and inevitably related to a migrant subject position. Moreover, experiences of social spaces vary not only between migrant groups (Bruneau, 2010; Dahinden, 2010; Glick Schiller et al., 1995; Portes, Fernández-Kelly et al., 2009; Slade, 2010), but also between individual subjects. Based on these observations, I would consider subjective experience as a key dimension of analysis in any "methodologically cosmopolitan" (Beck, 2006) study of migration and media.

My interviewees construct social spaces at various scales, referring, for example, to neighborhoods, cities, territories, and the world. They spatially distinguish and integrate their corporeal and mediated experiences. My interviewees demonstrate an awareness of the "affordances" (Gibson, 2014[1979]) of various environments when they compare these environments based on temporal dynamics (e.g., simultaneous experience and speed of communication) and social contexts (e.g., private, public, personal, anonymous, one-to-one, mass, state, corporate, and grassroots).

We can empirically substantiate complex models of media and space (Adams, 2010; Couldry and McCarthy, 2004) by identifying how Singaporean students in Melbourne configure media and space. How do these students define media environments, spaces represented in media, media spaces of representation, and spaces of interactive discourse?

Let me simplify the illustration by focusing on one dimension of media space: media environment. My interviewees perceive a variety of interrelated media environments, such as domestic, territorial, and online environments. In and from these media environments, my interviewees open up access to media, through media. Migration informs how my interviewees view different media-space configurations with reference to one another. For example, when someone migrates from Singapore to Melbourne (territorial media environment), he/she may depart from the family place of residence (domestic media environment) and lose existing access to cable television. He/she may compensate for this loss of access by entering an online media environment in and from which he/she opens up access to televisual content made available online, through a video streaming platform such as YouTube.

At an empirical level, then, we can understand how people actually experience social spaces and relate these spaces to one another, by observing the "cartographies" that they construct and reconstruct in response to changes such as migration:

> Place (and "home" in particular) is vital to how we both construct and understand the world, but the cartographies of struggle that we construct are not imprisoned in any fixed space (if only because, as we move house from, for example, country to city, we often encounter radically different experiences and understandings of the world as we change locations). Furthermore, solidarities and alliances . . . can be and are built across space, turning fixed boundaries into porous borders in such a way as to realise . . . struggles through the uneven geographical development of political dynamics.
>
> (Harvey, 2009, p. 50)

"Cartography" is the construction of the social in terms of the global (e.g., "world"), general locality (e.g., "place"), and special locality (e.g., "home"). Our cartographies are often informed by migration and media, which we experience at various levels, not necessarily across nations and states but also from rural to urban spaces, from "country to city." In considering subjective experience as a key dimension of analysis in a "methodologically cosmopolitan" (Beck, 2006) study of migration and media, I would focus on subjective cartographies.

The results of my interviews validate that it is fruitful to be open to the extensive plurality of spaces people construct as social contexts (cf. Warf and Arias, 2008). For knowledge about and from the social, we access global and general local spaces of information, news, entertainment, and interactive discourse. We network social relations in global and general local spaces oriented not only around combinations of communication spatialities, networks, and modes (CSNM), but also around topics of collective interest, impact, and experience. We appreciate the importance of "home" (a type of special locality) as a territory of concern, as we define it as the place of residence for our loved ones, the social relations we especially value.

We usually construct these spaces through "ways of being" ("social relations and practices"), rather than "ways of belonging" that aim to perform identity (cf. Levitt and Glick Schiller, 2004, p. 1010). This means that empirical research that focuses only on specific relations of belonging such as identity and community (Georgiou, 2006; Morley, 2000) will not capture the diversity of our relations to social spaces. Since our perceptions of the social inform our constructions of space, I would conceptualize spaces less specifically as "spaces of identity" (cf. Georgiou, 2006; Morley, 2000; Morley and Robins, 1995) and more generally as "social spaces" (Faist, 2006) and "social fields" (Levitt and Glick Schiller, 2004). Instead of viewing spaces through a specific "imagined community paradigm" (p. 152), I would analyze how they interplay with "sociality, one based on social networks and nexuses" (Robins, 2007, p. 156).

As we experience migration and media in contemporary globalization, it is worth thinking about how we relate space to "cosmopolitan sociability," how we use communication to develop various spatial patterns of social relations across different social boundaries in the world (Glick Schiller, Darieva, and Gruner-Domic, 2011).

In a "methodologically cosmopolitan" (Beck, 2006) study of migration and media, I propose that "subjective cartographies of the social" is a key dimension of analysis.

Social Spaces between the Global and the Local

In our experiences of migration and media, the global and the local are the horizons for constructing social spaces.

At a macrolevel, globalized social spaces are complex networks where individuals relate to the global and the local, the supranational and the subnational (Castells, 2010; R. Robertson, 1992; Sassen, 2006; Tomlinson, 1999; Volkmer, 2009). Chapters 4 and 5 detail how social spaces are constructed in empirical reality, with reference to both the global and the local, at the microlevel of subjective experience. For example, the local experience of global warming resonates because "it's the world I'm living in, it's so day-to-day" (Nicole, Female).

A "cosmopolitan outlook" (Beck, 2006) is prevalent, both encouraged by and encouraging the "globalization of biography" (Beck, 2000d). This "cosmopolitan outlook" (Beck, 2006) refers to the reflexive negotiation between the global and the local in social life. For my interviewees, "cosmopolitan outlook" (Beck, 2006) is reflected in the coordination of worldwide personal relations through diverse CSNM; in the creation of academic and professional migration plans based on a progressively revised understanding of the global structuring of education and employment opportunities across different local social spaces; as well as in the construction of personal and global hierarchies of news that are expressed in different ways depending on current events. The reflexive negotiation between the global and the local in social life is not just an idea in cosmopolitan theories of ethics and governance (cf. Appiah, 2006; Brown and Held, 2010), but a major empirical reality that calls for analysis through "methodological cosmopolitanism," a corresponding social scientific perspective (Beck, 2006, 2012).

My interview results indicate that "banal globalism" (Urry, 2000) is prevalent. But they also suggest that "banal globalism" is not simply a way of imagination cultivated through media representation, that "media images and narratives have developed" (cf. Urry, 2000, p. 4), but a way of life. It is a way of life because through migration and media, we now construct social relations among a worldwide distribution of locally situated, global actors.

The Singaporean students I have interviewed experience migration across a global, locally differentiated "field"; global migration is not just a macro-, aggregate level phenomenon (cf. Beck and Beck-Gernsheim, 2009; Castles and Miller, 2009; Glick Schiller and Çağlar, 2009; Global Commission on International Migration (GCIM), 2005; Papastergiadis, 2000; Solimano, 2010). By conceptualizing the migrant subject position as a type of "global subject" position (cf. Bayart, 2007, p. 186), we can discern how migration across local spaces reflects location and positioning in the global. Migration does not mean that places are abstracted from a distance rather than lived from within (cf. Ong, 2008; Szerszynski and Urry, 2006); rather, migration reflects lived experience in both the global and the local.

I view the global not just as a space that is represented and imagined in and from the local, but also as a locally differentiated "field" (Glick Schiller and Çağlar, 2009; R. Robertson, 1992) in which subjects live and act. As parameters for our lived experience of media and migration, the global and the local do not correspond to fixed scales; rather, we reflexively negotiate them based on our notions of "universalism" and "particularism." Similar to Appadurai's concept of "locality," I understand the global and the local as

> primarily relational and contextual rather than as scalar or spatial . . . a complex phenomenological quality, constituted by a series of links between the sense of social immediacy, the technologies of interactivity, and the relativity of contexts.
>
> (cf. Appadurai, 1996, p. 178)

The global extends in the first instance to the boundaries of the "world as a whole" (R. Robertson, 1992, p. 8). When we study migration and media, we usually focus on a specific form of "universalized particularism" (R. Robertson, 1992, p. 103; Tomlinson, 2001) such as a particular national/ethnic/diasporic imagination or media/social network on a worldwide scale (Giulianotti and Robertson, 2007; Naficy, 2003; Tsagarousianou, 2004). However, the Singaporean students I interviewed do not primarily imagine or relate to a worldwide Singaporean diaspora. For them, the global is not a worldwide network of co-nationals or co-ethnics, but a much broader, global realm of society, governance, and public engagement. Within this "cosmopolitan society" (Beck, 2002), their countries of origin (Singapore) and residence (Australia) are not necessarily evident or prominent.

Diverse Configurations of State, Nation, and Society

My interviewees distinguish between state, society, and nation, and they are conscious that these types of social space are globalized. This finding challenges the "methodologically nationalist" assumption that there is congruence between state, society, and nation, and that we can clearly separate the global and the local dimensions of social space (cf. Beck, 2006).

We negotiate the relationship between state and society. On the one hand, my interviewees view states as political representatives who lead, speak, and act on behalf of particular societies. This relationship of political representation coheres state/society configurations such as Singapore, Australia, and the United States. Since my interviewees recognize that states represent societies, they pay attention to official statements on the websites of news organizations, government, and social media, especially during events when acts of governance are more visible than usual (e.g., the National Day rally and the swine flu pandemic). My interviewees express their support for the roles and viewpoints of the state and its political leaders.

On the other hand, my interviewees often question the extent to which states act as political representatives of their societies. When we focus on the politics between states and minorities in media spaces of representation (Echchaibi, 2011; Sakr, 2008; Silverstone, 2001; Sinclair and Cunningham, 2001; Sun et al., 2011), we risk assuming that the congruence between state and national/majority spaces of representation is less problematic. For example, Sinclair and Cunningham (2001) state that it is difficult for public service broadcasting to represent minorities within a multicultural society because there is no critical mass of minority audiences. But ratings suggest that public service broadcasting does not represent a national/majority audience, but an elite, highly literate minority. My interviewees demarcate state and civic spaces more than they do state and minority spaces. For instance, they distinguish between "official," state-managed spaces of mass representation and "unofficial," grassroots civic spaces of interactive discourse.

Singaporean students in Melbourne discriminate between Singaporean state and civic spaces, aware that the online public sphere offers an alternative to the state-managed, mainstream news media space (C. Soon and Cho, 2011). Since both state-managed and civic spaces (political websites and spaces of general discourse such as the Hardware Zone forum and #singapore on Twitter) are online, Singaporeans in Melbourne can sustain connections to distinct Singaporean state and civic spaces while residing outside Singapore territory. Somewhat similarly, my interviewees also differentiate the state and society dimensions of other authoritarian state/society configurations such as Iran, Afghanistan, and Myanmar as these state/society configurations are given civic representation through Twitter. Are the boundaries between state and society clearer in authoritarian state-society configurations? Perhaps we can explore the empirical diversity of nation-states and societies by observing variations in how people relate states and societies (cf. Beck and Grande, 2010; Brubaker, 2005).

We can discern between state and societal spaces when we compare how states and societies experience globalization. For example, my interviewees think that the Singapore state-managed media space is externally oriented, presenting a public image of Singapore (but not Singaporean society) for a regional and global audience. They praise Singapore's news media for its coverage of world news. At the same time, they criticize it for covering up issues and events that concern Singaporean society. In contrast, my interviewees perceive that Singaporean civic media spaces are internally oriented, publicizing private pictures of Singapore for a domestic audience. As Singapore state-managed media spaces open up to the world, they are fragmented from Singaporean civic media spaces. Similarly, an interviewee notes that there are political differences in the globalization experiences of the American state and a segment of American society. The American state acts in global governance (the war in Iraq) while a segment of American society expresses a political position that is aligned with the position of the global public, in opposition to the position of the American state.

Singaporean students in Melbourne draw distinctions not only between state and society, but also between society and nation. Most of the societies they construct are multinational. In their corporeal and media experiences, in neighborhoods, cities (e.g., Singapore, Melbourne, and Shanghai), and territories (e.g., Australia), my interviewees interact with people whom they associate with different Asian countries (e.g., Malaysia, China, Japan, Hong Kong, Taiwan, the Philippines, and Kazakhstan) and other countries (e.g., Australia, the United States, the United Kingdom, Sweden, Iran, and Italy).

My interviewees perceive geographical places as multinational social spaces, aware of the "internal cosmopolitanization" of societies (Beck, 2006) as "place, whether it be Manhattan or East Prussia, Malmö or Munich, becomes the locus of encounters and interminglings" (Beck, 2006, p. 10). How much more, then, shall we as social scientists conceptualize these places as distinctive spaces of "transcultural diversity" (Robins, 2007), "spaces of juxtaposition and mixture, spaces where disparate cultures converge, collide, and grapple with each other" (Inda and Rosaldo, 2008, p. 5)?

We might believe that most of us experience cultural diversity mainly through media and that only some of us encounter cultural diversity in our first-hand experiences of migration (Hannerz, 1996; Tomlinson, 1999). However, my interviewees often construct national spaces through mass media and interact with different nationalities within "territorial cultures" (cf. Hannerz, 1996) of corporeal experience. Although contemporary cities can be spaces where we are indifferent to one another and clearly segregate differences (Sennett, 2002), my interviews show that we can often enjoy, appreciate, negotiate, and incorporate national differences within environments of corporeal interaction.

We not only perceive that societies are multinational, but also experience multiple nationalities in groups of personal relations such as families, friends, and communities. My interviewees associate their intimate social relations with different nationalities and locate them in different national territories. "Global families" (Beck, 2012)

> with dual-nationality...may embody the tensions between two countries or between the majority and minority communities in those countries, while migrant families may incorporate the tensions between the centre and the periphery.
>
> (Beck, 2012, p. 9)

In contrast, my interviewees are comfortable with international relations and public diplomacy at both societal and personal levels. Some of them also value "trans-ethnic" religious communities (Werbner,

2004, p. 900). These communities may comprise minorities of different nationalities, extend nationally (e.g., Christians in Australia) and globally (e.g., Christian and Atheist communities centered in the United States). The Stoics conceptualized moral communities as concentric spheres that extend from particular to universal social relations in the following order: family, neighbors, fellow city residents, co-nationals and other particular communities, and humanity (Nussbaum, 1994). My interview results show that we can experience multiple nations in each of these types of social spaces. Moreover, the distinction between nation and society can be comfortable and less problematic than we acknowledge.

Social Spaces as Relational Glocalities

In chapter 5, I have identified units of social spaces alternative to "nation" and "state," based on my analysis of the interview responses of Singaporean university students in Melbourne, Australia. I applied my concept of "relational spaces" to the empirical data and analyzed how we construct social spaces in three dimensions: spaces constructed *through* social *relations* (social spaces), *relations between* social spaces, and *relations to* social spaces. Now, I would like to discuss how we construct social spaces as different types of "relational glocalities" in empirical reality. Informed by Roland Robertson's concept of the "universalism-particularism nexus" (R. Robertson, 1992, Chapter 6), I identify two main types of "relational glocalities": connective contexts of access and comparative cultures of awareness.

Connective Contexts of Access

The results of my study reveal how we connect contexts and contextualize connections through migration and media. We articulate the connection-contexts dialectic in two forms: convergence-CSNM and deterritorialization-localities.

Convergence-CSNM

Although convergence is an established concept, it is worth exploring how convergence is relevant for contemporary experiences of social space (Jansson and Falkheimer, 2006). Media convergence is a key form of *universal* connection to *particular* contexts of access. My study finds that we value the distinctive "affordance"[1] of the Internet in opening up a *universal* space that is "transmedial, i.e., . . . articulated by the meshing of very different media" (Hepp, 2009a, p. 330). My interviewees associate a wide range of media technologies with *particular* spaces of access. These spaces include *particular* spaces *in* which my interviewees access *particular* media technologies and *particular* spaces they access *through particular* media technologies. However, my interviewees use the distinctive convergent technology of the Internet to open up a *universal*, "transmedial" (Hepp, 2009a, p. 330) space of access that replaces *particular* spaces of access.

At the same time, we access *universal* connections in *particular* contexts through different combinations of CSNM. My interviewees and their communication partners construct *particular* communication geographies and spacetimes as they negotiate the geographical and relational distances between them through different CSNM. The geographical and relational distances that influence the selection of different CSNM vary between relationships and change through the migration of one or more communication partners. My interviewees also associate different CSNM with different social dynamics. Within the space of *universal* connections, we differentiate many *particular* contexts of social relations, communication, and interaction. These social spaces are the specific outcomes of complex negotiation between a wide range of factors: different CSNM, the relative positions of communication partners, and the relationships between communication partners.

Through the interplay between technological and social factors, we differentiate online space not only in terms of "genre" (Siapera, 2007), but also in terms of communication geographies and spacetimes. Siapera associated different "genres" of online space (website, portal, weblog, and forum) with different ways of relating transnational/translocal imagination and thought to local experience and action (Siapera, 2007). Her empirically supported concept of different "genres" of online space as different types of "universalism-particularism" (R. Robertson, 1992) offers a comparative framework that we can use when we synthesize studies that focus on a single "genre" of online space, such as forums (Androutsopoulos, 2006; Parham, 2004), weblogs (Alinejad, 2011), and online magazines (Qiu, 2003). However, rather than categorizing social spaces prior to empirical research, I prefer to be open to how my research participants define their social spaces. The openness I have brought to my study has enabled me to discern a much wider diversity of *particular* communication geographies and spacetimes, both within and beyond online space.

Deterritorialization-localities

My study finds that convergence encourages deterritorialization, which I view as another form of *universal* connection to *particular* contexts of access. Using the terms "universal" and "particular," I would define "deterritorialization" as the construction of a *universal* space of culture or meaning across and beyond *particular* territories (cf. Hepp, 2009a; Tomlinson, 1999). My interviewees perceive that content is often enclosed within *particular* geocultural territories when they access it through technologies other than and apart from the Internet. Through the technological convergence of the Internet, however, they can access territorially associated content in a *universal*, "deterritorial" (cf. Hepp, 2009a, p. 328) space. In this way, technological convergence encourages "telemediatization," "deterritorialization" through media (cf. Tomlinson, 2007).

"Telemediatization" (Tomlinson, 2007) and convergence are related as "media do not merely enable their audiences to 'be in two places at once' but effectively give them the opportunity of producing *new spaces* where remote localities and their experiences come together and become 'synchronised'" (cf. Tsagarousianou, 2004, p. 62, original emphasis). Although "synchronization" here refers to "temporal convergence" (Tsagarousianou, 2004, p. 62), it is technological convergence that enables the convergence of time. We can observe how convergence facilitates "telemediatization" (Tomlinson, 2007) in the following spaces of collective experience: interactive discourse on the Singapore National Day rally expands a space around #ndrsg on the Twitter microblogging social networking service; a person supports an international soccer team as he watches their geographically distant matches live on public and private television screens, and online.

But even though my interviewees value the experience of "telemediatization" (Tomlinson, 2007), sometimes they think that it is too expensive (e.g., they are unwilling to pay a subscription fee to access content). "Telemediatization" (Tomlinson, 2007) is also limited by technological challenges (e.g., difficulties streaming the National Day parade and the National Day rally live). Although *universal* connection is theoretically possible, it may require time (e.g., staying up to watch a soccer match live because of the time difference between where the match is played and where it is watched), money, and technological capability/proficiency. These factors depend on which *particular* territories are involved (e.g., territories that are represented, territorial centers of events, territories of residence and reception) and how these *particular* territories are related.

Diaspora is "deterritorial" (Hepp, 2009a, p. 328). Societies and individuals may be strongly invested in viewing diaspora as a "deterritorialized" version of nation, as "deterritorialized nation" (Karim, 2007; see also Kim, 2011). However, experiences of "telemediatization" (Tomlinson, 2007) are not limited to "self-imagination as a diaspora" (Tsagarousianou, 2004, p. 63). My interviewees experience "telemediatization" (Tomlinson, 2007) as they use instant messaging platforms and MMS to communicate with peers for purposes that are not explicitly related to the expression of diasporic collective identity. As one interviewee speaks concerning MMS communication: "even friends who are overseas, 'cos it's live, they get it immediately." If we start with the idea that all spaces are constructed through "universalism-particularism" (R. Robertson, 1992), we can analyze how we negotiate the dynamics of "universalism" and "particularism" through CSNM.

As technological convergence complements and contributes to "temporal convergence" (Tsagarousianou, 2004, p. 62), we can continue to access content as we migrate across *particular* territories of residence. For example, through technological convergence, my interviewees can view Taiwanese programs on television in Singapore and on YouTube in Melbourne. As technological convergence facilitates "temporal convergence" (Tsagarousianou, 2004, p. 62), my interviewees can watch the National Day parade live on television in Singapore and online in Melbourne.

While we establish *universal* connections across territories, we construct localities as *particular* contexts of access to these *universal* connections. Localities are phenomenological contexts that emerge from geographically specific associations between media and the social (cf. Appadurai, 1996, p. 178). Localities emerge in our subjective experiences as we draw associations between the multiple geographical reference points of our media technologies and social relations. We create "spatiotemporal orders" from the "partial imbrication" of the "digital" and the "non-digital," the "global," the "national," and the "subnational" (Sassen, 2006, Chapter 8). For example, "online territories" reflect "extensions and reconfigurations of pre-existing means of territorialization" (Christensen et al., 2011, p. 5).

"Localities of everyday media appropriation" are "material aspects of translocal-mediated networking" to "diasporic communicative spaces" (Hepp, 2009a, p. 328). We access *universal* (not just diasporic) "deterritorial" spaces of content in *particular* "analog" media environments (cf. Volkmer, 2006) that vary in their material, territorial, and social dimensions. My interviewees define their media environments by whether they share or don't share corporeal access with others (social dimension), and they view these places as the geographical locations of different media technologies (material dimension) that are associated with different territories (territorial dimension). For example, Andrew (Male) rents a worldwide range of global and local mainstream films from DVD shops and watches nonmainstream films associated with different countries at film festivals. Similarly, Will (Male) accesses Australian and Singapore newspapers at different places on campus (such as the library and the Overseas Student Lounge).

We access the *universal* through different technologies (such as cable television) as the cost and personal flexibility associated with these technologies are influenced by whether these technologies are geographically located in family or nonfamily domestic environments. Whereas Hepp views the "domestic world" as a locality where boundaries between the private and the family are organized through media (Hepp, 2009a), international students often incorporate nonfamily members such as housemates into domestic environments (see Beck, 2012), with social implications for *particular* access to the *universal.*

Comparative Cultures of Awareness

We can distinguish cultures as forms of awareness of social spaces. What social spaces are we aware of? How are we aware of these social spaces?

We can compare these cultures based on how they reflect *particular* configurations of *universal* modes of experience. We understand social spaces through different configurations of corporeal and mediated modes of experience.

Rantanen clearly distinguishes between corporeal and mediated modes of experience when she delineates "five zones of everyday cosmopolitanism": "media and communications," "learning another language," "living/working abroad or having a family member living abroad," "living with a person from another culture," and "engaging with foreigners in your locality or across a frontier" (Rantanen, 2005, pp. 123–130). However, my interviews show that we become aware of *particular* social spaces through complex configurations of corporeal and mediated modes of experience. We know social spaces first hand as we experience them corporeally or through media (its associated media or media associated with a different social space). We also experience social spaces second hand through corporeal or mediated relationships with others who have had corporeal or mediated experiences of the social space.

My interviewees are aware of a single globalized world as this world is routinely represented and revised in news media discourse. This finding empirically supports theories that contemporary globalized experiences distinctively reflect "consciousness of the world as a whole" (R. Robertson, 1992, p. 8) or "perceived or reflexive world society" (Beck, 2000d, p. 10). Our subjective consciousness of the world is socialized as global news (Beck, 2000d, p. 10) and foreign news (Hannerz, 2004) are experienced as forms of "banal globalism" (Urry, 2000). Whereas John Urry's concept of "banal globalism" points to the "flagging of the global" through "global imagery" (Urry, 2000, pp. 4–6), my interviewees perceive the world less through images of the *universal* and more through discourse of the *particular in the universal.*

Through news, the *particular* is discursively related *in the universal* in two ways. First, my interviewees are aware of the relations between *particular* societies in *universal* society through news representations of interstate relations. News brings to awareness the actions and responses of states in relation to one another, as well as their collaboration and conflict. These interstate relations are reflected in subjective experiences of *particular* sets of bilateral and multilateral relations within "global domestic politics" (Beck, 2006, p. 2).

Second, news of *universal* society is constituted through the juxtaposition of news of *particular* societies. The results of my study with Singaporean students in Melbourne support Chouliaraki's argument that we construct "hierarchies of place and human life" through news discourse (Chouliaraki, 2006, p. 8). However, the results suggest that we rank *particular* societies based on their *universal* influence rather than according to hierarchies of "safety" and "suffering" (cf. Chouliaraki, 2006). Moreover, although my interviewees rely heavily on the discourse of news media organizations when they construct hierarchies of societal spaces, these hierarchies are influenced more by how my interviewees position themselves within their social relations and less by discourse. My interviewees rank societies first in personal hierarchies, then in global hierarchies.

Within the *universal* discursive space of news journalism in general, we construct *particular* discursive spaces around *particular* news media organizations. These *particular* spaces reveal *particular* views of *universal* society. With this awareness, my interviewees construct the world across the spaces of multiple news media organizations. Alexa Robertson argues that we view the world and global events differently through national lenses, having observed that there are similarities across the discourses of nationally situated domestic and global broadcasters as well as the perceptions of foreign correspondents and national publics (A. Robertson, 2010). This is an argument that *particular* discursive spaces reveal *particular* views of *universal* society. My interviews support this argument, but they show that these discursive spaces are organizational rather than national spaces of news media discourse.

Although we construct *universal* spaces through our experiences of migration and media, we hierarchically associate these spaces with *particular* geographical places.

This book is an invitation to reflect in a new way on our experiences of migration and media. To facilitate this reflection, I have proposed a new conceptual approach of "glocal cosmopolitanism," in which I redefine social spaces as "relational glocalities": "glocal" spaces that are locally and unequally differentiated in relation to one another within a "global field."

This book offers conceptual, methodological, and empirical contributions to our understanding of migration and media. It helps researchers to think beyond "methodological nationalism" and to develop a "methodologically cosmopolitan" approach to our study of migration and media (Beck, 2006, 2012). Rather than conceptualizing social spaces with reference to "nation" and "state," I encourage us to explore how we configure global-local spaces. I have refined Beck's approach of "methodological cosmopolitanism" (Beck, 2006) with reference to Robertson's concept of "glocality" as a "universalism-particularism nexus" (R. Robertson, 1992, 1995) to analyze the dialectic between "universalism" and "particularism" that has been critiqued as a strength of Beck's concept but a weakness in his analysis (see Harvey, 2009, pp. 81–82).

This book also shows how we can discover and analyze subjective cartographies of the social. I have included methodological details in Appendix 2. Half of the book offers in-depth insight into the experiences of Singaporean university students in Melbourne, Australia, as examples of how we view life, migration, and media in contemporary globalization.

As we think about how we position ourselves in the world, we might consider defining our personal ethics of responsibility in relation to the people we engage with in and across our global-local spaces.

The "transferability" (Bertrand and Hughes, 2005, pp. 63–68) of the results of my study is limited by my choices of case study and sample. For example, Singapore is distinctive as a globalized city-state (see chapter 3). I have interviewed 21 self-identified Singaporean university students in Melbourne, Australia (see Appendices 1 and 2 for the details of my interviewees and methodological approach). However, these are "critical cases": cases in which particular ideas, themes, and characteristics of phenomena are revealed in high visibility (see Deacon, Pickering, Golding, and Murdock, 1999, p. 53). This study has illuminated diverse configurations of the social, space, and media, the global and the local. In doing so, it contributes to "an understanding of space as an ongoing process, which has to be *made strange* in order to reach beyond commonsense-based associations of communication and space, culture and territory" (Jansson, 2009, p. 307, original emphasis).

Appendix 1: List of Interviewees

Interviewee		*Demographic characteristics*				*Locality context*		*Cultural capital*			*Mobility*					
#	Pseudonym	Gen	Age	Ethnic	Religion	Legal Status	Kin	Lang.	Education		Localities	Summary	A	B	C	D
									U/G	P/G						
P1		F		Chinese	Christian											
P2		M		Chinese	Christ.				BSc							
1	Clara	F		Chinese					BSc	HSc	Singapore → Vancouver → Brisbane → Singapore → Vancouver → Melbourne	B1, D1		1		1
2	Isabel	F		Chinese			Mother 'shuttles' between Singapore and Australia	Japan.	BA	Arts	Singapore ↔ *Melbourne* → Japan?	C1, D1			1	1
3	Naomi	F		Chinese	Christ.	PR	Immediate family in Australia		BCom/ LLB		Singapore → Melbourne	D1				1
4	Nicole	F		Chinese	Christ.	PR			BA	HSc	Singapore → *Melbourne* → Singapore? → Canada/London/other Western country?	C1, C2, D1			1, 2	1

5	Jamie	F		Chinese				BSc	Singapore → Perth → Singapore → Melbourne → Germany? -> Singapore	A2, C1, C2, D1	2		1, 2	1
6	Wendy	F	21	Chinese				BA	Singapore → Melbourne → Singapore?/Germany?	C1, C2			1, 2	
7	Lisa	F	25	Chinese				BA	Singapore → Melbourne → Texas → Washington D.C. → Melbourne → Singapore?	B2, C2		2	2	
8	Zach	M	23	Chinese				IS	Singapore → *Melbourne*					
9	Timothy	M	22	Burmese		PR	Parents are Burmese, mother is in Australia	BCom	Singapore → *Melbourne*	D1				1
10	KoT	M	21	Chinese	Free-thinker			HSc	Singapore ↔ Malaysia → Singapore → Melbourne	A2	2			
11	Thornton	M	25	Chinese			Sister studied in Melbourne, married a Singaporean, and is working in Melbourne	BEng	Singapore ↔ *Melbourne* → Singapore?	C2, D1			2	1

continued

Interviewee		Demographic characteristics				Locality context		Cultural capital			Mobility					
#	Pseudonym	Gen	Age	Ethnic	Religion	Legal Status	Kin	Lang.	Education		Localities	Summary	A	B	C	D
									U/G	P/G						
12	Peter	M	22	Chinese					HSc		Singapore → Melbourne → Singapore?	C2			2	
13	Will	M	21	Chinese					HSc		Chengdu → Singapore → Melbourne	A1	1			
14	Zack	M	22	Chinese					BCom		Singapore → *Melbourne* ↔ Singapore ↔ Malaysia					
15	Andrew	M	25	Chinese					BCom	Arts	Singapore → Melbourne → Japan?	C1			1	
16	Rachel	F	21	Chinese	Christ.				BA		Singapore → London → Singapore → Shanghai → Singapore → Melbourne	B1		1		
17	Stryker	M	26	Chinese	Christ.				BA		Singapore → Brunei → Singapore → Melbourne	B1		1		
18	Sally	F	24	Chinese			Married sister in London		BA		Singapore → *Melbourne* → Singapore ↔ London	B2, D1		2		1

19	Mark	M	24	Chinese			BCom	Singapore ↔ Melbourne			
20	Ivan	M	20	Chinese	Atheist	Russ-ian	BA	Singapore → Melbourne			
21	Natasha	F	21	Chinese	Christ.		BA	Hong Kong (UK) → Singapore ↔ *Shanghai* → Singapore → Melbourne	A1, B1	1	1

Notes:
Languages:
All participants are likely to be able to speak English, Mandarin Chinese, and possibly a Chinese dialect.
Mobility Classification:
A-C: Mobility in Biography
A: Childhood mobility
A1: Born in a locality other than Singapore and moved to Singapore as a child
A2: Born in Singapore and moved to a locality other than Singapore as a child
B: Postchildhood mobility
B1: Moved to one or more localities other than a childhood locality before moving to Melbourne
B2: Moved to one or more localities other than a childhood locality after moving to Melbourne
C: Future mobility
C1: Intends to move to a new locality
C2: Intends to return to a previous locality
C3: No intention to move in future (not indicated)
D: Other mobility
D1: Family-related mobility postchildhood

Appendix 2: Methodological Details

It takes years of training and practice to learn how to design a research project that is worth investing in, and to apply a methodological approach to systematically discover and analyze a specific aspect of the world we live in. This book is the outcome of years of PhD research training (extensive reading and writing enriched by generous supervision, mentoring, and collegial support), months of interviews, and two years of data analysis. Given the time and energy we researchers invest to develop proficiency in any type of research method, we tend to focus our individual practice on a particular type of method (e.g., quantitative or qualitative, survey or interview) and collaborate on multimethod research. I hope that chapters 4 and 5 encourage us all (researchers with different methodological orientations and members of the public who enable our research through public funding) to appreciate the depth of insight we can gain through qualitative research and the rigor we aim for when we interpret interview data.

I include the methodological details of my study in this Appendix for three reasons:

- To communicate transparently to fellow researchers and the public how I have obtained my results and to invite necessary reflection and constructive criticism on the soundness, value, and limitations of my study
- To explain how my research is informed by particular methodological approaches (e.g., qualitative paradigm, multistep sampling, semi-structured interviews, phenomenology, and hermeneutic interpretation) that may be unfamiliar to the readers of this book, including other researchers of migration and media
- To give students an example of research design, what we might consider when developing a methodological approach, how we can justify our methodological decisions, and how we can communicate our process of research.

Qualitative Approach

Although approaches to qualitative research are diverse, we can distinguish qualitative research by its research aim, empirical context, and the role of the researcher (Jensen, 2002, p. 236). Qualitative research aims to explore the relationship between meaning and action, it analyzes phenomena in their "*naturalistic contexts*," and it considers the researcher to be responsible for the "global and continuous…interpretation" of results (Jensen, 2002, p. 236, original emphasis).

Being an "iterative" process, qualitative research allows us to flexibly engage theoretical concepts with empirical contexts (Jensen, 2002, p. 236). My empirical research is oriented toward "emic" analysis: the exploration of "global[ ]" phenomena through "local experiences" (Jensen, 2002, pp. 236–237). By analyzing specific experiences, I can best understand diversity and complexity in the experiences of Singaporean university students in Melbourne, Australia.

The interview is a process of "purposive conversation" (Bertrand and Hughes, 2005, p. 74) which the interviewer guides to reveal aspects of the respondents' worldviews which the respondents may not be conscious of (Berger, 1991, p. 57), but which are relevant to the research objectives.

Interviews diverge based on the level of structure and the number of respondents in one interview (Bertrand and Hughes, 2005, pp. 77–80; Jensen, 2002, pp. 240–242). I use semi-structured interviews because this type of interview is distinctively flexible (Priest, 1996, pp. 107–109)—it allows me to adapt questions to individual respondents (R. D. Wimmer and Dominick, 1997, p. 100), but it is also focused by a basic structure that facilitates the management of time (Bertrand and Hughes, 2005, p. 79) and data. The fluid structure of semi-structured interviews promotes cross-subjective interpretation since I can compare individual narratives in relation to common parameters of discourse.

Interview Questions

I structured my interview questions into three sections. My interview questions explore how my interviewees perceive:

- the media environments in their biographical present and past;
- public communities (their significance, participation in them, and the relevance of media);
- public issues and/or events (their significance, interest in them, and the relevance of media).

Other researchers have explored how these topics are perceived in generational memories of news (Volkmer, 2006), and "mediated public connection" in the United Kingdom (Couldry, Livingstone, and Markham, 2010).

I designed the interview guide (Table A2.1) based on my research question (Priest, 1996, p. 108): How do we construct social spaces

Table A2.1 Links between conceptual framework and interview questions

Conceptual framework	*Interview questions*
• Experiences of migration and media (chapter 1) • Media and cosmopolitanism (chapter 2)	1. Media environment • Which media are most important to you? Why? • How is your media use similar to/different from when you were a teenager?
• Critique of the concept of "imagined communities" (cf. Anderson, 1991; Robins, 2007)	2. Public communities • Which public communities are most important to you? Why? • Have there been times when certain public communities became more important to you than others? If so, how did this happen? • Is there any relationship between your media use and your participation in these communities?
Studies of mediated perceptions of public events (Couldry et al., 2010; Volkmer, 2006) Public events in experiences of migration and media • Conflict events in the country of origin (Kolar-Panov, 1997) • Global conflict events such as September 11 (e.g., Gillespie, 2006) The Singapore context of public issues/events • List of major public issues and events in Singapore in 2009 (D. Soon, 2010) • Public events as case studies of strategic public relations (T. Lee, 2008)	3. Public Issues/Events • Which public issues/events are most important to you? Why? • Have there been times when certain public issues/events became more important to you than others? If so, how did this happen? • Is there any relationship between your media use and your interest in these issues/events?

in our experiences of migration and media? Through the first interview question, I explore how my respondents construct social spaces through diverse media and changing media environments. Through the interview questions on public communities, issues, and/or events, I discover how my respondents variously define the "social" in relation to space. Rather than focusing on specific instances of public communities, issues, and/or events, such as major political changes in the country of origin (Kolar-Panov, 1997) and global conflict events such as September 11 (Gillespie, 2006), I kept myself open to the social relations, spaces, and experiences that my respondents find meaningful.

When I conducted my interviews in 2009, public communication in Singapore revolved around the following topics (D. Soon, 2010):

- local experiences of the global economic recession;
- changes in the regulation of political practices (e.g., representation, election, the use of the Internet for campaigning and political expression);
- local concern about "foreign talent";
- incompatible worldviews, divisions in public opinion, and fragmentation of society, especially in

> [t]he saga surrounding the Association of Women for Action and Research (AWARE) [which] was regarded as a watershed in civil society development in terms of the intensity of public debate that contrasts with the common perception that Singaporeans are politically apathetic.
>
> (D. Soon, 2010, p. 6)

Fieldwork

The University of Melbourne Culture and Communication Human Ethics Advisory Group approved the fieldwork (Ethics Application 0829731).

I conducted two pilot interviews to test and revise the interview questions. For the main study, I conducted 21 interviews over two stages in 2009. The pilot interviews and the first five interviews took place in February and the other 16 interviews in August and September. Sampling and interviewing over different time periods broadens the variation in data and enables me to explore changes in my interviewees' experiences of media and society (e.g., current issues and events). I conducted the interviews just before and at the beginning of the two academic semesters. Perhaps the Singaporean students I interviewed might have recently returned from overseas and be conscious of fresh experiences of migration and social space. As assessment would not be due for some time, the students could also take time to share their experiences.

I conducted most of the interviews in rooms at the University of Melbourne. These spaces are where university students regularly share their experiences with academics over an extended time with minimal distractions and interruptions. The interview venue is relevant for the quality of the interview data and I would choose a classroom rather than my office to encourage "interactional symmetry" or balance in the relative power of the interviewer and the interviewee (Schrøder, et al., 2003, pp. 150–151).

Since Singaporean university students and I are proficient in English, I have conducted the interviews in English. It is consistent to use a common language to interpret data, and comparative studies have been challenged by the use of diverse languages (Livingstone and Lemish, 2001, p. 40). However, my respondents have felt comfortable using colloquial terms and other languages occasionally.

The interview recordings are 98 minutes long on average. The shortest recording was 73 minutes long and the longest was 139 minutes long. To obtain in-depth insight into the respondents' experiences, it is best to interview for at least an hour and not less than half an hour (Priest, 1996, p. 108). However, the length of interviews varies widely between studies depending on the studies' research aims and practical contexts (Jensen, 2002, p. 241).

I digitally recorded all interviews (including pilot interviews) with the interviewee's permission. I transcribed the 21 interviews, resulting in nearly 600 pages of transcripts in total.

At the end of transcription, I emailed my interviewees in April 2010, thanking them again for their participation in my study and advising them that transcripts were available for checking upon request. I emailed them the transcripts upon request and made minor changes to the data based on my interviewees' responses to their transcripts.

Sampling

I selected the sample of this study through "non-probability sampling." Nonprobability sampling refers to the selection of the sample according to specific criteria (Deacon et al., 1999, p. 50). As such, some researchers refer to nonprobability sampling and purposive sampling interchangeably (Deacon et al., 1999, p. 50; Schrøder, Drotner, Kline, and Murray, 2003, p. 159), although others consider nonprobability sampling as a broader set of methods of which purposive sampling is but one type (Bertrand and Hughes, 2005, p. 68).

The relevant contexts for the construction of social spaces and my interpretation include

- *political* contexts: nationalities, legal statuses (e.g., citizenship and residency);
- *cultural* contexts: age, gender, ethnicity, religion, languages of proficiency;
- *social* contexts: places of present and previous residence, levels and courses of education;
- *biographical* contexts: the geographical distribution of family members (genealogical and biographical), migration histories and aspirations;
- *discursive* contexts: the interview.

I would conduct multiple rounds of sampling to sense what contexts are potentially relevant, and to progressively focus data collection and interpretation in specific contexts as particular contexts are revealed to be especially relevant. By sampling over multiple rounds, I express the idea that

> [t]he qualitative research process amounts to a continuous operationalization and refinement of theoretical concepts with reference to empirical evidence generated through several analytical stages.
>
> (Jensen, 2002, p. 238)

I selected my sample over three rounds: the recruitment of potential interviewees, the selection of recruits for interview, and the selection of interview texts for close analysis. "Multi-step sampling" is consistent with the "contextual orientation" of qualitative research, which expects the researcher both to sample and to interpret in context (Jensen, 2002, p. 238).

Nonprobability sampling gives the researcher greater flexibility to sharpen theoretical knowledge and empirical observation in relation to each another. Nonprobability or nonrandom sampling is especially associated with qualitative research (Deacon et al., 1999, p. 50) in general and it is typical of interview research (Schrøder et al., 2003, p. 159) in particular. Nonprobability sampling is suitable for constructivist approaches that aspire to achieve "transferability": to relate observations of particular "cases" and "instances" of "cases" to the understanding of more universal phenomena (Bertrand and Hughes, 2005, pp. 63–68).

My decisions on sampling method are based on my theoretical interests and practical constraints, specifically the "transferability" of results, the suitability of the sampling method for the research question, the effort required to recruit research participants, and empirical research expenses (Bertrand and Hughes, 2005, p. 66).

I selected my sample through the nonprobability sampling method of theoretical sampling. Theoretical sampling is the selection of a sample that the researcher judges to best further or challenge theoretical understanding (Deacon et al., 1999, p. 52).

I recruited 55 potential interviewees, selected 21 recruits for interview, and chose seven interview transcripts (texts) for the first round of close analysis. After this first round of interpretation, I interpreted the 21 texts.

Qualitative samples are "illustrative" rather than "representative" (Deacon et al., 1999, p. 43). Research which does not intend to generalize is not constrained by any standard regulation regarding sample size; instead, decisions on sample size are based on the research objectives and sample size may be as small as a single "information-rich" case (Bertrand and Hughes, 2005, pp. 65–66). Although the optimum sample size may be at "saturation point" when data appears to be recurring, qualitative research may not always aim for "saturation point" (Deacon et al., 1999, p. 43). Particularly in hermeneutical research, I would argue that the notion of "saturation point" is impossible to know or reach.

Recruitment and Selection of Interview Participants

In the Call for Participants, I specified four criteria: participants would be aged between 20 and 26 years old, self-identified Singaporeans, students at a university in Melbourne, and media users.

I initially specified an age range of 20–24 years after considering how the United Nations, Singapore, and Australia define youth, and reviewing the methodological details of research on migration and media. However, I revised the upper limit of the age range to 26 years old to account for the fact that Singaporean males enter university later than females because of Singapore's compulsory military service regulations.

I recruited my research participants through Melbourne-based Singaporean university student networks, university networks, Asian Australian research networks, and my personal networks. In the recruitment process, I received responses from 55 individuals.

Selection of Interview Participants

From the 55 recruits, I selected a sample of 21 interviewees through the theoretical sampling of critical cases.

Although theoretical sampling and critical-case sampling are distinct sampling methods (Deacon et al., 1999, p. 53), a theoretical sample may include critical cases (Jensen, 2002, p. 239). Critical cases are cases in which particular ideas, themes, and characteristics of phenomena are revealed in high visibility (see Deacon et al., 1999, p. 53). I can select critical cases through theoretical sampling because they contribute to theoretical advancement by prominently showcasing theoretically relevant empirical details, thereby facilitating my analysis of these details.

To those who responded to the Call for Participants, I emailed a request for biographical details including date of birth, educational background, places of (present and previous) residence, and time spent in each place. Collecting preliminary demographic information enables me to observe any association between demographic categories and interview findings (Berger, 1991, p. 61). Since my research is theoretically concerned about how we construct social spaces in our experiences of migration and media, I selected interviewees based on the number of places of residence they specified.

I aimed for gender balance at all stages of sampling. In response to an initially low number of male recruits relative to females, I distributed an additional Call for Participants highlighting the need for males. I selected eleven males and ten females for interview, and chose the interview texts of four females and three males for the first round of interpretation.

So that my sampling would follow specific criteria aimed at a "diversity of discursive repertoires" (Schrøder et al., 2003, p. 160), I aimed for diversity in the following areas when I selected interviewees and interview texts:

- demographic characteristics: age and religion;
- cultural capital: languages of proficiency, education contexts (including educational pathways, courses, and funding arrangements);
- biographical experiences of migration: significant places (number of places, type of place, duration of residence, and the names of these places), migration in relation to life stage (e.g., childhood, postchildhood, intention to migrate), and family migration.

Interpretation

Within extensive theoretical traditions, my interpretive method is based on Gadamer's hermeneutical approach and Schutz's phenomenological approach.

A hermeneutical approach understands the "whole" in terms of its "parts," and vice versa, in a perpetual, concentric circular process

(Gadamer, 1982 [1975], pp. 258–259). Understanding aims toward the ideal of synchronized meaning between the interpreter and the text, as well as between the "whole" and the "parts" of the text (Gadamer, 1982 [1975], pp. 260–261).

In Heidegger's existential concept, tradition and interpretation are related in the "hermeneutic circle," which is "an ontological structural element in understanding" (Gadamer, 1982 [1975], p. 261). Understanding is a permanent process in which I refine meaning by continuously projecting and confirming possible meanings with reference to what I aim to understand (Gadamer, 1982 [1975], p. 237). I project meaning based on tradition (Gadamer, 1982 [1975], p. 261).

According to Gadamer, the "hermeneutic situation" is the situation of the interpreter in relation to tradition, and it coordinates the "horizon" or "range of vision" (Gadamer, 1982 [1975], p. 269). Understanding is self-positioning within "a process of tradition, in which past and present are constantly fused" (Gadamer, 1982 [1975], p. 258). As the interpreter, I position myself in the space between foreignness and familiarity in relation to the text, and this liminal position enables me to reflect on "prejudices" or untested preconceptions which are essential for understanding and misunderstanding (Gadamer, 1982 [1975], pp. 262–263).

The awareness of the "hermeneutical situation" is always partial given that the interpreter is situated historically (Gadamer, 1982 [1975], p. 269). In the "hermeneutic situation," I continuously achieve a higher "horizon of the present" from which to view the text and myself (Gadamer, 1982 [1975], p. 272). "Effective-historical consciousness" involves both the distinction and "fusion of horizons": the "horizon" of the text is not only projected as different from the "horizon of the present," but it is also merged with it in the process of understanding (Gadamer, 1982 [1975], pp. 272–273). Interpretation reveals the text in relation to the historical and continuously changing situation in which the text is understood (Gadamer, 1982 [1975], pp. 274–276).

In hermeneutics-oriented audience research, the historical and cultural locations which inform interpretation are "multiple intersecting spaces that make up an individual life-world" (Harindranath, 2009, p. 81). As such, interpretative frameworks may diverge among subjects whose interpretations converge (Harindranath, 2009, p. 81).

As in Figure A2.1, my interpretation process involves a continuous deepening of insight through the dialogical engagement of theoretical and empirical forms of understanding. I progressively question and refine my conceptual framework of "glocal cosmopolitanism" in relation to the empirical data (Figure A2.1).

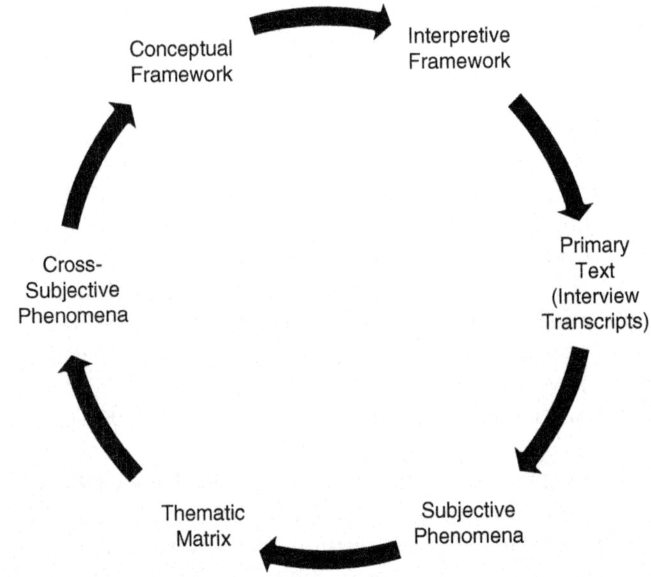

Figure A2.1 Stages of interpretation

I defined the interpretation of each interview transcript (text) as a "whole." This interpretation of subjective phenomena formed the basis for cross-subjective interpretation: the interpretation of each text as "part" of the "whole" corpus of texts.

Phenomenological Approach

My interpretive framework is informed by a phenomenological approach that helps me to reconstruct structures of subjective experience (see D. W. Smith, 2011). Phenomenology is the study of "phenomena" or the meaning of "things" as they are structured in reflection or first-person experience (D. W. Smith, 2011). These "phenomena" include forms of experience such as the perception of space, awareness of the self and others, as well as the meaning of action and communication as these are experienced in culture (D. W. Smith, 2011). Phenomena are "intended" or given meaning as a result of "conditions" including the biographical, social, and cultural situations of the subject (D. W. Smith, 2011).

In the "natural attitude" of the "life-world" where social experience and action are conducted, I assume the existence of the "life-world" and the stability of: the structure of the world, the truth of my experience of the world, and my capacity to act upon and in the world (Schutz, 1966, p. 116).

According to Schutz, the "life-world" is layered spatio-temporally into three "zones": "zones of actual, restorable and obtainable reach" (Schutz, 1966, p. 118). The "zone" of "actual" reach is the world I may immediately perceive, be impacted by and act upon; the "zone" of "restorable" reach is the world which has been, is not, and which may be brought back within my "actual" reach, possibly in a different version; and the "zone" of "obtainable" reach is the world which has never been but which may be brought within my "actual" reach (Schutz, 1966, p. 118). The world within my "obtainable" reach is the world within your "actual" or "restorable" reach (Schutz, 1966, p. 118). Although I have not experienced this world and will experience it differently to you because of my "biographical situation," I am "familiar" with it because I assume that it is similarly structured to the worlds I have experienced (Schutz, 1966, p. 118).

We can divide the "social world" into four types based on the extent to which we experience other subjects as within reach and action. I experience "fellow-men" as within mutual reach and action in the world of "direct social experience," where our worlds overlap in space and time (Schutz, 1966, pp. 118–119). This world is encircled by the world of "contemporaries" including previous and potential "fellow-men," who are also experienced as within mutual reach and action, but who share only time and not space (Schutz, 1966, p. 119). In addition, the world of "predecessors" may act upon me but not vice versa, whereas I may act upon the world of "successors" but not vice versa (Schutz, 1966, p. 119).

The "stock of knowledge" is the collection of all experiences of previously defining "situation" (Schutz, 1966, p. 123). The "stock of knowledge" comprises two basic elements: the "limitation" of the subjective "situation" in the world, and the "spatial, temporal and social" organization of subjective experience (Schutz, 1966, p. 101). Although all subjects share the basic elements of the "stock of knowledge," the "situation," experience, and the "stock of knowledge" are all "biographically articulated" (Schutz, 1966, pp. 109, 111–113).

> To the experiencing subject's mind, the elements singled out of the pregiven structure of the world always stand in sense-connections, connections of orientation as well as of mastery of thought or action.
>
> (Schutz, 1966, p. 122)

My interpretation focuses on revealing the subjective associations through which significant social spaces emerge in perception and are given meaning.

Scoping Approach

Since my interpretation of the first interview text would inform my interpretation of subsequent texts, I ranked the texts based on the order in which I planned to interpret them. I ranked the texts after interpreting the 21 texts as a whole. The texts that I judged to hold the greatest potential for theoretical advancement, I interpreted first.

I interpreted the texts through what I would call a scoping approach, in which I interpreted the most in-depth phenomena first in order to develop initial understanding of both subjective and cross-subjective patterns. I identified phenomena and themes from the first text, and progressively refined these phenomena and themes when interpreting the second and third texts. I then developed an interpretation template and used this template to focus my interpretation of four additional texts.

The interpretation template outlines the main foci of the interpretation of each text: holistic understanding of the text in relation to the conceptual framework (meaning of the "whole"), a pivotal quote which opens up the interpretation of the text (meaning of the "part"), phenomena, the relevance of media in phenomena, and themes.

Guided by the template, I followed these steps when interpreting each text:

- I grouped quotes from the text and interpreted them with reference to the phenomena
- I coded the interpretation with the themes
- I wrote phrase-length and paragraph-length summaries of each text
- I cited pivotal quotes

The outcome of my subjective interpretation is a written interpretation, averaging 20–25 pages per interview text.

The seven subjective interpretation texts (which show the selection, grouping and ordering of quotes, as well as their interpretation) formed the basis for the cross-subjective interpretation. I compared the subjective interpretation texts within the themes. Based on the interpretation of seven interview texts across five themes (Norms, Proximity, Community, Proficiency, and Agency), I interpreted 21 interviews in relation to the theme of Proximity.

Notes

1 Migration, Media, and Social Space

1. Along with transnationalism, assimilation is one of the two dominant paradigms in migration studies. The Chicago School introduced classical assimilation theory in the 1920s to think about European migration to the United States. Refining classical assimilation theory, the differentiated model of "segmented assimilation" was developed in the 1990s to understand the more recent Latin, African, and Asian migration to the United States (Portes, Fernández-Kelly, and Haller, 2009). As transnationalism emerged in the 1990s as an alternative paradigm to assimilation, migration studies began to consider the relationship between assimilation and transnationalism (Portes, Escobar, and Arana, 2009).

4 Geographies

1. While analytical distinctions can be made between "absolute," "relative," and "relational" conceptions of space, "absolute" space can be perceived in experiences of "relational" space (Harvey, 2009).
2. I use the terms "migration" and "migrate" to refer to a change in the social context in which one lives. In contrast, I use "mobility," "move," and "travel" to refer to a change in the social context in which one is located. I distinguish between these two sets of terms to refer to different experiences of social space rather than to different lengths of time in a different social context. That said, compared to mobility, migration tends to be associated with a longer period of residence in a different social context. For example, migration could range from the three months of an academic semester to the years of a university course.
3. At KoT's request, I am especially careful not to mention details specific to his migration background, for confidentiality reasons.
4. Interestingly, places other than Singapore are mentioned in passing (e.g., Hong Kong) or implied.
5. Although Will also mentions the *BBC* and *The Age* (Australian newspaper) as news sources, he downplays the everyday significance of these news sources: the *BBC* is used "just occasionally...really occasional," during "really important international" events, whereas use

of *The Age* is unplanned, "just only whenever I come across it," for example, at the library.

6. *Lianhe Zaobao* is one of the two mainstream Chinese-language national broadsheets in Singapore.
7. *Channel NewsAsia* is a Singapore-based regional news organization that offers 24 hour news on television and a news website that is non-subscription-based (in contrast to the *Straits Times*).
8. The Saturday print edition of the *Straits Times* is available at the Melbourne University Overseas Student Service lounge.
9. At KoT's request for confidentiality, I have protected specific personal details.
10. In Naomi's case, the age of migration is not explicitly stated, but can be inferred from the personal details provided by the respondent.
11. Naomi visits her friends in Singapore and her friends from Singapore visit her in Melbourne.
12. Hiller and Franz do not discuss chain migration in their work on virtual diasporic communities. However, their distinction between subjects at different stages of migration experience ("pre-migrant," "post-migrant," and "settled migrant") and their research on these subjects' different uses of social networking within diasporic community can facilitate thinking about chain migration.
13. That is, relations with "a friend of a friend" (Hiller and Franz, 2004, p. 738).
14. Here, overseas is viewed relative to the location before trans-state migration, for example, Singapore (Thornton; Jamie) but also Vancouver, Canada (Clara).
15. Nicole has been granted permanent residency (PR) under General Skilled Migration. At the time of her visa application, having a partner was not a requirement for the granting of PR.
16. Her mother has applied for what Nicole describes as business-related professional skilled migration.
17. At the time of the interview.
18. Given the parameters of this study, all 21 trajectories cut across Singapore and Melbourne. However, as I show in this comparative overview of subjective geographies, multiple places other than Singapore and Melbourne are relevant in experiences of migration. In the context of this overview, and at this point in the analysis in particular, I highlight divergence in trajectories of independent migration.
19. These include the newspaper, radio, phone, television, cinema, and video.
20. For example, the respondents read world news through the websites of global news organizations, not just the world content incorporated in national newspapers. They converse through Skype, not just through the phone. They watch audiovisual content originally produced for broadcast (such as movies and shows) through video streaming platforms such as YouTube.

21. For example, a campus Rotary Club (Clara, Female), the Singapore Students' Society (Jamie, Female), and church (Zach, Male).
22. Examples of these include Singaporean and Asian societies, Christian and Atheist societies, Law, Commerce, and international students societies, as well as sport, fanfiction, photography, and music societies.
23. Public communities that are perceived as socially significant during events include worldwide and local social movements such as the Iran election protests (Lisa, Female), as well as the AWARE (Lisa, Female) and pink dot (Sally, Female) events in Singapore.
24. For example, Atheist websites, video streaming of Manchester United soccer matches, blogging and instant messaging with friends in the community, and discourses around the Iran election protests on Twitter.
25. "Locals" may be viewed as others with whom the subjects perceive shared corporeal location and common interests. With reference to the subjects, "locals" may be corporeally located in the same country of residence (e.g., Australia), university or church. They may also have similar professional, educational, and leisure interests.
26. For example, a Facebook Group or Page, and through the professional social networking platform LinkedIn.
27. I have not made a clear distinction between issues and events, considering that events are often oriented around issues and issues are often raised by events. In addition, some respondents use the terms "issues" and "events" interchangeably.
28. I have briefly classified important issues/events not in objective terms, but in terms of how they are sociospatially experienced by respondents. I elaborate on these sociospatial experiences below.
29. With the exception of the Singapore general elections which occurred in 2006. The National Day Parade is an annual event.
30. For example, conditions in which self-expression is limited (Nicole, Female).
31. For example, gender and/or sexuality-related marginalization in Singapore (Lisa, Female; Sally, Female).
32. For example, terrorist attacks (e.g., September 11, the Mumbai bombings), the Iran election protests, soccer matches, the US Presidential debate, and the National Day Parade.
33. Involving semi-structured interviews interpreted through hermeneutical and phenomenological approaches, this study is clearly and deeply situated in qualitative research traditions. In this context, I use the term "quantitative" here to refer to the idea that a multiplicity of places—and not just one place or two places—are relevant for experiences of (media and) migration.
34. Subjects are often sociospatially defined primarily in relation to these places, for example, in official public (e.g., immigration) or enrolment records.

5 Cartographies

1. For example, linguistic, political, national, ethnic, and religious.
2. I interpret "someone," "everybody," and "anyone" as interchangeable, discursive forms of sociospatial boundary definition.
3. Communication spatialities include reach and portability of communication, enabled by online and mobile technologies. Networks include groups of personalized contacts organized around social networking platforms such as Facebook and LinkedIn, instant messaging platforms such as MSN, as well as the Skype voice-over-Internet Protocol service. Modes include video, audio, or textual modes of communication. I use the acronym CSNM to refer to configurations of communication spatialities, networks, and modes, such as audio-visual communication with geographically distant family through Skype.
4. The respondents only communicate online with some friends.
5. For example, adolescent pregnancy, violence, and murder.
6. For example, similarities in ethnic appearance (which may be associated with cultural similarity), experiences, values, ways of thinking or "wavelength," lifestyle, and work style.
7. For example, differences in linguistic and media preferences, perspective, and lifestyle.
8. Citizens may refer to Singaporeans that are not acting as state representatives, rather than to those who hold Singapore citizenship in the legal sense.
9. As Timothy phrases it, this "all on one" capability refers to the capability to converge all technologies onto one technological platform.
10. For example, the university newsagent where an Australian newspaper can be personally picked up upon display of a student discount subscription card.
11. I infer this point from Andrew's interview as a whole. Andrew expresses very high usage of music and television, as well as keen interest in exploring new content.
12. For example, Yahoo!, Sky Sports, as well as the University of Melbourne Student Portal and Learning Management System (LMS).
13. Singapore and Australia were affected in the worldwide swine flu pandemic.
14. For example, natural disaster, accident, "national" violence, and "international" war.
15. The "Zimbabwe situation" likely refers to the 2008 postelection violence by ruling party leaders and supporters against opposition leaders and supporters.
16. A respondent may perceive multiple "home territories." For example, a respondent who has migrated with his Burmese mother to Australia uses "home" to refer to Singapore, Australia, and (to a certain extent) Burma.

17. In circular migration, the temporal markers "past," "present," and "future" may not be permanently and exclusively fixed to place. For example, a place of return migration may be a place of both past and future residence. However, as I elaborate in the text, the temporal markers may be relevant for perceptions of and relations to place.
18. See the discussion on "heartland" relations below.
19. Clara completed her undergraduate studies in Canada before graduate studies and employment in Melbourne.
20. Singlish for "rowdy, wild, undisciplined" ("A Dictionary of Singlish and Singapore English").
21. For example, Japan in Japanese anime fanfiction, and the Manchester United soccer team which plays in the United Kingdom and Europe.
22. One respondent watches the National Day Parade when she is in Singapore only because her father "forces" the family to do so.
23. "Home" here tends to refer to the respondent's "home" (Singapore). However, it may also refer to a family heritage territory that is described as "not really my home, it's my parents' home, it's my family home."
24. "kampong" means "village" in Malay.
25. Andrew refers to Singapore but not Japan as "home," as Singapore is where his family and close friends reside. However, Singapore has not been chosen as home and he would otherwise "gladly not be a Singaporean."

Bibliography

Adams, P. C. (2010). A taxonomy for communication geography. *Progress in Human Geography 35*(1), 1–21.

Ahmed, S. (2006). The media consumption of young British Muslims. In E. Poole and J. E. Richardson (eds.) *Muslims and the News Media* (pp. 167–175). London; New York: I.B. Tauris.

Aksoy, A., and Robins, K. (2003a). Banal transnationalism: the difference that television makes. In K. H. Karim (ed.) *The Media of Diaspora* (pp. 89–104). London: Routledge.

Aksoy, A. and Robins, K. (2003g). The enlargement of meaning: social demand in a transnational context. *Gazette: The International Journal for Communication Studies 65*(4–5), 365–388.

Albizu, J. A. (2007). Geolinguistic regions and diasporas in the age of satellite television. *International Communication Gazette 69*(3), 239–261. DOI: 10.1177/1748048507076578.

Alia, V. and Bull, S. (2005). *Media and Ethnic Minorities.* Edinburgh: Edinburgh University Press.

Alinejad, D. (2011). Mapping homelands through virtual spaces: Transnational embodiment and Iranian diaspora bloggers. *Global Networks 11*(1), 43–62. DOI: 10.1111/j.1471-0374.2010.00306.x.

Aly, A. (2007). Australian Muslim responses to the discourse on terrorism in the Australian popular media. *Australian Journal of Social Issues 42*(1), 27–40.

Anderson, B. (1991). *Imagined Communities: Reflections on the Origin and Spread of Nationalism* (Rev. and extended ed.). London; New York: Verso.

Anderson, B. (1992). *Long-Distance Nationalism: World Capitalism and the Rise of Identity Politics.* Amsterdam: Centre for Asian Studies Amsterdam.

Anderson, B. (1998). Nationalism, identity, and the world-in-motion: On the logics of seriality. In P. Cheah and B. Robbins (eds.) *Cosmopolitics: Thinking and Feeling Beyond the Nation* (pp. 117–133). Minneapolis: University of Minnesota Press.

Androutsopoulos, J. (2006). Multilingualism, diaspora, and the Internet: Codes and identities on German-based diaspora websites. *Journal of Sociolinguistics 10*(4), 520–547.

Ang, I. and Stratton, J. (1995). The Singapore way of multiculturalism: Western concepts/Asian cultures. *Sojourn: Journal of Social Issues in Southeast Asia 10*(1), 65–89.

Appadurai, A. (1996). *Modernity at Large: Cultural Dimensions of Globalization* (Vol. 1). Minneapolis; London: University of Minnesota Press.

Appadurai, A. and Morley, D. (2011). Decoding diaspora and disjuncture: Arjun Appadurai in dialogue with David Morley. *New Formations 73*(3), 43–55. DOI: 10.3898/NEWF.73.03.2011.

Appiah, K. A. (2006). *Cosmopolitanism: Ethics in a World of Strangers*. New York; London: W. W. Norton and Company.

Arcioni, E. (2006). *Representation for the Italian diaspora Discussion Paper* (Vol. 37, pp. 1–8). Democratic Audit of Australia, Australian National University.

Australian Broadcasting Corporation. (2015). Australia-Singapore CSP: Tony Abbott, Lee Hsien Loong sign agreement formalising defence, economic ties. *ABC News*. Retrieved from: http://www.abc.net.au/news/2015-06-29/australia-singapore-announce-comprehensive-strategic-partnership/6581334.

Australian Education International. (2011). *Study Pathways of International Students in Australia*. Retrieved from: https://www.aei.gov.au/research/Research-Papers/Documents/20110520_Pathways.pdf.

Australian Government Department of Immigration and Border Protection. Arrivals SmartGate. Retrieved July 16, 2015, from: http://www.border.gov.au/Trav/Ente/Goin/Arrival/Smartgateor-ePassport.

Bailey, O. G. (2007). Transnational identities and the media. In O. G. Bailey, M. Georgiou, and R. Harindranath (eds.) *Transnational Lives and the Media: Re-imagining Diasporas [electronic resource]* (pp. 212–230). Basingstoke: Palgrave Macmillan.

Bailey, O. G., Georgiou, M., and Harindranath, R. (2007). Introduction: Exploration of diaspora in the context of media culture. In O. G. Bailey, M. Georgiou, and R. Harindranath (eds.) *Transnational Lives and the Media: Re-imagining Diasporas [electronic resource]* (pp. 1–8). Basingstoke: Palgrave Macmillan.

Banaji, S. and Al-Ghabban, A. (2006). 'Neutrality comes from inside us': British-Asian and Indian perspectives on television news after 11 September. *Journal of Ethnic and Migration Studies 32*(6), 1005–1026. DOI: 10.1080/13691830600761495.

Basch, L., Glick Schiller, N., and Szanton Blanc, C. (1994). *Nations Unbound: Transnational Projects, Postcolonial Predicaments, and Deterritorialized Nation-States*. London; New York: Routledge.

Bauböck, R. (2010). Studying citizenship constellations. *Journal of Ethnic and Migration Studies 36*(5), 847–859.

Bayart, J.-F. (2007). *Global Subjects: A Political Critique of Globalization* (A. Brown, Trans.). Cambridge: Polity.

Bearce, M. Super Commuter Couples. Retrieved May 5, 2015, from: http://supercommutercouples.com.

Beck, U. (2000a). The cosmopolitan perspective: Sociology of the second age of modernity. *British Journal of Sociology 51*(1), 79–105.

Beck, U. (2000d). *What Is Globalization?* (P. Camiller, Trans.). Malden, MA: Polity.

Beck, U. (2002). The cosmopolitan society and its enemies. *Theory, Culture and Society 19*(1–2), 17–44. DOI: 10.1177/026327640201900101.

Beck, U. (2006). *The Cosmopolitan Vision* (C. Cronin, Trans.). Cambridge, UK; Malden, MA: Polity.

Beck, U. (2012). Redefining the sociological project: the cosmopolitan challenge. *Sociology 46*(1), 7–12. DOI: 10.1177/0038038511425562.

Beck, U. and Beck-Gernsheim, E. (2009). Global generations and the trap of methodological nationalism for a cosmopolitan turn in the sociology of youth and generation. *European Sociological Review 25*(1), 25–36.

Beck, U., Bonss, W., and Lau, C. (2003). The theory of reflexive modernization. *Theory, Culture and Society 20*(2), 1–33. DOI: 10.1177/0263276403020002001.

Beck, U. and Grande, E. (2010). Varieties of second modernity: The cosmopolitan turn in social and political theory and research. *The British Journal of Sociology 61*(3), 409–442.

Beck, U. and Sznaider, N. (2006). Unpacking cosmopolitanism for the social sciences: A research agenda. *The British Journal of Sociology 57*(1), 1–23. DOI: 10.1111/j.1468-4446.2006.00091.x.

Berger, A. A. (1991). *Media Research Techniques.* Newbury Park, CA: Sage.

Bertrand, I. and Hughes, P. (2005). *Media Research Methods: Audiences, Institutions, Texts.* New York: Palgrave Macmillan.

Billig, M. (1995). *Banal Nationalism.* London; Thousand Oaks, CA: Sage.

Bloemraad, I., Korteweg, A., and Yurdakul, G. (2008). Citizenship and immigration: Multiculturalism, assimilation, and challenges to the nation-state. *Annual Review of Sociology 34*(1), 153–179. DOI: 10.1146/annurev.soc.34.040507.134608.

Boltanski, L. (1999). *Distant Suffering: Morality, Media and Politics* (G. Burchell, Trans.). Cambridge: Cambridge University Press.

Bonfadelli, H., Bucher, P., and Piga, A. (2007). Use of old and new media by ethnic minority youth in Europe with a special emphasis on Switzerland. *Communications 32*(2), 141–170. DOI: 10.1515/COMMUN.2007.010.

Brah, A. (1996). *Cartographies of Diaspora: Contesting Identities.* London; New York: Routledge.

Breckenridge, C. A., Chakrabarty, D., Bhabha, H., and Pollock, S. (2000). Cosmopolitanisms. *Public Culture 12*(3), 577–589.

Brown, G. W. and Held, D. (2010). Editors' introduction. In G. W. Brown and D. Held (eds.) *The Cosmopolitanism Reader* (pp. 1–14). Cambridge; Malden: Polity.

Brubaker, R. (2005). The 'diaspora' diaspora. *Ethnic and Racial Studies 28*(1), 1–19. DOI: 10.1080/0141987042000289997.

Bruneau, M. (2010). Diasporas, transnational spaces and communities. In R. Bauböck and T. Faist (eds.) *Diaspora and Transnationalism: Concepts,*

Theories and Methods (pp. 35–49). Amsterdam: Amsterdam University Press.

Calhoun, C. (2010). Beck, Asia and second modernity. *The British Journal of Sociology 61*(3), 597–619. DOI: 10.1111/j.1468-4446.2010.01328.x.

Castells, M. (2000). Materials for an exploratory theory of the network society. *British Journal of Sociology 51*(1 (January/March)), 5–24.

Castells, M. (2004). Informationalism, networks, and the network society: A theoretical blueprint. In M. Castells (ed.) *The Network Society: A Cross-Cultural Perspective.* Northampton, MA: Edward Elgar.

Castells, M. (2007). Communication, power and counter-power in the network society. *International Journal of Communication 1*(1), 238–266.

Castells, M. (2008). The new public sphere: Global civil society, communication networks, and global governance. *The ANNALS of the American Academy of Political and Social Science 616*(1), 78–93.

Castells, M. (2009). *The Power of Identity [electronic resource]* (2nd ed.). Malden, MA: Wiley-Blackwell.

Castells, M. (2010). *The Rise of the Network Society [electronic resource]* (2nd ed.). Chichester, West Sussex; Malden, MA: Wiley-Blackwell.

Castles, S. and Miller, M. J. (2009). *The Age of Migration: International Population Movements in the Modern World* (4th ed.). New York: Guilford Press.

Cenite, M. (2006). Too much legislation, too little expression. In K. Seneviratne and S. Singarayar (eds.) *Asia's March Towards Freedom of Expression and Development.* Singapore: Asian Media Information & Communication Centre.

Chan, K.-b. (2005). *Migration, Ethnic Relations and Chinese Business.* London; New York: Routledge.

Chang, K.-S. (2010). The second modern condition? Compressed modernity as internalized reflexive cosmopolitization. *The British Journal of Sociology 61*(3), 444–464. DOI: 10.1111/j.1468-4446.2010.01321.x.

Cheng, H. L. (2005). Constructing a transnational, multilocal sense of belonging: An analysis of Ming Pao (West Canadian Edition). *Journal of Communication Inquiry 29*(2), 141–159.

Cheong, P. H. (2008). The young and techless? Investigating internet use and problem-solving behaviors of young adults in Singapore. *New Media & Society 10*(5), 771–791. DOI: 10.1177/1461444808094356.

Chernilo, D. (2006). Social Theory's methodological nationalism: Myth and reality. *European Journal of Social Theory 9*(1), 5–22. DOI: 10.1177/1368431006060460.

Chernilo, D. (2007). *A Social Theory of the Nation-State: The Political Forms of Modernity beyond Methodological Nationalism.* London; New York: Routledge.

Chitty, N. (2010). Mapping Asian international communication. *Asian Journal of Communication 20*(2), 181–196. DOI: 10.1080/01292981003693377.

Choi, J. (2010). Of the East Asian cultural sphere: Theorizing cultural regionalization. *The China Review 10*(2 (Fall)), 109–136.

Chong, Z. L. (June 30, 2015). Abbott seeks to grow Australia's ties with Singapore. *The Straits Times*. Retrieved from: http://www.straitstimes.com/singapore/abbott-seeks-to-grow-australias-ties-with-singapore.

Choo, H., Gentile, D. A., Sim, T., Li, D., Khoo, A., and Liau, A. K. (2010). Pathological video-gaming among Singaporean youth. *Annals Academy of Medicine Singapore 39*, 822–829.

Chouliaraki, L. (2006). *The Spectatorship of Suffering*. London; Thousand Oaks, CA: Sage.

Chouliaraki, L. (2008a). The media as moral education: mediation and action. *Media, Culture & Society 30*(6), 831–852. DOI: 10.1177/0163443708096096.

Chouliaraki, L. (2008c). The mediation of suffering and the vision of a cosmopolitan public. *Television & New Media*. DOI: 10.1177/1527476408315496.

Chouliaraki, L. (2011). 'Improper distance': Towards a critical account of solidarity as irony. *International Journal of Cultural Studies 14*(4), 363–381. DOI: 10.1177/1367877911403247.

Chouliaraki, L. and Orgad, S. (2011). Proper distance: mediation, ethics, otherness. *International Journal of Cultural Studies 14*(4), 341–345. DOI: 10.1177/1367877911403245.

Christensen, M. (2011). Online mediations in transnational spaces: cosmopolitan (re)formations of belonging and identity in the Turkish diaspora. *Ethnic and Racial Studies 35*(5), 888–905. DOI: 10.1080/01419870.2011.628039.

Christensen, M., Jansson, A., and Christensen, C. (2011). Globalization, mediated practice and social space: Assessing the means and metaphysics of online territories. In M. Christensen, A. Jansson, and C. Christensen (eds.) *Online Territories: Globalization, Mediated Practice and Social Space*. New York; Bern; Berlin; Bruxelles; Frankfurt am Main; Oxford; Vienna: Peter Lang.

Christiansen, C. C. (2004). News media consumption among immigrants in Europe. *Ethnicities 4*(2), 185–207. DOI: 10.1177/1468796804042603.

Chua, B. H. (2006). Gossips about stars—newspaper and pop culture China. In W. Sun (ed.) *Media and the Chinese Diaspora: Community, Communications and Commerce*. London: Routledge.

Couldry, N., Livingstone, S., and Markham, T. (2010). *Media Consumption and Public Engagement: Beyond the Presumption of Attention*. Basingstoke: Palgrave Macmillan.

Couldry, N. and McCarthy, A. (2004). Introduction: Orientations: mapping MediaSpace. In N. Couldry and A. McCarthy (eds.) *MediaSpace: Place, Scale and Culture in a Media age*. London; New York: Routledge.

Cunningham, S. (2001). Popular media as public 'sphericules' for diasporic communities. *International Journal of Cultural Studies 4*(2), 131–147. DOI: 10.1177/136787790100400201.

Curtin, M. (2007). *Playing to the World's Biggest Audience: The Globalization of Chinese Film and TV*. Berkeley: University of California Press.

D'Haenens, L. and Ogan, C. (2007). Introduction to the special issue: Media and ethnic minorities in Europe. *Communications 32*(2), 137–140. DOI: 10.1515/COMMUN.2007.009.

Dahinden, J. (2010). The dynamics of migrants' transnational formations: Between mobility and locality. In R. Bauböck and T. Faist (eds.) *Diaspora and Transnationalism: Concepts, Theories and Methods.* Amsterdam: Amsterdam University Press.

Dahms, H. F. (2008). Retheorizing global space in sociology: Towards a new kind of discipline. In B. Warf and S. Arias (eds.) *The Spatial Turn [electronic resource]: Interdisciplinary Perspectives* (pp. 88–101). Hoboken: Taylor & Francis.

Dayan, D. (2007). On morality, distance and the other: Roger Silverstone's *Media and Morality. International Journal of Communication* 1, 113–122.

Dayan, D. and Katz, E. (1994, c1992). *Media Events: The Live Broadcasting of History.* Cambridge, MA: Harvard University Press.

Deacon, D., Pickering, M., Golding, P., and Murdock, G. (1999). *Researching Communications: A Practical Guide to Methods in Media and Cultural Analysis.* London: Arnold.

de Blij, H. (2009). *The Power of Place: Geography, Destiny, and Globalization's Rough Landscape [electronic resource].* Oxford; New York: Oxford University Press.

de Block, L. and Buckingham, D. (2007). *Global Children, Global Media: Migration, Media and Childhood [electronic resource].* Basingstoke: Palgrave Macmillan.

de Leeuw, S. and Rydin, I. (2007a). Diasporic mediated spaces. In O. G. Bailey, M. Georgiou, and R. Harindranath (eds.) *Transnational Lives and the Media: Re-imagining Diasporas [electronic resource]* (pp. 175–194). Basingstoke: Palgrave Macmillan.

de Leeuw, S. and Rydin, I. (2007e). Migrant children's digital stories. *European Journal of Cultural Studies 10*(4), 447–464. DOI: 10.1177/1367549407081948.

A Dictionary of Singlish and Singapore English. Retrieved July 24, 2012, from www.singlishdictionary.com.

Echchaibi, N. (2011). From audio tapes to video blogs: The delocalisation of authority in Islam. *Nations and Nationalism 17*(1), 25–44. DOI: 10.1111/j.1469-8129.2010.00468.x.

Elias, N. (2008). *Coming Home: Media and Returning Diaspora in Israel and Germany.* Albany: State University of New York Press.

European Commission. (2014). *Erasmus—Facts, Figures* and *Trends.* Brussels: European Commission.

Faist, T. (2006). The transnational social spaces of migration. *Working Papers—Center on Migration, Citizenship and Development.* Retrieved from: http://www.uni-bielefeld.de/tdrc/ag_comcad/downloads/workingpaper_10.pdf.

Faist, T. (2010a). Diaspora and transnationalism: What kind of dance partners? In R. Bauböck and T. Faist (eds.) *Diaspora and Transnationalism: Concepts, Theories and Methods* (pp. 9–34). Amsterdam: Amsterdam University Press.

Faist, T. (2010c). Towards transnational studies: World theories, transnationalisation and changing institutions. *Journal of Ethnic and Migration Studies 36*(10), 1665–1687.

Faist, T. and Fauser, M. (2011). The migration-development nexus: Toward a transnational perspective. In T. Faist, M. Fauser, and P. Kivisto (eds.) *The Migration-Development Nexus: A Transnational Perspective*. Baskingstoke, England; New York: Palgrave Macmillan.

FIFO Families. Retrieved May 5, 2015, from: http://www.fifofamilies.com.au.

Fox, J. (2005). Unpacking "transnational citizenship." *Annual Review of Political Science 8*(1), 171–201. DOI: 10.1146/annurev.polisci.7.012003.104851.

Friedmann, J. (1986). The world city hypothesis. *Development and Change 17*(1), 69–83. DOI: 10.1111/j.1467-7660.1986.tb00231.x.

Frosh, P. (2006). Telling presences: Witnessing, mass media, and the imagined lives of strangers. *Critical Studies in Media Communication 23*(4), 265–284. DOI: 10.1080/07393180600933097.

Frum, D. (2015). Does immigration harm working Americans? *The Atlantic*. Retrieved from: http://www.theatlantic.com/business/archive/2015/01/does-immigration-harm-working-americans/384060/.

Fujita, Y. (2004). Young Japanese 'cultural migrants' and the construction of their imagined West. *Westminster Papers in Communication and Culture 1*(1), 23–37.

Gadamer, H.-G. (1982 [1975]). *Truth and Method*. New York: Crossroad.

Gallup, I. (2015). Immigration. Retrieved March 3, 2015, from: http://www.gallup.com/poll/1660/Immigration.aspx.

GaWC Research Network. (April 13, 2010). The world according to GaWC 2008. Retrieved from: http://www.lboro.ac.uk/gawc/world2008t.html.

George, C. (2014). Moving on. Retrieved from: https://cheriangeorge.wordpress.com/.

Georgiou, M. (2005a). Diasporic media across Europe: Multicultural societies and the universalism–particularism continuum. *Journal of Ethnic and Migration Studies 31*(3), 481–498. DOI: 10.1080/13691830500058794.

Georgiou, M. (2005e). Mapping diasporic media cultures: A transnational cultural approach to exclusion. In R. Silverstone (ed.) *From Information to Communication: Media, Technology and Everyday Life in Europe* (pp. 33–53). London: Ashgate.

Georgiou, M. (2006). *Diaspora, Identity and the Media: Diasporic Transnationalism and Mediated Spatialities*. Cresskill, NJ: Hampton Press.

Georgiou, M. (2007a). Cities of difference: Cultural juxtapositions and urban politics of representation. *International Journal of Media and Cultural Politics 2*(3), 283–298. DOI: 10.1386/macp.2.3.283/1.

Georgiou, M. (2007c). Transnational crossroads for media and diaspora: Three challenges for research. In O. G. Bailey, M. Georgiou, and R. Harindranath (eds.) *Transnational Lives and the Media: Re-imagining Diasporas [electronic resource]* (pp. 11–32). Basingstoke: Palgrave Macmillan.

Georgiou, M. (2008). Urban encounters: Juxtapositions of difference and the communicative interface of global cities. *International Communication Gazette 70*(3–4), 223–235. DOI: 10.1177/1748048508089949.

Gibson, J. J. (2014[1979]). The theory of affordances. In J. J. Gieseking, W. Mangold, C. Katz, S. Low, and S. Saegert (eds.) *The People, Place, and Space Reader*. New York; Oxfordshire, England: Routledge.

Gillespie, M. (1995). *Television, Ethnicity and Cultural Change*. London; New York: Routledge.

Gillespie, M. (2006). Transnational television audiences after September 11. *Journal of Ethnic and Migration Studies 32*(6), 903–921. DOI: 10.1080/13691830600761511.

Gillespie, M. (2009). 'Anytime, anyplace, anywhere'. *Journalism 10*(3), 322–325. DOI: 10.1177/1464884909102575.

Gillespie, M., Pinkerton, A., Baumann, G., and Thiranagama, S. (2010). Introduction—South Asian diasporas and the BBC World Service: contacts, conflicts, and contestations. *South Asian Diaspora 2*(1), 3–23. DOI: 10.1080/19438190903541911.

Giulianotti, R. and Robertson, R. (2007). Forms of glocalization: Globalization and the migration strategies of Scottish football fans in North America. *Sociology 41*(1), 133–152.

Glick Schiller, N. (2010). Old baggage and missing luggage: A commentary on Beck and Sznaider's 'Unpacking cosmopolitanism for the social sciences: a research agenda'. *The British Journal of Sociology 61*, 413–420. DOI: 10.1111/j.1468-4446.2009.01297.x.

Glick Schiller, N., Basch, L., and Szanton Blanc, C. (1995). From immigrant to transmigrant: Theorizing transnational migration. *Anthropological Quarterly 68*(1), 48–63.

Glick Schiller, N. and Çağlar, A. (2009). Towards a comparative theory of locality in migration studies: Migrant incorporation and city scale. *Journal of Ethnic and Migration Studies 35*(2), 177–202.

Glick Schiller, N., Darieva, T., and Gruner-Domic, S. (2011). Defining cosmopolitan sociability in a transnational age. An introduction. *Ethnic and Racial Studies 34*(3), 399–418. DOI: 10.1080/01419870.2011.533781.

Global Commission on International Migration (GCIM) (2005). *Migration in an Interconnected World: New Directions for Action*. Geneva: The Commission.

Granovetter, M. S. (1973). The strength of weak ties. *American Journal of Sociology 78*(6 (May)), 1360–1380.

Gumpert, G. and Drucker, S. J. (2008). Communicative cities. *The International Communication Gazette 70*(3–4), 195–208.

Hafez, K. (2007). *The Myth of Media Globalization* (A. Skinner, Trans.). Cambridge: Polity.

Hall, S. (2003[1990]). Cultural identity and diaspora. In J. E. Braziel and A. Mannur (eds.) *Theorizing Diaspora: A Reader* (Kindle ed., pp. 233–246). Malden, MA; Oxford; Melbourne, Victoria; Berlin: Blackwell.

Hall, S. and Werbner, P. (2008). Cosmopolitanism, globalisation and diaspora, Stuart Hall in conversation with Pnina Werbner. In P. Werbner (ed.) *Anthropology and the New Cosmopolitanism: Rooted, Feminist and Vernacular Perspectives.* Oxford; New York: Berg.

Han, K. (2013). A tenure rejection with many implications. Retrieved from The Diplomat website: http://thediplomat.com/2013/03/a-tenure-rejection-with-many-implications/.

Han, S.-J. and Shim, Y.-H. (2010). Redefining second modernity for East Asia: A critical assessment. *The British Journal of Sociology 61*(3), 465–488. DOI: 10.1111/j.1468-4446.2010.01322.x.

Hanafi, S. (2005). Reshaping geography: Palestinian community networks in Europe and the new media. *Journal of Ethnic and Migration Studies 31*(3), 581–598. DOI: 10.1080/1369183050005870 3.

Hannerz, U. (1996). *Transnational Connections: Culture, People, Places.* London; New York: Routledge.

Hannerz, U. (2004). *Foreign News: Exploring the World of Foreign Correspondents.* Chicago; London: University of Chicago Press.

Harindranath, R. (2007). Refugee communities and the politics of cultural identity. In O. G. Bailey, M. Georgiou, and R. Harindranath (eds.) *Transnational Lives and the Media: Re-imagining Diasporas [electronic resource]* (pp. 133–148). Basingstoke: Palgrave Macmillan.

Harindranath, R. (2009). *Audience-Citizens: The Media, Public Knowledge and Interpretive Practice.* Los Angeles: Sage.

Harvey, D. (2009). *Cosmopolitanism and the Geographies of Freedom.* New York; Chichester, West Sussex: Columbia University Press.

Held, D. (2002). Culture and political community: national, global, and cosmopolitan. In S. Vertovec and R. Cohen (eds.) *Conceiving Cosmopolitanism: Theory, Context, and Practice* (pp. 48–58). New York: Oxford University Press.

Held, D., McGrew, A., Goldblatt, D., and Perraton, J. (2003). Rethinking globalization. In D. Held and A. McGrew (eds.) *The Global Transformations Reader* (2nd ed., pp. 67–74). Cambridge: Polity.

Hepp, A. (2008). Translocal media cultures: Networks of the media and globalization. In A. Hepp, F. Krotz, S. Moores, and C. Winter (eds.) *Connectivity, Networks and Flows: Conceptualizing Contemporary Communications.* Cresskill, NJ: Hampton Press.

Hepp, A. (2009a). Localities of diasporic communicative spaces: Material aspects of translocal mediated networking. *The Communication Review 12*(4), 327–348.

Hepp, A. (2009b). Transculturality as a perspective: Researching media cultures comparatively. *Forum Qualitative Sozialforschung/Forum: Qualitative Social Research 10*(1), 1–14.

Hiller, H. H. and Franz, T. M. (2004). New ties, old ties and lost ties: The use of the internet in diaspora. *New Media & Society, 6*(6), 731–752. DOI: 10.1177/1461444804044327.

Ho, E. L.-E. (2008a). Citizenship, migration and transnationalism: A review and critical interventions. *Geography Compass 2*(5), 1286–1300.

Ho, E. L.-E. (2008d). "Flexible citizenship" or familial ties that bind? Singaporean transmigrants in London. *International Migration 46*(4), 145–175. DOI: 10.1111/j.1468-2435.2008.00475.x.

Höijer, B. (2004). The discourse of global compassion: The audience and media reporting of human suffering. *Media, Culture & Society 26*(4), 513–531. DOI: 10.1177/0163443704044215.

Hooks, G., Lobao, L. M., and Tickamyer, A. R. (2007). Conclusion: An agenda for moving a spatial sociology forward. In L. M. Lobao, G. Hooks, and A. R. Tickamyer (eds.) *The Sociology of Spatial Inequality* (pp. 253–263). Albany: State University of New York Press.

Hsu, C. Y. (2010). Diaries and diaspora identity: Rethinking Russian emigration in China. *Kritika: Explorations in Russian and Eurasian History 11*(1), 127–144.

Hubbard, P., Kitchin, R., and Valentine, G. (2004). Editors' introduction. In P. Hubbard, R. Kitchin, and G. Valentine (eds.) *Key Thinkers on Space and Place* (pp. 1–15). London; Thousand Oaks; New Delhi: Sage.

Inda, J. X. and Rosaldo, R. (2008). Tracking global flows. In J. X. Inda and R. Rosaldo (eds.) *The Anthropology of Globalization: A Reader* (2nd ed., pp. 3–46). Malden; Oxford; Carlton: Blackwell.

Iwabuchi, K. (2010). De-Westernization and the governance of global cultural connectivity: A dialogic approach to East Asian media cultures. *Postcolonial Studies 13*(4), 403–419. DOI: 10.1080/13688790.2010.518349.

Jansson, A. (2009). Beyond "other spaces": Media studies and the cosmopolitan vision. *Communication Review 12*(4), 305–312. DOI: 10.1080/10714420903346613.

Jansson, A. and Falkheimer, J. (2006). Towards a geography of communication. In J. Falkheimer and A. Jansson (eds.) *Geographies of Communication: The Spatial Turn in Media Studies* (pp. 9–25). Göteborg: Nordicom.

Jenkins, H. (2004). Pop cosmopolitanism: Mapping cultural flows in an age of media convergence. In M. M. Suárez-Orozco and D. B. Qin-Hilliard (eds.) *Globalization: Culture and Education for a New Millennium* (pp. 114–140). Berkeley: University of California Press.

Jensen, K. B. (2002). The qualitative research process. In K. B. Jensen (ed.) *A Handbook of Media and Communication Research: Qualitative and Quantitative Methodologies* (pp. 235–253). London; New York: Routledge.

Johnson, M. (2010). Exporting exile on TV Martí. *Television & New Media 11*(4), 293–307. DOI: 10.1177/1527476410365710.

Karanfil, G. (2007). Satellite television and its discontents: Reflections on the experiences of Turkish-Australian lives. *Continuum 21*(1), 59–69. DOI: 10.1080/10304310601103968.

Karim, K. H. (2007). Media and diaspora. In E. Devereux (ed.) *Media Studies: Key Issues and Debates*. London: Sage.

Karim, K. H. (2010). Re-viewing the 'national' in 'international communication' through the lens of diaspora. In D. K. Thussu (ed.) *International Communication: A Reader* (pp. 393–409). New York: Routledge.

Katz, E. and Liebes, T. (2007). 'No more peace!': How disaster, terror and war have upstaged media events. *International Journal of Communication 1*(1), 157–166.

Kearney, A. T. (2010). The Urban Elite: A.T. Kearney Global Cities Index 2010. Retrieved from: http://www.atkearney.com/images/global/pdf/Urban_Elite-GCI_2010.pdf.

Kenyon, A. T. (2010). Investigating chilling effects: News media and public speech in Malaysia, Singapore, and Australia. *International Journal of Communication 4*, 440–467.

Khoo, S.-E. and Mak, A. (2003). Career and family factors in intention for permanent settlement in Australia. In M. W. Charney, B. S. A. Yeoh, and C. K. Tong (eds.) *Chinese Migrants Abroad: Cultural, Educational, and Social Dimensions of the Chinese Diaspora*. Singapore: Singapore University Press; World Scientific.

Kim, Y. (2011). Diasporic nationalism and the media. *International Journal of Cultural Studies 14*(2), 133–151. DOI: 10.1177/1367877910382184.

King, R. (2010). The dynamics of international student circulation in a global context; and students, staff and academic mobility in higher education. *Journal of Ethnic and Migration Studies 36*(8), 1355–1357. DOI: 10.1080/1369183x.2010.498720.

King, R. and Mai, N. (2009). Italophilia meets Albanophobia: paradoxes of asymmetric assimilation and identity processes among Albanian immigrants in Italy. *Ethnic and Racial Studies 32*(1), 117–138. DOI: 10.1080/01419870802245034.

Kleingeld, P., and Brown, E. (2011). Cosmopolitanism. In E. N. Zalta (ed.) *The Stanford Encyclopedia of Philosophy*. Stanford: The Metaphysics Research Lab, Center for the Study of Language and Information, Stanford University. Retrieved from: http://plato.stanford.edu/archives/spr2011/entries/cosmopolitanism/.

Kleinschmidt, H. (2006). *Migration and the Making of Transnational Social Spaces*. Paper presented at the seminar of the Australian Centre.

Knott, K. and McLoughlin, S. (2010). Introduction. In K. Knott and S. McLoughlin (eds.) *Diasporas: Concepts, Intersections, Identities*. London; New York: Zed Books.

Koh, A. (2004). Newspaper literacy: An investigation of how Singaporean students read the Straits Times. *English Teaching: Practice and Critique 3*(3), 43–60.

Koh, A. (2012). Tactics of interventions: Student mobility and human capital building in Singapore. *Higher Education Policy 25*(2 (June)), 191–206. DOI: 10.1057/hep.2012.5.

Kolar-Panov, D. (1997). *Video, War, and the Diasporic Imagination.* London; New York: Routledge.

Kononova, A., Alhabash, S., and Cropp, F. (2011). The role of media in the process of socialization to American politics among international students. *International Communication Gazette 73*(4), 302–321. DOI: 10.1177/1748048511398592.

Kosnick, K. (2004). 'Speaking in one's own voice': Representational strategies of Alevi Turkish migrants on open-access television in Berlin. *Journal of Ethnic and Migration Studies 30*(5), 979–994. DOI: 10.1080/1369183042000245651.

Kosnick, K. (2007). Ethnic media, transnational politics: Turkish migrant media in Germany. In O. G. Bailey, M. Georgiou, and R. Harindranath (eds.) *Transnational Lives and the Media: Re-imagining Diasporas [electronic resource]* (pp. 149–172). Basingstoke: Palgrave Macmillan.

Krossa, A. S. (2012). Why 'European Cosmopolitanism'? In R. Robertson and A. S. Krossa (eds.) *European Cosmopolitanism in Question* (pp. 6–24). Houndsmill, Basingstoke, Hampshire, UK; New York: Palgrave Macmillan.

Krotz, F. (2008). Media connectivity: Concepts, conditions, and consequences. In A. Hepp, F. Krotz, S. Moores, and C. Winter (eds.) *Connectivity, Networks and Flows: Conceptualizing Contemporary Communications.* Cresskill, NJ: Hampton Press.

Kuek, J. (March 9, 2013). Dr Cherian George denied tenure. Retrieved July 16, 2015, from: https://storify.com/kuekj/denial-of-tenure-sparks-furore.

Lacatus, C. (2007). What is a blatte? Migration and ethnic identity in contemporary Sweden. *Journal of Arab & Muslim Media Research 1*(1), 79–92. DOI: 10.1386/jammr.1.1.79/1.

Latino Decisions. (2014). New poll results: National poll finds overwhelming support for executive action on immigration. Retrieved from: http://www.latinodecisions.com/blog/2014/11/24/new-poll-results-nat…ll-finds-overwhelming-support-for-executive-action-on-immigration/.

Lee, H. L. (2006). *National Day Rally Speech.* Singapore: Prime Minister's Office, Singapore Government.

Lee, H. L. (2015). *Transcript of Prime Minister Lee Hsien Loong's Speech at the Ho Rih Hwa Leadership in Asia Public Lecture Series on 30 June 2015.* Singapore: Government of Singapore. Retrieved from: http://www.pmo.gov.sg/mediacentre/transcript-prime-minister-lee-hsien-loongs-speech-ho-rih-hwa-leadership-asia-public.

Lee, T. (2005). Gestural politics: civil society in "new" Singapore. *Sojourn: Journal of Social Issues in Southeast Asia 20*(2), 132–154. DOI: 10.1353/soj.2005.0009.

Lee, T. (2006). Creativity and cultural globalisation in suburbia: mediating the Perth-Singapore 'network'. *Australian Journal of Communication 33*(2–3), 21–42.

Lee, T. (2008). Gestural politics: Mediating the "new" Singapore. In K. Sen and T. Lee (eds.) *Political Regimes and the Media in Asia*. London; New York: Routledge.

Levitt, P. and Glick Schiller, N. (2004). Conceptualizing simultaneity: A transnational social field perspective on society. *International Migration Review 38*(3), 1002–1039. DOI: 10.1111/j.1747-7379.2004.tb00227.x.

Levitt, P. and Jaworsky, B. N. (2007). Transnational migration studies: Past developments and future trends. *Annual Review of Sociology 33*, 129–156.

Lin, J.-H., Peng, W., Kim, M., Kim, S. Y., and LaRose, R. (2012). Social networking and adjustments among international students. *New Media & Society 14*(3), 421–440. DOI: 10.1177/1461444811418627.

Lin, T. T. C. and Liu, Y.-l. (2011). The development of mobile broadcasting TV: A socio-technical comparison of Singapore and Taiwan. *Asian Journal of Communication 21*(1), 4–24. DOI: 10.1080/01292986.2010.496862.

Lin, W.-Y., Cheong, P. H., Kim, Y.-C., and Jung, J.-Y. (2010). Becoming citizens: Youths' civic uses of new media in five digital cities in East Asia. *Journal of Adolescent Research 25*(6), 839–857. DOI: 10.1177/0743558410371125.

Lin, W.-Y., Song, H., and Ball-Rokeach, S. (2010). Localizing the global: Exploring the transnational ties that bind in new immigrant communities. *Journal of Communication 60*(2), 205–229. DOI: 10.1111/j.1460-2466.2010.01480.x.

Livingstone, S. and Lemish, D. (2001). Doing comparative research with children and young people. In S. Livingstone and M. Bovill (eds.) *Children and Their Changing Media Environment: A European Comparative Study*. Mahwah, NJ: Lawrence Erlbaum Associates.

Luscombe, S. (2015). The legacy of empire in Singapore. *britishempire.co.uk*. Retrieved May 6, 2015, from: http://www.britishempire.co.uk/maproom/singapore/legacysingapore.pdf.

Madianou, M. (2005). Contested communicative spaces: Rethinking identities, boundaries and the role of the media among Turkish speakers in Greece. *Journal of Ethnic and Migration Studies 31*(3), 521–541. DOI: 10.1080/13691830500058760.

Madianou, M. and Miller, D. (2012). Polymedia: Towards a new theory of digital media in interpersonal communication. *International Journal of Cultural Studies 16*(2), 169–187.

Madianou, M. and Miller, D. (2013). *Migration and New Media [electronic resource]: Transnational Families and Polymedia*. London: Routledge.

Mai, N. (2004). 'Looking for a more modern life…': The role of Italian television in the Albanian migration to Italy. *Westminster Papers in Communication and Culture 1*(1), 3–22.

Mai, N. (2005). The Albanian diaspora-in-the-making: Media, migration and social exclusion. *Journal of Ethnic and Migration Studies 31*(3), 543–561. DOI: 10.1080/13691830500058737.

Mainsah, H. (2011). 'I could well have said I was Norwegian but nobody would believe me': Ethnic minority youths' self-representation on social network sites. *European Journal of Cultural Studies 14*(2), 179–193. DOI: 10.1177/1367549410391926.

Massey, D. (1993). Power-geometry and a progressive sense of place. In J. Bird, B. Curtis, T. Putnam, G. Robertson, and L. Tickner (eds.) *Mapping the Futures: Local Cultures, Global Change* (pp. 60–70). London: Routledge.

Massey, D. (2005). *For Space*. London: Sage.

McLuhan, M. (2011[1962]). *The Gutenberg Galaxy*. Toronto; Buffalo; London: University of Toronto Press.

McQuire, S. (2008). *The Media City: Media, Architecture and Urban Space*. Los Angeles; London: Sage.

Meld Magazine. (2015). About. Retrieved July 16, 2015, from: http://www.meldmagazine.com.au/about/.

Meyrowitz, J. (2005). The rise of glocality: New senses of place and identity in the global village. In K. Nyíri (ed.) *A Sense of Place: The Global and the Local in Mobile Communication* (pp. 21–30). Vienna: Passagen Verlag.

Molloy, K. (October 2003–October 2004). Literature in the Irish diaspora: The New Zealand case, 1873–1918. *Journal of New Zealand Studies* (2/3), 87–128.

Moores, S. (2007). Media and senses of place: On situational and phenomenological geographies. *MEDIA@LSE Electronic Working Papers*. Retrieved from: http://www2.lse.ac.uk/media@lse/research/mediaWorkingPapers/pdf/EWP12.pdf.

Morawska, E. (2008). The recognition politics of Polish Radio MultiKulti in Berlin. *Journal of Ethnic and Migration Studies 34*(8), 1323–1335. DOI: 10.1080/13691830802364882.

Morley, D. (2000). *Home Territories: Media, Mobility and Identity*. London; New York: Routledge.

Morley, D. and Robins, K. (1995). *Spaces of Identity: Global Media, Electronic Landscapes and Cultural Boundaries*. London; New York: Routledge.

Naficy, H. (2003). Narrowcasting in diaspora: Middle Eastern television in Los Angeles. In K. H. Karim (ed.) *The Media of Diaspora* (pp. 51–62). London: Routledge.

National Population and Talent Division. (2015). Resources. Retrieved April 21, 2015, from: http://population.sg/resources/.

Nickels, H. C., Thomas, L., Hickman, M. J., and Silvestri, S. (2009). A comparative study of the representations of 'suspect' communities in multi-ethnic Britain and of their impact on Irish communities and Muslim communities—Mapping newspaper content. *ISET Working Paper Series*. Retrieved from: http://www.londonmet.ac.uk/londonmet/fms/MRSite/Research/iset/Working%20Paper%20Series/WP13%20.pdf.

Nussbaum, M. (1994). Patriotism and cosmopolitanism. *Boston Review*. Retrieved from: http://bostonreview.net/martha-nussbaum-patriotism-and-cosmopolitanism.

Obama, B. (2014). Transcript: Obama's immigration speech. *The Washington Post.*

Ogan, C. (2001). *Communication and Identity in the Diaspora: Turkish Migrants in Amsterdam and Their Use of Media.* Lanham: Lexington Books.

Ong, A. (1999). *Flexible Citizenship: The Cultural Logics of Transnationality.* Durham, NC: Duke University Press.

Ong, A. (2005). Ecologies of expertise: Assembling flows, managing citizenship. In A. Ong and S. J. Collier (eds.) *Global Assemblages: Technology, Politics, and Ethics as Anthropological Problems* (pp. 337–353). Malden, MA; Oxford: Blackwell Publishing.

Ong, A. (2008). Cyberpublics and diaspora politics among transnational Chinese. In J. X. Inda and R. Rosaldo (eds.) *The Anthropology of Globalization: A Reader* (2nd ed.). Malden; Oxford; Carlton: Blackwell.

Orgad, S. (2011). Proper distance from ourselves: The potential for estrangement in the mediapolis. *International Journal of Cultural Studies 14*(4), 401–421. DOI: 10.1177/1367877911403249.

Overseas Singaporean Portal. (2015). Retrieved July 16, 2015, from: http://overseassingaporean.sg/.

Overseas Singaporean Unit. (2015). About us. *Overseas Singaporean Portal.* Retrieved May 6, 2015, from: http://www.overseassingaporean.sg/about-us.

Papastergiadis, N. (2000). *The Turbulence of Migration: Globalization, Deterritorialization, and Hybridity.* Malden, MA: Polity.

Papastergiadis, N. (2010). Understanding hybrid identities: From mechanical models to complex systems. *World Futures 66*(3–4), 243–265. DOI: 10.1080/02604021003680487.

Parham, A. A. (2004). Diaspora, community and communication: Internet use in transnational Haiti. *Global Networks 4*(2), 199–217.

Parker, D., and Song, M. (2007). Inclusion, participation and the emergence of British Chinese websites. *Journal of Ethnic and Migration Studies 33*(7), 1043–1061. DOI: 10.1080/13691830701541564.

Philo, G. (2002). Television news and audience understanding of war, conflict and disaster. *Journalism Studies 3*(2), 173–186. DOI: 10.1080/14616700220129955.

Portes, A., Escobar, C., and Arana, R. (2009). Divided or convergent loyalties? The political incorporation process of Latin American immigrants in the United States. *International Journal of Comparative Sociology 50*(2), 103–136. DOI: 10.1177/0020715208101595.

Portes, A., Fernández-Kelly, P., and Haller, W. (2009). The adaptation of the immigrant second generation in America: A theoretical overview and recent evidence. *Journal of Ethnic and Migration Studies 35*(7), 1077–1104. DOI: 10.1080/13691830903006127.

Portes, A., Guarnizo, L. E., and Landolt, P. (1999). The study of transnationalism: Pitfalls and promise of an emergent research field. *Ethnic and Racial Studies 22*(2), 217–237.

Priest, S. H. (1996). *Doing Media Research: An Introduction*. Thousand Oaks, CA: Sage.

Qiu, H. (2003). Communication among knowledge diasporas: Online magazines of expatriate Chinese students. In K. H. Karim (ed.) *The Media of Diaspora* (pp. 148–161). London: Routledge.

QS. (2015). QS Best Student Cities 2015. Retrieved May 5, 2015, from: http://www.topuniversities.com/city-rankings/2015#sorting=rank+custom=rank+order=desc+search=.

Ragazzi, F. and Balalovska, K. (2011). Diaspora politics and post-territorial citizenship in Croatia, Serbia and Macedonia. *CITSEE Working Paper Series 2011*(18). Retrieved from: http://www.law.ed.ac.uk/file_download/series/338_diasporapoliticsandpostterritorialcitizenshipincroatiaserbiaandmacedonia.pdf.

Rantanen, T. (2003). The new sense of place in 19th-century news. *Media, Culture & Society 25*(4), 435–449. DOI: 10.1177/01634437030254001.

Rantanen, T. (2005). *Media and Globalization*. London: Sage.

Rantanen, T. (2007). The cosmopolitanization of news. *Journalism Studies 8*(6), 843–861. DOI: 10.1080/14616700701556765.

Robbins, B. (1998). Introduction part I: Actually existing cosmopolitanism. In P. Cheah and B. Robbins (eds.) *Cosmopolitics: Thinking and Feeling beyond the Nation* (pp. 1–19). Minneapolis; London: University of Minnesota Press.

Robertson, A. (2010). *Mediated Cosmopolitanism: The World of Television News*. Cambridge, UK; Malden, MA: Polity.

Robertson, R. (1992). *Globalization: Social Theory and Global Culture*. London: Sage.

Robertson, R. (1994). Globalisation or glocalisation? *The Journal of International Communication 1*(1), 33–52.

Robertson, R. (1995). Glocalization: time-space and homogeneity-heterogeneity. In M. Featherstone, S. Lash, and R. Robertson (eds.) *Global Modernities* (pp. 25–44). London; Thousand Oaks, CA: Sage.

Robertson, R. (2003). The conceptual promise of glocalization: commonality and diversity. *ART-e-FACT: Strategies of Resistance 4*. Retrieved from: http://artefact.mi2.hr/_a04/lang_en/theory_robertson_en.htm.

Robins, K. (2007). Transnational cultural policy and European cosmopolitanism. *Cultural Politics 3*(2), 147–174. DOI: 10.2752/174321907x194002.

Rouse, R. (1991). Mexican migration and the social space of postmodernism. *Diaspora 1*(1), 8–23.

Sabry, T. (2004). Editorial. *Westminster Papers in Communication and Culture 1*(1), 1–2.

Sakr, N. (2008). Diversity and diaspora: Arab communities and satellite communication in Europe. *Global Media and Communication 4*(3), 277–300. DOI: 10.1177/1742766508096082.

Sassen, S. (2006). *Territory, Authority, Rights: From Medieval to Global Assemblages*. Princeton, NJ: Princeton University Press.

Sassen, S. (2007). *Sociology of Globalization*. New York: W.W. Norton.

Scannell, P. (1996). *Radio, Television and Modern Life: A Phenomenological Approach*. Oxford: Blackwell.

Schlesinger, P. (2007). A cosmopolitan temptation. *European Journal of Communication 22*(4), 413–426. DOI: 10.1177/0267323107083059.

Schrøder, K., Drotner, K., Kline, S., and Murray, C. (2003). *Researching Audiences: A Practical Guide to Methods in Media Audience Analysis*. London: Arnold.

Schutz, A. (1966). Some structures of the life-world. In I. Schutz (ed.) *Collected Papers III—Studies in Phenomenological Philosophy* (pp. 116–132). The Hague: Martinus Nijhoff.

Sennett, R. (2002). Cosmopolitanism and the social experience of cities. In S. Vertovec and R. Cohen (eds.) *Conceiving Cosmopolitanism: Theory, Context, and Practice* (pp. 42–47). New York: Oxford University Press.

SG50 Programme Office. (2015). SG50. Retrieved May 6, 2015, from: https://www.singapore50.sg/en.aspx.

Sheller, M. and Urry, J. (2006). The new mobilities paradigm. *Environment and Planning A 38*(2), 207–226.

Shi, Y. (2005). Identity construction of the Chinese diaspora, ethnic media use, community formation, and the possibility of social activism. *Continuum 19*(1), 55–72. DOI: 10.1080/1030431052000336298.

Shi, Y. (2009). Re-evaluating the 'alternative' role of ethnic media in the US: The case of Chinese-language press and working-class women readers. *Media, Culture & Society 31*(4), 597–616. DOI: 10.1177/0163443709335219.

Siapera, E. (2007). Transnational Islam and the Internet. In O. G. Bailey, M. Georgiou, and R. Harindranath (eds.) *Transnational Lives and the Media: Re-imagining Diasporas [electronic resource]* (pp. 97–114). Basingstoke: Palgrave Macmillan.

Siapera, E. (2010). *Cultural Diversity and Global Media: The Mediation of Difference*. Malden, MA: Wiley-Blackwell.

Silverstone, R. (2001). Finding a voice: minorities, media and the global commons. *Emergences: Journal for the Study of Media & Composite Cultures 11*(1), 13–27. DOI: 10.1080/10457220120044648.

Silverstone, R. (2003). Proper distance: Towards an ethics for cyberspace. In G. Liestol, A. Morrison, and T. Rasmussen (eds.) *Digital Media Revisited* (pp. 469–491). Cambridge, MA: MIT Press.

Silverstone, R. (2007). *Media and Morality: On the Rise of the Mediapolis*. London: Polity.

Silverstone, R. and Georgiou, M. (2005). Editorial introduction: Media and minorities in multicultural Europe. *Journal of Ethnic and Migration Studies 31*(3), 433–441. DOI: 10.1080/13691830500058943.

Sinclair, J. and Cunningham, S. (2001). Diasporas and the media. In S. Cunningham and J. Sinclair (eds.) *Floating Lives: The Media and Asian Diasporas* (pp. 1–24). Lanham, MD: Rowman & Littlefield.

Singapore-Western Australia Network. About SWAN. Retrieved July 16, 2015, from: http://swan.org.au/about-swan/.

Singapore 21 Committee. (1999). *Singapore 21 Report*. Singapore.

Singapore Economic Development Board. (September 29, 2014). The Millennium. Retrieved May 6, 2015, from: https://www.edb.gov.sg/content/edb/en/why-singapore/about-singapore/our-history/2000s.html.

Singapore High Commission in Canberra. (July 16, 2015). Singapore High Commission in Canberra Facebook page. Retrieved July 16, 2015, from: https://www.facebook.com/pages/Singapore-High-Commission-in-Canberra/741302032574362?sk=timeline&ref=page_internal.

Singh, J. (2008). Singapore Country Report. In I. Banerjee and S. Logan (eds.) *Asian Communication Handbook 2008*. Singapore: Asian Media Information and Communication Centre.

Slade, C. (2010). Media and citizenship: Transnational television cultures reshaping political identities in the European Union. *Journalism 11*(6), 727–733. DOI: 10.1177/1464884910379709.

Smith, D. W. (2011). Phenomenology. In E. N. Zalta (ed.) *The Stanford Encyclopedia of Philosophy* (Fall 2011 ed.). Retrieved from: http://plato.stanford.edu/archives/fall2011/entries/phenomenology/.

Smith, S. J., Pain, R., Marston, S. A., and Jones, J. P., III (2010). Introduction: Situating social geographies. In S. J. Smith, R. Pain, S. A. Marston, and J. P. Jones III (eds.) *The Sage Handbook of Social Geographies*. Los Angeles; London: Sage.

Solimano, A. (2010). *International Migration in the Age of Crisis and Globalization [electronic resource]: Historical and Recent Experiences*. New York: Cambridge University Press.

Soon, C. and Cho, H. (2011). Flows of relations and communication among Singapore political bloggers and organizations: the networked public sphere approach. *Journal of Information Technology & Politics 8*(1), 93–109. DOI: 10.1080/19331681.2010.514538.

Soon, D. (2010). Singapore: year in review 2009. Retrieved from: http://www.spp.nus.edu.sg/ips/docs/enewsletter/Feb2010/Debbie_Soon_Singapore_Year_in_Review_2009_022010.pdf.

Stevenson, N. (2000). The future of public media cultures. *Information, Communication & Society 3*(2), 192–214. DOI: 10.1080/13691180050123703.

Stevenson, N. (2003). *Cultural Citizenship: Cosmopolitan Questions*. Maidenhead: Open University Press.

The Straits Times Print Edition. (July 16, 2015). Retrieved July 16, 2015, from: http://www.straitstimes.com/print-edition.

Sun, W., Yue, A., Sinclair, J., and Gao, J. (2011). Diasporic Chinese media in Australia: A post-2008 overview. *Continuum 25*(4), 515–527. DOI: 10.1080/10304312.2011.576751.

SWAN. (2015). Singapore Film Festival Australia. Retrieved July 16, 2015, from: http://singaporefilmfestival.org/.

Szerszynski, B. and Urry, J. (2006). Visuality, mobility and the cosmopolitan: Inhabiting the world from afar. *The British Journal of Sociology 57*(1), 113–131.

Tan, E. S. (2005). Globalisation, nation-building and emigration: The Singapore case. In B. P. Lorente, N. Piper, H.-H. Shen, and B. S. A. Yeoh (eds.) *Asian Migrations: Sojourning, Displacement, Homecoming and Other Travels* (pp. 87–98). Singapore: Asia Research Institute.

Tan, T. (October 14, 2012). 200,000 S'poreans living abroad; 27% rise in number of citizens overseas since 2003, with Australia the top draw. *The Straits Times.* Retrieved from: http://lkyspp.nus.edu.sg/ips/wp-content/uploads/sites/2/2013/06/ST_200000-Singaporeans-living-abroad_141012.pdf.

Teo, C. W. (2015). S'poreans praised for boosting China ties. *The Straits Times.* Retrieved from: http://www.straitstimes.com/asia/sporeans-praised-for-boosting-china-ties.

Tey, T. H. (2008). Confining the freedom of the press in Singapore: A "pragmatic" press for "nation-building"? *Human Rights Quarterly 30*(4), 876–905. DOI: 10.1353/hrq.0.0034.

Tomlinson, J. (1999). *Globalization and Culture.* Chicago: University of Chicago Press.

Tomlinson, J. (2001). Vicious and benign universalism. In F. J. Schuurman (ed.) *Globalization and Development Studies: Challenges for the 21st Century.* London; Thousand Oaks, CA: Sage.

Tomlinson, J. (2007). Globalization and cultural analysis. In D. Held and A. McGrew (eds.) *Globalization Theory: Approaches and Controversies* (pp. 148–168). Cambridge, UK; Malden, MA: Polity.

Tomlinson, J. (2011). Beyond connection: Cultural cosmopolitan and ubiquitous media. *International Journal of Cultural Studies 14*(4), 347–361. DOI: 10.1177/1367877911403246.

Transient Workers Count Too. (September 18, 2011). Advocacy. Retrieved July 16, 2015, from: http://twc2.org.sg/what-we-do/advocacy/.

Transient Workers Count Too. (July 11, 2015a). Transient Workers Count Too Facebook page. Retrieved July 16, 2015, from: https://www.facebook.com/transientworkerscount2.

Transient Workers Count Too. (July 13, 2015c). Transient Workers Count Too home page. Retrieved July 16, 2015, from: http://twc2.org.sg/.

Trebbe, J. (2007). Types of integration, acculturation strategies and media use of young Turks in Germany. *Communications, 32*, 171–191. DOI: 10.1515/COMMUN.2007.011.

Tsagarousianou, R. (2004). Rethinking the concept of diaspora: Mobility, connectivity and communication in a globalised world. *Westminster Papers in Communication and Culture 1*(1), 52–65.

UNESCO Institute for Statistics. (2014). *Global Flow of Tertiary-Level Students.* Retrieved May 6, 2015, from: http://www.uis.unesco.org/Education/Pages/international-student-flow-viz.aspx.

Urry, J. (2000). The *Global Media and Cosmopolitanism*. Retrieved from: http://www.lancs.ac.uk/fass/sociology/papers/urry-global-media.pdf.

Urry, J. (2007). *Mobilities*. Cambridge, UK; Malden, MA: Polity.

Van Leuven, J. K. (1996). Public relations in South East Asia from nation-building campaigns to regional interdependence. In H. M. Culbertson and N. Chen (eds.) *International Public Relations: A Comparative Analysis*. Mahwah, NJ: Erlbaum.

Vertovec, S. (1999). Conceiving and researching transnationalism. *Ethnic and Racial Studies 22*(2), 447–462.

Vertovec, S. (2004). Cheap calls: The social glue of migrant transnationalism. *Global Networks 4*(2), 219–224. DOI: 10.1111/j.1471–0374.2004.00088.x.

Vertovec, S. and Cohen, R. (2002). Introduction: Conceiving cosmopolitanism. In S. Vertovec and R. Cohen (eds.) *Conceiving Cosmopolitanism: Theory, Context, and Practice* (pp. 1–22). New York: Oxford University Press.

Volkmer, I. (ed.). (2006). *News in Public Memory*. New York: Peter Lang.

Volkmer, I. (2008). Conflict-related media events and cultures of proximity. *Media, War & Conflict 1*(1), 90–98.

Volkmer, I. (2009). Globalization theories. In S. W. Littlejohn and K. A. Foss (eds.) *Encyclopedia of Communication Theory* (pp. 444–448). Thousand Oaks: Sage.

Wang, C. K. J., Liu, W. C., Chye, S., and Chatzisarantis, N. L. D. (2011). Understanding motivation in internet gaming among Singaporean youth: The role of passion. *Computers in Human Behavior 27*(3), 1179–1184. DOI: 10.1016/j.chb.2010.12.012.

Warf, B. and Arias, S. (2008). Introduction: The reinsertion of space into the social sciences and humanities. In B. Warf and S. Arias (eds.) *The Spatial Turn [electronic resource]: Interdisciplinary Perspectives* (pp. 1–10). Hoboken: Taylor & Francis.

Weiss, M. L. and Ford, M. (2011). Temporary transnationals: Southeast Asian students in Australia. *Journal of Contemporary Asia 41*(2), 229–248. DOI: 10.1080/00472336.2011.553042.

Werbner, P. (2004). Theorising complex diasporas: purity and hybridity in the South Asian public sphere in Britain. *Journal of Ethnic and Migration Studies 30*(5), 895–911. DOI: 10.1080/1369183042000245606.

"What is Singapore 21." Retrieved August 25, 2012, from: http://www.singapore21.org.sg/introduction.html.

Williams, A. M. and Baláž, V. (2008). *International Migration and Knowledge*. London; New York: Routledge.

Wimmer, A., and Glick Schiller, N. (2003). Methodological nationalism, the social sciences, and the study of migration: An essay in historical epistemology. *International Migration Review 37*(3), 576–610. DOI: 10.1111/j.1747–7379.2003.tb00151.x.

Wimmer, R. D. and Dominick, J. R. (1997). *Mass Media Research: An Introduction*. Belmont, CA: Wadsworth Pub.

Witteborn, S. (2011). Constructing the forced migrant and the politics of space and place-making. *Journal of Communication 61*(6), 1142–1160. DOI: 10.1111/j.1460-2466.2011.01578.x.

Wong, K. Y. (2015). International students pay tribute to Singapore's Lee Kuan Yew. *Meld Magazine*. Retrieved from: http://www.meldmagazine.com.au/2015/03/students-pay-tribute-to-lee-kuan-yew/.

Wong, L. (2003). Belonging and diaspora: The Chinese and the Internet. *First Monday 8*(4). Retrieved from: http://firstmonday.org/ojs/index.php/fm/article/view/1045/966.

World Economic Forum. (2015). *Global Information Technology Report 2015.*

Yeoh, B. and Lin, W. (2012). Rapid growth in Singapore's immigrant population brings policy challenges. *Migration Information Source*. Retrieved from: http://www.migrationpolicy.org/article/rapid-growth-singapores-immigrant-population-brings-policy-challenges.

Yeoh, B. S. A. and Willis, K. (2005). Singaporean and British transmigrants in China and the cultural politics of 'contact zones'. *Journal of Ethnic and Migration Studies 31*(2), 269–285. DOI: 10.1080/1369183042000339927.

Zhou, M. and Cai, G. (2002). Chinese language media in the United States: Immigration and assimilation in American life. *Qualitative Sociology 25*(3), 419–441.

Zolo, D. (2001). The "Singapore model": democracy, communication, and globalization. In K. Nash and A. Scott (eds.) *The Blackwell Companion to Political Sociology* (pp. 407–416). Malden, MA: Blackwell.

Zubrzycki, J. (1958). The role of the foreign-language press in migrant integration. *Population Studies 12*(1), 73–82.

Index

Tables and figures are denoted by *t* and *f* respectively.

9/11 terrorist attacks, 111

Abbott, Tony, 25, 28
absolute space, 193n1 (Ch.4)
accessibility through networking platforms, 119–20
accommodation, as glocalization project, 49
Afghanistan, state vs. civic spaces, 164
The Age, as news source, 138–9, 141
amnesty from deportation, 11
analytical-empirical cosmopolitanism, 64
Anderson, Benedict, 12–13, 19, 20–1, 24, 40
Appadurai, Arjun, 40, 43, 162
Arcioni, E., 19–20
Asian vs. Western culture, 142–3
assimilation, 3–4, 14–15, 93, 193n1 (Ch.1)
Association of Women for Action and Research (AWARE), 151–3, 195n23
Australia
  Asian vs. Western cultures of origin, 143
  defense partnership with Singapore, 25
  dual citizenship recognition, 28
  labor market, Singaporeans' success in, 83–4
  Singapore students in, 25, 81–2, 82*t*
  See also Singaporean students in Melbourne
AWARE (Association of Women for Action and Research) controversy, 151–3, 195n23
awareness of distant places, methods for, 146–8

Baláž, V., 106
banal globalism, 60, 162, 171
BBC
  BBC World Service, South Asian heimat and, 23
  as news source, 138, 140, 154
  on student migration regulation, 2
biographical glocalization, 56–7, 113–14
birthplace awareness for migrant children, 91–4
blogospheres, 116–17, 129, 131, 140
Bloomberg, as news source, 139–40
"both/and" logic of inclusive differentiation, 69
Brah, Avtar, 9
brain drain, 80–1
Buckingham, D., 50
Bulgarians, economic migration to UK, 3

Çağlar, A., 48
Cai, G., 14

cartographies, 115–55
vs. geographies, 8–9
relational spaces, 115–48
social cartographies, subjective, 158–61
social spaces, 115–29
subjective social cartographies, 158–61
See also communication spatialities, networks, and modes
Cartographies of Diaspora (Brah), 9
Castells, M., 122–3
cell phones. *See* mobile connectivity
centralized global broadcasting, 23–4
chain migration, 30–1, 97–9, 194n11
Champions League soccer match, 111
Channel NewsAsia
as official channel, 129
as Singapore news source in Australia, 32, 92–3, 138–40, 148–9, 194n7
Cheng, H. L., 57–8
children
birthplace awareness for migrants, 91–3
forced migration and media experiences, 50, 51
home, perception of, 91–4
interest in current events, 92–5
migration experiences, 91–5
China
labor market, Singaporeans' success in, 84
student migration to UK, 2
Chinese media in US, 29
Chouliaraki, L., 171
circular migration, 109, 141, 197n17
cities, communication levels of, 55
citizenship, 15, 28, 35, 196n8
city-scale, 48
classical (Stoic) cosmopolitanism, 62
climate change, 109–10
cluster, as community space, 45
CNBC, as news source, 138, 140
CNN, as news source, 138, 140
co-development, 27
communication/communicative cities, 55
communication geography, 53
communication spatialities, networks, and modes (CSNM)
convergence-CSNM, 166–7
cosmopolitan outlook and, 161
defined, 196n3
personal presence vs. absence in, 124
relational configurations of, 115, 120–4
social relations networks, 160
communicative deterritorialization, 44
communities of practice (CoPs), 78, 106–7
community, new definition, 45–6
comparative theory of locality, 48
Comprehensive Strategic Partnership (CSP), 25
compressed modernization in East Asia, 75
connective contexts of access, 166–70
connectivity of network society, 47–8
contemporary cosmopolitanism, 62
convergence-CSNM, 166–7
CoPs, 78, 106–7
corporeal mobility, 21–2
cosmopolitanism
classical (Stoic) cosmopolitanism, 62
cosmopolitan approach to relational spaces, 62–9
cosmopolitan concepts, 62, 64
cosmopolitan gaze, 70–1
cosmopolitan outlook, contributing factors, 161–2
cosmopolitan paradigm, 66

cosmopolitan vision, 71–2
cultural cosmopolitanism, 62–4, 95
enlightenment cosmopolitanism, 62
Euro-American perspectives, 73–4
vs. methodological cosmopolitanism, 64
national media cultures of, 60
zones, 170
cosmopolitanization
vs. methodological cosmopolitanism, 64
universalism-particularism nexus in, 69–70
countries of origin
birthplace awareness for migrant children, 91–4
exilic imagination of, 23
media representation, 20–1
nonreciprocal relations to, 21
postmigration familiarity to, 31–3
transnational fields incorporating, 27–30
countries of settlement
minority media in, 13–15
minority paradigm orientation, 4
national imagination in, 20
"neither/nor" loyalty choices, 69, 93
stability from family presence, 96–9
transnational fields incorporating, 27–30
transnational paradigm and, 25
crisis events, cross-territorial mobility during, 134
Croatia, transnational citizenship definitions, 28–9
cross-territorial spaces of mobility, 134–5
CSNM. *See* communication spatialities, networks, and modes
CSP (Comprehensive Strategic Partnership), 25
culture
comparative cultures of awareness, 170–3
cultural cosmopolitanism, 62–4, 95
cultural cosmopolitanism as cultural project, 95
cultural deterritorialization, 44
cultural diversity through media vs. migration experiences, 165
cultural identity, 67–8
culturally homogenous local communities, 127
of real virtuality, 48
as shared vision, 44
Culture and Communication Human Ethics Advisory Group (University of Melbourne), 184
Cunningham, S., 163–4

DBS (Digital Broadcasting Satellite), 42
de Blij, H., 101
de Block, L., 50, 51
decentralized global narrowcasting, 23–4
de-mythologization, process of, 32–3
deportation, amnesty from, 11
deterritorialization, diaspora as, 4, 40, 44–5, 169
deterritorialization-localities, 168–70
diasporas
as bound series, 40
as category of practice, 39
as deterritorialized nations, 4, 40, 44–5, 169
diaspora paradigm, 4, 33–7
diaspora television, 23–4
diasporic communicative spaces, 35–6
diasporic function of transnational media, 30–1
diasporic nationalism, 33–5
diasporic space, 58

diasporas—*Continued*
diasporic vs. national spaces, 35–7
digital diasporas, 115
global diaspora, 33
growing visibility of, 26
national vs. diasporic spaces, 35–7
as segment of national population, 3
Singaporean diaspora, 80–1
as social figurations of their own, 36
Digital Broadcasting Satellite (DBS), 42
digital diasporas, 115
dis-embedding and re-embedding capacities, 34–5
displaced broadcast television, 32
The Diving Bell and the Butterfly (French film), 136
dual citizenship, 28

East Asia
compressed modernization in, 75
Internet use by youths for civic engagement, 86
views of global society, 73–7
East Asian Cultural Sphere, 75
embedded and encultured knowledge, 78
embeddedness, simultaneous, 25, 94–5
English language and international students, 82
enlightenment cosmopolitanism, 62
Erasmus, 33
ethical glocalist perspectives, 50
ethnic media in countries of origin and settlement, 29–30
ethnic television, 23–4
ethnicization and long distance nationalism, 18–24
ethnoscapes, 42–3
European space, 59–60
events vs. issues, 195n27, 195n28
exclusionary discourses among minority groups, 17–18
exclusive vs. inclusive differentiation between cultural spaces, 142–5
exilic imagination of country of origin, 23

Facebook, 119–20, 122–4, 140
Faist, Thomas, 37
family migration in childhood, 91–5
family migration in young adulthood, 95–7
fandom communities, 104–5
film industry, 136
fly-in fly-out (FIFO) families, 22
foreigners with local experience, 125–6
Franz, T. M., 97, 194n11
friends
accessibility through networking platforms, 119–20
as public communities, 104–7

Gadamer, H.-G., 188–9
Gallup polls on illegal immigrants becoming citizens, 15
General Skilled Migration applications, 194n15
geographical distance, 29–30
geographies, 89–114
biographical glocalization and place polygamy, 113–14
vs. cartographies, 8–9, 90
chain migration in young adulthood, 97–9
family migration in childhood, 91–5
family migration in young adulthood, 95–7
glocal biographies, 90–101
independent migration in young adulthood, 99–101
media environment and public communities, 102–13
migration experiences, 91*f*
public communities, 104–7
public issues/events, 107–13
second-hand migration experiences, 101–2

geolinguistic region as translocal media culture, 44–5
George, Cherian, 21
Georgiou, M., 40, 89, 93
gestural politics, 85
Gillespie, M., 115
Glick Schiller, N., 48
global and local spaces, relational glocalities and, 41–51
global connectivity, deterritorialization and, 44
global diaspora, 33
global ethnoscapes, 49
global financial crisis, 149, 151
global/globalized cities, 66
global interdependencies, 4–5
global issues and events defined by interviewees, 107–12
global landscapes of flow and local neighborhoods, 42–4
global networks of connectivity and deterritorialized localities, 44–8
global news from news organizations, 138
global warming, 109–10
global wealth distribution, 65
global worldviews, professional development and, 135–6
globalism (banal globalism), 60, 162, 171
globalization
  as complex connectivity, 44
  defined, 42
  Singapore news and civic media, 164
  social relations and, 24
  social spaces and, 37
globals, as category, 49
glocal biographies, 90–101
glocal cosmopolitanism, 157–73
  of migration and media, 172
  social spaces as relational glocalities, 166
  social spaces through, 158–66
  transmedial context of migration and, 5–7
glocality defined, 49–51
Google, 131
The Guardian
  as news source, 138
  on student migration regulation, 2

Hannerz, U., 126
Hardware Zone forum, 129, 151, 164
havoc, 143, 197n20
heartland, 153–4
Heidegger, Martin, 188
Held, D., 14, 95
Hepp, Andreas, 35–6, 59, 170
hermeneutic situation, 188–9
hierarchies of place and human life, 171–2
hierarchies of places in media, 135–7
Hiller. H. H., 97, 194n11
home (space)
  emotional investment in, 152–5
  as family heritage territory, 197n23
  as fluid, 160
  home territories, 196n16
  vs. overseas relations, 149–52
  perception of, 58, 91–4
  perception of Singapore as, 152–3
  as relational glocality, 148–55
  as territorial society, 148–9
  view of future, 153
hybridization, 49
hyper-space-biased communication, 53

imagined communities, 12–13, 39–40
imagined heimat, 19–20, 23
inclusive differentiation of social spaces, 68–9
inclusive vs. exclusive differentiation between cultural spaces, 142–5
independent migration in young adulthood, 99–101
India, student migration to UK, 2

Innis, Harold, 53
internalization of social spaces, 67–8
international students
  in Australia, home countries of, 83*t*
  English language and, 82
  transnational paradigm and, 25
  use of media for knowledge expansion, 78
  See also interviewees' experiences; Singaporean students in Melbourne
Internet
  blogospheres, 116–17
  convergence-CSNM, 166–7
  deterritorialization, 168–70
  as environment of connectivity, 34
  events, experiencing globally, 107–13
  gaming, 86
  geographic proximity and distance, 117–18
  incorporation of media technologies, 194n20
  internet genres, 118–19
  irrelevance of corporeal location, 130–1
  as medium of choice for news, entertainment, and research, 102–6, 130–3
  mobile connectivity, 118
  online sociospatial experience, 115
  online space genres, 167
  public discourse and social relations, 116–17
  See also communication spatialities, networks, and modes (CSNM)
interviewees' demographics and personal details, 176–9
interviewees' experiences
  chain migration, 97–9
  children, 91–5
  of global issues and events, 107–12, 135–7
  global mobility, 146–8
  home vs. overseas, 149–55
  independent migration in young adulthood, 99–101
  Internet use, 130–3, 137–8, 150–1
  maintaining connectivity, 119–24
  mass self-communication, 122–3
  media environment and public communities, 102–6
  Melbourne's transcultural society, 126–7
  of national issues and events, 112–13
  news sources and organizations, 138–41
  preconceived ideas of US not borne out, 127–8
  second-hand migration, 101–2
  on sociospatial boundaries of online discourse, 115–19
  views of globalized world, 171
  young adults in families, 95–8
Iran, state vs. civic spaces, 164
Irish in New Zealand, 23
issues vs. events, 195n27, 195n28
Italian Parliament and outside electorates, 19–20

Japan, emotional investment in, 154–5
Japan Times, as news source, 139, 154
Johnson, M., 99

kampong (village), 154, 197n24
Kim, Youna, 34
knowledge migration, 78
Korean media in US, 29

language as signifier of ethnicity, 17
Latino media in US, 29
Leadership in Asia Public Lecture, 11–12
Lee Hsien Loong, 12
Lee Kuan Yew, 18–19

Lianhe Zaobao (newspaper)
as Chinese-language news source in Singapore, 194n6
as news source, 93
Pop Culture China coverage, 75
local communities, transcultural equality and cultural homogeneity in, 126–7
local cultures, 69
local perspectives, multiple, 144–5
localities of media appropriation, 36
locality, production of, 43
locals, as category, 49, 125–6, 195n25
long distance nationalism
Anderson on, 19
and ethnicization, 18–24
media and communication use in, 23
nonreciprocal relations to country of origin, 21

Macedonia, transnational citizenship definitions, 28–9
Mai, Nick, 99
Malaysia, Western-local cultural tension in, 76
maritime migration, unauthorized, 41
mass self-communication, 122–3
mass vs. minority imaginations, 16–17
May, Theresa, 1, 2–3, 6
McLuhan, Marshall, 13
media
awareness of distant places through, 147–8
in community creation, 46
embedded and encultured knowledge, 78
imagined places/communities and, 6–7, 12–13
media cities, 55
media convergence, 60–1
media environments, 102–13, 159–60
media types across multiple societies, 25–7
mediascapes, 42
mediated networking, 119
mediatization, globalization and, 41
migration and polymedia relationship, 6
vs. network society, 47–8
for Singaporean audiences, 75
telemediatization, 168–70
transboundary networks and formations and, 51
transmigrants' use of, 36
unofficial Singaporean channels, 129
use by international students, 78
as used by transmigrants, 36
views of migration and, 1–2
media and social space, 11–40
convergence-CSNM, 166–7
diaspora paradigm, 33–7
diasporic nationalism, 33–5
diasporic vs. national spaces, 35–7
long distance nationalism and ethnicization, 18–24
methodological nationalism, 37–40
minority paradigm, 13–24
postmigration familiarity to country of origin, 31–3
premigration aspirations to resettlement countries, 30–1
scales of, 159
transnational fields incorporating countries of origin and settlement, 27–30
transnational paradigm, 25–33
MediaCorp Online Broadband Television (MOBTV), 150
MediaSpace, space-communication nexus and, 53–4
meeting people on the ground (relationship establishment), 129
Melbourne, Australia, student city ranking, 8

Meld Magazine
 on Lee Kuan Yew's death, 19
 as minority media for Singaporean students in Melbourne, 15–16
methodological cosmopolitanism
 "both/and" logic of inclusive differentiation, 69
 vs. cosmopolitanism, 64
 vs. cosmopolitanization, 64–5
 social networks across globalized cities, 67
 universalism-particularism nexus and, 172
methodological details, 181–92
 fieldwork, 184–5
 interview participant selection, 187–8
 interview questions, 182–4, 183*t*
 phenomenological approach, 190–2
 qualitative research approach, 182–5
 sampling, 185–7
 scoping approach to text interpretation, 192
 study interpretations, 188–92, 189–90*f*
methodological nationalism, 3, 37–40, 158–9
Meyrowitz, Joshua, 50
migrant children. *See* children
migrant subject positions, 158–9
migration
 aspiration to migrate, transnational media effect on, 30–1
 circular migration, 109, 141
 continuity toward places of, 140–2
 cross-cultural personal relations, development of, 125, 127–8
 definitions and distinctions, 52–3
 embedded and encultured knowledge, 78
 global wealth distribution and, 65
 as lived global and local experience, 162
 media affecting views of, 1–2
 media and relation to social spaces, 68
 migration experiences, 91*f*
 reasons for, 36–7
 Singapore's management of, 76
 social space and, 193n2
 television and multiple sense of place, 56
 terminologies, 9
 territories' relevance for identity, 145
 transcultural diversity and, 59
 UK migration policies, 1–2
 See also interviewees' experiences
minority paradigm, 13–24
 centralized global broadcasting, 23–4
 corporeal mobility, 21–2
 country of origin, media representation of, 20–1
 decentralized global narrowcasting, 23–4
 ethnic television, 23–4
 ethnicization and long distance nationalism, 18–24
 exclusionary discourses among minority groups, 17–18
 imagined heimat, 19–20, 23
 language as signifier of ethnicity, 17
 limited self-representation of minorities, 16
 long distance nationalism, 19, 21, 22–3
 mass media, imagined communities and, 12–13
 mass vs. minority imaginations, 16–17
 minority media and assimilation, 3–4
 minority media infrastructures, 13–15

minority representation, problems with, 16
minority television, 23–4
misrepresentations, 16
networking, worker mobility and, 22
nonreciprocal relations to country of origin, 21
overseas voting, 19–20
stereotypical misrepresentation of minorities, 16
mixed spatio-temporal assemblages, glocalities as, 51
mobals, as category, 49
mobile connectivity, 103, 118, 121–2
mobile phone multimedia messaging service (MMS), 121
mobilities paradigm, 43–4
moral community, concentric spheres of, 166
"Mr Brown" blog, 129
MSN sphere, 121–2
multiethnic place scales, 126
Myanmar
state vs. civic spaces, 164
view of future, 153

Nanyang Technological University (NTU), 21
narrowcasting, 23–4
nation, state, and society configurations, 163–6
national issues and events defined by interviewees, 112–13
National Population and Talent Division of Singapore Public Service, 81
national vs. diasporic spaces, 35–7
nation-state, varied definitions of, 38–9
neighborhoods as ethnoscapes, 42–3
networking, worker mobility and, 22
New York Times, as news source, 138
news constellations, cultural spatial differentiation, 138–40
news distribution, 66, 136–7
news media, hierarchies of place and human life, 171
news sources and organizations, 138–40, 193–4n5
Nickels, H. C., 17
nomadic theory of social life, 52
nonreciprocal relations to country of origin, 21
nonrepresentation of minorities, 16
NTU (Nanyang Technological University), 21

Obama, Barack
global news from, 140
immigration reform, 11, 12, 18
social equity of actions, 17
on US as nation of immigrants, 15
Ong, A., 100–1
online media. *See* Internet
online sociospatial experience, 115
overseas, defined, 149–50
Overseas Christian Fellowship, 143
Overseas Singaporeans
emigration countries, 81–2, 82*t*
identification with and emotional attachment to Singapore, 78–9, 151–2
migration experiences, 7–8
Overseas Singaporean organizations, 18–19
Overseas Singaporean Portal, 34
Overseas Singaporean Unit (OSU), 81
overseas voting, 19–20

partial denationalization, 51
particular within universal, 171
permanent settlement vs. pragmatic sojourn, 141–2
physical deterritorialization, 44
place polygamy, 56–7

politics of pity and global compassion, 61
polymedia, 6
postmigration familiarity to country of origin, 31–3
post-territorial nationalism, 28–9
power geometry of time-space compression, 48–9, 51
pragmatic sojourn vs. permanent settlement, 141–2
premigration aspirations to resettlement countries, 27–30
professional development, 135–6
proper distance (media) and distant suffering, 61
public communities, 104–7
public discourse, 116–17, 137–8
public issues/events, 107–13

qualitative and quantitative research approaches, 195n33

radio, as closed around national culture, 131
Rantanen, T., 170
reflexive modernization, 64, 74–5
refugee children. *See* children
relational comfort, ethnicity vs. nationality, 127
relational consciousness of neighborhoods, 56
relational glocalities, 41–72
  cosmopolitan approach to relational spaces, 62–9
  cosmopolitan gaze, 70–1
  cosmopolitan vision, 71–2
  global and local spaces, 41–51
  global landscapes of flow and local neighborhoods, 42–4
  global networks of connectivity and deterritorialized localities, 44–8
  glocality, 49–51
  inclusive differentiation of social spaces, 68–9
  internalization of social spaces, 67–8
  relational spaces, 51–8
  social networks across globalized cities, 66–7
  social spaces as, 5–7
  transcultural relativity, 59–62
  unequal differentiation of social spaces, 48–9
  universal-particularism nexus, 69–72
relational spaces, 51–8, 115–48
  accessibility through networking platforms, 119–20
  Asian vs. Western cultures, 142–3
  awareness of distant places, methods for, 146–8
  circular migration, 141
  cross-territorial spaces of mobility, 134–5
  CSMN and, 115, 120–4
  digital diasporas, 115
  exclusive vs. inclusive differentiation between cultural spaces, 142–5
  hierarchies of places in media, 135–7
  home as relational glocality, 148–55
  home as territorial society, 148–9
  local perspectives, multiple, 144–5
  mass self-communication, 122–3
  multiethnic place scales, 126
  online sociospatial experience, 115
  permanent settlement vs. pragmatic sojourn, 141–2
  public discourse and social relations, 116–17
  relations between social spaces, 130–7
  relations to social spaces, 137–48
  relationship establishment (meeting people on the ground), 129

social networks, subgroups and corporeal experience, 133
social relations, public discourse and, 116–17
social spaces, 115–29
television, as closed to transnational cultural diversity, 131
territorial differences and similarities, 144–5
transcultural equality in culturally diverse local society, 126–7
as tripartite concept, 58
unequal sociopolitical relations and, 55–6
world politics, importance of, 135
relativization, 49
resettlement countries, premigration aspirations to, 30–1
residency as legal membership form, 28
residentialism, 52, 158–9
Reuters, as news source, 138
Robertson, Alexa, 171–2
Robertson, Roland
on biographical glocalization and place polygamy, 56–7, 113
on cosmopolitan gaze, 70–1
on cosmopolitan vision, 71–2
on global and local interconnectedness, 89
on global families, 94
on glocality as universalism-particularism nexus, 5
on methodological cosmopolitanism, 5, 62
methodological cosmopolitanism, 65
on methodological nationalism, 38
on reference points in global field, 71
on universalism-particularism nexus, 89
Rudd, Kevin, 140
Rumanians, economic migration to UK, 3
Russian-language media, Jews in Israel and, 14
Russians in China, 23

Sassen, Saskia, 46
satellite television in diasporic communication, 44–5
SBS (Special Broadcasting Service, Australia), 20, 111
Schutz, A., 188, 191
scientific observations on methodological nationalism, 37–8
SCV (Singapore Cable Vision), 84
second-hand migration experiences, 101–2
sedentarist theory of social life, 52
segmented assimilation, 193n1 (Ch.1)
Selamat, Mas, 149
self-representation of minorities, limited, 16
September 11 terrorist attacks, 111
Serbia, transnational citizenship definitions, 28–9
settler colonialism, 24
shared time, perception of, 111–12
Siapera, E., 167
Silverstone, R., 122
simultaneous dis-embedding and re-embedding capacities, 34–5
simultaneous embeddedness, 25, 94–5
Sinclair, J., 163–4
Singapore
academic freedom in, 21
connectedness with, 150
cultures of migration and media, 7–8
defense partnership with Australia, 25
dual citizenship recognition, 28
emigrants' participation from geographical distance, 21

Singapore—*Continued*
emigration vs. immigration, 81
as global city, 75–6
history of migration, 77
immigration debate, 11–12
increased patriotism for, 151
independence (1965), 76
international education in Australia, 25
Internet use by youths for civic engagement, 86
mass media and migration, 13
multiculturalism in, 77
news sources for, 140
religion and public policy, 145
restrictive media and communication law, 85, 129
SG50, 7, 76
society and heartware, 80
as territorial home, 148–50
Transient Workers Count Too (TWC2), 18
as young society, 144
Singapore 21, 79–80
#singapore (Twitter), 148–9, 164
Singapore Cable Vision (SCV), 84
Singapore Film Festivals, 26
Singapore High Commission in Canberra, on Lee Kuan Yew's death, 19
Singapore National Day, 80, 152, 168–9
Singapore Students Societies, 16
#singaporean (Twitter), 34
Singaporean cultures of migration and media, 73–87
East Asia views of global society, 73–7
international students in Australia, home countries, 83*t*
Overseas Singaporeans, emigration countries, 82*t*
Singapore media environment, 84–7
Singaporean international student countries, 83*t*
Singaporean students in Melbourne, 77–84
Singaporean diaspora, 80–1
Singaporean students in Melbourne
cosmopolitan society, view of, 163
global family relationships, 165–6
as high media users, 87
internal cosmopolitization of societies, 164–5
interviewees' demographics and personal details, 176–9
Singaporean cultures of migration and media, 77–84
social networks of, 67
social spaces through media experiences, 54
state vs. civic spaces, 164
support for state and political leaders, 163
See also interviewees' experiences
Singaporeans
keeping up with news, 129
Singaporean junior college students, 85
Singaporeans of Victoria, 16
Singapore-Western Australia Network (SWAN), 26
Sky News as news source, 139, 154
Skype sphere, 121–2
social cartographies, subjective, 158–61
social fields, defined, 27
social media. *See* media; media and social space
social networks, 66–7, 133
social relations, public discourse and, 116–17
social spaces, 115–29
cultures as awareness of, 170–3
between global and local, 161–3
through glocal cosmopolitanism, 158–66
inclusive differentiation of, 68–9
internalization of, 67–8

methodological nationalism and, 37–8
migrant subject positions, 158–9
migration and, 37
perspectives of, 55
as relational glocalities, 166
relationships to, 61–2
in transmedial environments, 102
unequal differentiation of, 48–50
society, state, and nation configurations, 163–6
space, dialectical relationships between media and, 53
space conceptualizations, 52
space of flows, 46–7, 48
space-communication nexus, MediaSpace and, 53–4
spatial ambiguities, 53
spatiotemporal orders, 169
Special Broadcasting Service (SBS, Australia), 20, 111
speech pathology as career, 136
stability from family presence, 96–7
state, nation, and society configurations, 163–6
stereotypical misrepresentation of minorities, 16
stock of knowledge, 191
Stoic concentric spheres of moral community, 166
Straits Times (website and newspaper)
availability, 194n8
vs. *New Straits Times* (Malaysia news source), 94
for Singaporeans in Australia, 32, 92–3, 139, 148
Student Portal and Learning Management System (LMS; University of Melbourne), 196n12
study results, transferability of, 172–3
subjective geographies as individualized, 194n18
subjective social cartographies, 158–61
SWAN (Singapore-Western Australia Network), 26
synchronization of media forms, 46

Tan, Tony, 27–8
technological convergence, 168–70
telemediatization, 44–5, 168–70
television as closed to transnational cultural diversity, 131
territorial cultures, 69
territorial differences and similarities, 144–5
territorial multi-ethnicism, 28–9
Today (website), for Singaporeans in Australia, 32
Today Online as news source, 139–40
Tomlinson, John, 44, 110–11, 122
transcultural diversity, 59, 165
transcultural equality in culturally diverse local society, 126–7
transcultural relativity, 59–62
transferability of study results, 172–3
transformation, as glocalization project, 49
Transient Workers Count Too (TWC2), 18
translocal media cultures, 44–5
transmedial communicative spaces, 36, 102
transmigrants use of media, 36
transmigration as simultaneous embeddedness, 25
transnational paradigm, 25–33
citizenship definitions, 29
connections to countries of origin and settlement, 4
cultures, 69
economies between countries of origin and settlement, 29
expanded worldview through media, 48

transnational paradigm—*Continued*
place polygamy and, 56–7
transnational embodiment, 35
transnational fields in countries of origin and settlement, 27–30
transnational social spaces, 30, 97
transnational television, 23–4
transnationalism and assimilation, 29, 30–3, 193n1 (Ch.1)
travel advisories, responses to, 145
triangular spatial context of diasporic belonging, 33
Tsagarousianou, R., 40
TWC2 (Transient Workers Count Too), 18
Twitter, 34, 131, 140, 148–9, 164

undocumented immigrants and immigration reform, 11
United Kingdom, relationship to EU, 1–3
United States immigration, opinions on, 16–17
universalism-particularism nexus
cosmopolitanization and, 69–70
through CSNM, 169
methodological cosmopolitanism and, 172
online space genres, 167
relational glocalities and, 69–72
University of Melbourne Culture and Communication Human Ethics Advisory Group, 184
University of Melbourne Student Portal and Learning Management System (LMS), 196n12
unofficial channels of Singaporean media, 129
US presidential debates, 111

voice-over-Internet Protocol service, 121
voyeur aspect of mediated communication, 123

ways of being, 27, 160–1
ways of belonging, 27
Western vs. Asian cultures, 142–3
Williams, A. M., 106
worker mobility and networking, 22
World Economic Forum Global Information Technology Report (2015), 86
world economic maps, 2–3
world political maps, 3
world politics, importance of, 135

Yahoo! News as news source, 139–40, 154
yompies (young, outwardly mobile professionals), 100–1
YouTube, 129, 144–5, 160

Zimbabwe situation, 196n15
Zubrzycki, J., 14

CPSIA information can be obtained at www.ICGtesting.com
Printed in the USA
BVOW06*0221080716

454898BV00004B/25/P